JOHN WILSON'S

COARSE FISHING METHOD MANUAL

BOXTREE

First published in Great Britain in 1997 by Boxtree

an imprint of Macmillan Publishers Ltd
25 Eccleston Place, London, SW1W 9NF
and Basingstoke

Associated companies throughout the world

This edition published for Bookmart Ltd, 1998

ISBN 0 7522 1099 8

1 2 3 4 5 6 7 8 9 10

A CIP catalogue record for this book is available from the British Library.
Designed by Lovelock & Co.
Illustrations by David Batten
Printed in Italy by New Interlitho, S.P.A.– Milan

John Wilson's Coarse Fishing Method Manual by John Wilson

This book is for my best friend: my wife, Jo.

ACKNOWLEDGEMENTS

Compiling a book that includes 250 colour photos and diagrams can only be
accomplished with the help of friends. I should therefore like to thank regular
fishing companions for their help at the other end of the camera and my typist,
Jan Carver, who for over ten years has suffered my long hand and turned
Wilsonisms into English. But most of all, my sincere thanks and congratulations
go to a friend and fellow fisherman, Dave Batten, who throughout so many of my
books has drawn the illustrations. This time, as I am sure you will agree, he has
surpassed even his own past artistry.

CONTENTS

INTRODUCTION

While we all go fishing for very different reasons, some for pure relaxation, others for the kudos of putting a whopper on the bank, we must never lose sight of the fact that there is more than one way of skinning a cat. Which is why, after a lifetime spanning fifty years of freshwater fishing, including the penning of over twenty books on the subject, I have decided to write this particular volume.

Many of the following methods may already be known to you; some may seem strange, while others could appear downright ridiculous, outrageous even. But to my mind anglers who enjoy an entire spectrum of different methods at varying seasons throughout the year, often using a more traditional approach, will find their rewards all the more satisfying. For instance, take a sizeable carp living in a typical lakeland or gravel pit environment. Now

you could conceivably catch it, and all the others like it, using only one method. And as bolt-rig ledgering boilies has now become the accepted technique by the vast majority of carp anglers, you might well ask why you should try other methods.

But equally, would you really be content sitting down to lasagne or a roast dinner every single day of your life without change? Bolt-rig ledgering is certainly a very effective technique for hooking carp – probably the deadliest of all – but, and here's the rub, it is just one method among dozens. Or, in the context of this book, just one of thirty different methods. Variety is indeed the spice of life. And learning that carp, our most popular species, can often be more effectively caught by implementing the lift method – by freelining, quivertipping, stret pegging or even with a fly rod – a whole new world of thought will, I hope, be opened up to you.

The same could be said of quivertipping for barbel and chub using a block end feeder rig; it is unquestionably the deadliest and possibly the easiest technique for catching barbel in particular, due to the way in which they charge off downstream with your bait, virtually hooking themselves in the process.

Yet there are infinitely more skilful ways of fishing for barbel. And those who, with the help of this book, learn to fish the 'stick float' at close range or long trott using a waggler or loafer-style float or balsa trotter and centre pin reel combination, have much to look forward to. Good fishing.

John Wilson
Great Witchingham

John's favourite method, above all others,
is long trotting for dace, grayling, roach
or chub using a centre-pin reel.

ARTIFICIAL LURES

Far out in Lake Nasser, a big Nile perch
shakes its head angrily – having taken
John Jarvis's Rapala lure.

WORKING DIVING PLUGS

The strength of using plugs which dive is that, by carefully selecting a suitable pattern, virtually any freshwater situation and depth band can be explored. Of the two basic types, floating divers and sinking divers, the former are probably the most versatile artificial lure of all because their working range covers every depth from the surface down to at least 20 feet. Sinking divers are generally considered a more specialized lure used purposely to reach predators in deep locations by counting them down at around 1 foot per second, just like you would a large spoon, before starting the retrieve. However, sinking divers can, of course, also be effectively worked in quite shallow water through that clear layer of water between bottom weeds and the surface. So with pike, perch, zander and chub in mind, let's explore this fascinating method. First of all, however, let's consider the combinations of rods and reels required to get the best from these artificials.

RODS AND REELS

For the bulk of my plug fishing I use two entirely different outfits: a 9-foot two-piece snappy actioned, low-profile carbon rod (usually referred to as a spinning rod) and a smooth-running fixed-spool reel in the 2500–3000 format loaded to the lip with 10–12lb monofilament. I have in fact delved exhaustively into this subject at the beginning of Method 2, 'Working Spinners and Spoons', so rather than duplicating these technical details let me simply add that the second outfit consists of a 6-foot one-piece trigger-grip American-style baitcasting rod married to a baby left-handed multiplier loaded with 10lb test which has magnetic casting control (though this is not imperative) and a trip bar which disengages the spool through thumb pressure alone for superb single-handed casting. Incidentally a comprehensive rundown on baitcasting outfits is included in Method 3, 'Working Top-water Lures'.

Now the reason I go artificial lure fishing with these two entirely different outfits is simply that I enjoy using both. I suppose I do tend to use the longer rod more for working lures at greater distances and the baitcasting combo for close-range fun, which it certainly provides. In fact with a little single-handed outfit you certainly don't need big fish to appreciate its qualities of extremely accurate casting and snappy performance. But at the end of the day it's all about deriving pleasure from working diving plugs.

LINES AND TRACES

During the course of a day's lure fishing you could make hundreds and hundreds of casts, certainly more than is demanded by any other method within this manual. So do not in any way try to economize on your line which will tend to wear quickly due to the constant abrasion of coming into contact with rod rings, your reel's bale-arm roller, aquatic plants, gravel bars and the rigours of repetitive casting. I suggest, for instance, that you always cut off the last few yards to which the wire trace is tied at the end of every session because the constant casting and stretching of this section eventually weakens it.

For optimum casting performance the reel's spool should be filled to the lip with a good quality, abrasion-resistant monofilament in a neutral colour and should be replaced regularly, at least two or three times during a season's lure fishing. In recent years, due to their extremely low diameter and virtual nonstretch qualities, gel spun braided polyethylene reel lines have become popular with artificial lure enthusiasts. Personally I much prefer working lures using braid on a multiplying reel (as opposed to a fixed spool) because it is less inclined to 'bed in,' being wound across the spool by the level wind mechanism. Braid does however vastly improve hook setting regardless of which reel is used and tends also to cut through weeds more efficiently than monofilament. In addition, due to the reduced diameter of braid, you can use a substantially higher breaking strain as a safety margin to offset the inherent lack of elasticity should a big fish thrash or make a sudden getaway run when held on a short line. So if wishing to switch from 10–12lb monofilament, for instance, go up to an 18–20lb braided line. It's certainly not cheap but you may well finds its qualities to your liking, particularly if your lure rod has a softish tip. Superfast tips, powerful carbon rods (snooker-cue action) and braided reel lines are not recommended for general lure fishing.

Wire traces should not be overlong or kinking might result – 10–12 inches being quite sufficient. I use 15lb breaking strain braided alasticum for my traces because it can be quickly twisted around itself to attach the swivels without the need for crimps and crimping pliers. As can be seen from Diag. 1, Fig. A, a size 10 swivel is twisted on to accommodate the reel line and at the opposite end there is a size 5 Croslok snap swivel for rapid lure changing (Fig. C).

If you prefer to use the lower-diameter seven-strand type wire, secure with crimps as in Fig. B. Either way keep a watchful eye on your wire trace whilst fishing and replace immediately it looks worse for wear, shows signs of kinking or actually has a fractured strand. Any slight kink occurring in alasticum wire, if spotted straight away (which is why I like it), can easily be eradicated by gently unrolling and pulling at each end to straighten, whereas kinks in springy seven-strand type wire require instant replacement.

FLOATING DIVERS

To the newcomer working out which does what from the galaxy of artificial lures on display in tackle shops must seem a daunting, almost impossible task. Yet simply by studying each lure carefully you will glean what you want to know. With floating divers, which are called crank baits in the US because you need to crank them in fast to get them down quickly, lip size is everything. The bigger the lip, the deeper they dive. Those with small plastic or aluminium lips like Heddon's famous Meadow Mouse for instance will dive just a few feet, whereas at the opposite end of the scale Manns' 20+ or a Shadling deep diver will plough quickly down to 20 feet, compliments of their large angled diving vanes or lips to which the trace is attached. Naturally if you stop the retrieve at any time, the plug starts to float back up to the surface

American-style baitcasting outfits, which incorporate a baby multiplier reel, allow you to enjoy predators of all sizes while plug fishing.

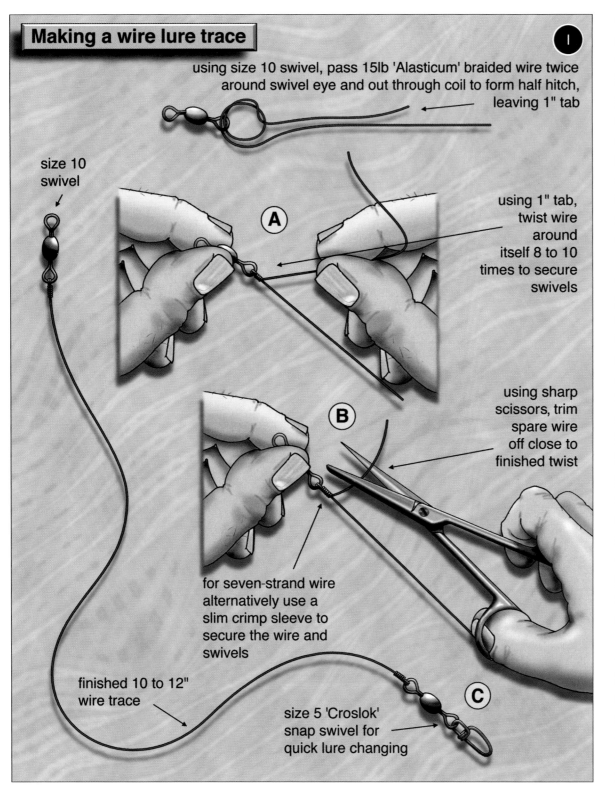

Making a wire lure trace

using size 10 swivel, pass 15lb 'Alasticum' braided wire twice around swivel eye and out through coil to form half hitch, leaving 1" tab

size 10 swivel

A

using 1" tab, twist wire around itself 8 to 10 times to secure swivels

B

using sharp scissors, trim spare wire off close to finished twist

for seven-strand wire alternatively use a slim crimp sleeve to secure the wire and swivels

finished 10 to 12" wire trace

size 5 'Croslok' snap swivel for quick lure changing

C

again. This is what makes floating divers the most attractive and versatile of all lures, because by varying the retrieve even the most irregular-bottomed fisheries can be searched. You crank the plug down to explore deep holes or gullies then stop the retrieve so its floats up over shallow bars, snags or weed beds, before working it down again through deep water in that tantalizing side-to-side chugging action. Some even have an extra attraction in the form of a built-in rattle, which produces a throbbing sound from a ball bearing vibrating within a hollow chamber.

There are indeed hundreds of different floating divers and so choice should be made according to the particular depth band in which you expect predators to be situated, which is only common sense. Obviously during the warmer months when perch, zander and pike are more active, working floating divers of varying patterns through different depth bands is the way of ascertaining at which level they are happy to attack. Sometimes the retrieve needs to be slow, sometimes fast, and sometimes erratic. And it's great fun putting your lure collection through its paces to this end. During some sessions a particular type of lure may outfish all others; on other occasions there seems to be little preference other than at which depth your plug is worked. Rarely is there a status quo, and of course this is the fascination of catching predators on lures. It is a working, searching, totally unpredictable method that is limited only by your thought pattern.

Winter plug fishing however is an entirely different ball game. Consider the cold water tactics in Diag. 2 for instance, which depicts in cross section a typical irregular-bottomed gravel pit where depths in the deepest holes and gullies shelve down to over 14 feet. Now as can be seen from cast C it is imperative to use a big lipped floating diver, like a Rapala Shadrap deep runner or a Manns' 10+, to

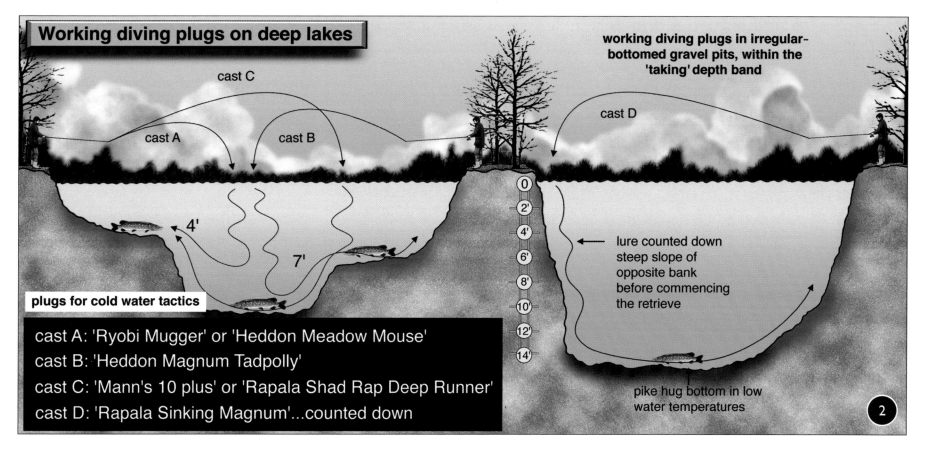

Working diving plugs on deep lakes

cast C

cast A   cast B

working diving plugs in irregular-bottomed gravel pits, within the 'taking' depth band

cast D

4'

7'

0
2'
4'
6'
8'
10'
12'
14'

lure counted down steep slope of opposite bank before commencing the retrieve

plugs for cold water tactics

cast A: 'Ryobi Mugger' or 'Heddon Meadow Mouse'
cast B: 'Heddon Magnum Tadpolly'
cast C: 'Mann's 10 plus' or 'Rapala Shad Rap Deep Runner'
cast D: 'Rapala Sinking Magnum'...counted down

pike hug bottom in low water temperatures

2

attract pike occupying the lowest depth band in a 12-foot deep hole. Such pike are often covered in double sucker leeches around their fin roots and on their gill covers during periods of really cold weather literally from lying amongst the bottom detritus. Unless your plug dives down to almost hit them on the snout they won't grab hold or even give chase. There is certainly little chance of a lure being taken at midwater which is commonplace during the warmer months when pike may follow a lure for many many yards and even chase it upwards from really deep water almost to the surface before making an attack. It is therefore critical that you choose the right plug for a particular depth band so the pike opens its jaws to secure its meal, almost without moving.

Conversely using a really deep diver, say on either casts A or B, would result in the plug's diving lip actually burying into the bottom stratum after just a few cranks of the reel. So learning exactly to what depth each lure is capable of diving is of paramount importance. Thus for cast A, a Ryobi Mugger which won't scrape the bottom in 5 feet would be a good choice, and for cast B, Heddon's Magnam Tad Polly or a Lazy Ike retrieved slowly will work nicely through that lowest layer in 7–8 feet of water just above the bottom.

Simply imagining each fishery in cross section, like in this diagram, and in say 2-foot thick layers helps enormously in your plan of attack, whether seeking pike, perch or zander. This is especially useful during the colder winter months when fish become inactive and lie dormant on the bottom all leeched up for week upon week.

Coldwater Bottom-Crawling Rig

To guarantee your floating diver (and other plugs) works within that all-important lowest layer and mere inches above the bottom, make up the crawling rig shown in Diag. 3 which incidentally works effectively in both still and running water. For this technique I use a longer 20-in 15lb alasticum trace with a bead and running bomb link above the swivel constructed from silicone tubing sleeved over a 6-inch length of 6lb monofilament (which breaks and jettisons the lead if snagged) holding a 1–2oz bomb (as Fig. D). This link ensures the plug works only within the very lowest layer of water immediately above the bottom stratum. As an alternative to constructing your own link, use a ready-made Fox ledger stem (Fig. E) which has a snap link swivel at the lower end to facilitate quick bomb changing (to suit varying lures and distances cast) and

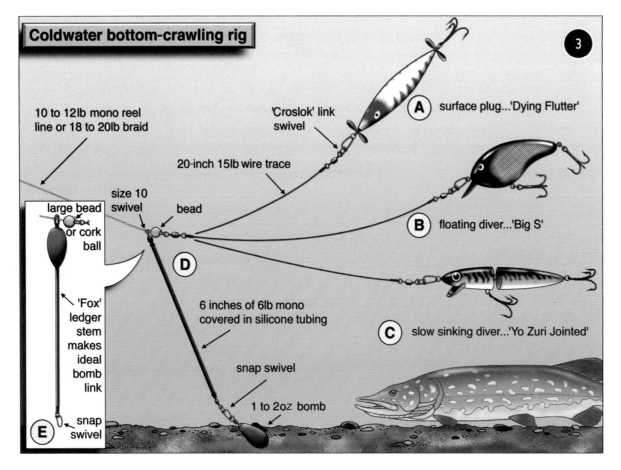

Coldwater bottom-crawling rig

10 to 12lb mono reel line or 18 to 20lb braid

'Croslok' link swivel

20-inch 15lb wire trace

size 10 swivel

bead

large bead or cork ball

'Fox' ledger stem makes ideal bomb link

6 inches of 6lb mono covered in silicone tubing

snap swivel

1 to 2oz bomb

snap swivel

A surface plug...'Dying Flutter'

B floating diver...'Big S'

C slow sinking diver...'Yo Zuri Jointed'

up your sleeve for those really prolonged periods of cold weather when predators simply won't leave the bottom. So wake them up but don't expect hits to be as aggressive as when plugs are worked higher up in the water. A pike already on the bottom can hardly crash dive and very often all that happens in the way of an indication is the rod tip nodding strangely. So be ready to start cranking fast and heaving the rod into a powerful strike at any unusual feeling transmitted up the line.

STRIKING

A few general words on striking are, I think, in order at this stage because a large proportion of plug-hooked predators, especially pike, will shake the trebles out due to the stretch in monofilament if you don't hold them hard enough. Moreover, endeavour to point the rod tip more or less directly at the plug during the retrieve and not angled over to one side as though you were quivertipping. This applies to working all types of plugs incidentally.

What can happen is that as a pike grabs hold and you attempt to strike with the rod tip angled side on (unless it is a real monster and goes charging off at speed in the opposite direction slamming the hooks home in the process) the sheer amount of stretch in monofilament (about 25 per cent) will allow those hooks to be shaken out before you have time to wind the rod tip into a bend and apply any pressure. But if the rod tip is pointed at the fish when you simultaneously strike (don't stop winding) and heave it back into a full bend, the hooks have far less chance of being thrown clear when the pike senses danger and starts that lovely flared-gill, head-shaking routine.

You will find that hooks penetrate more easily, particularly the large sized trebles which some manufacturers attach to their plugs, if you gently squeeze each barb down with a pair of pliers. Don't

a buoyancy foam body at the top with a large-diameter ring ensuring it slides easily above your trace swivel with a large bead or cork ball between.

After casting out watch for the line falling momentarily slack after the bomb touches bottom, then start the retrieve which should be slow and erratic. Only trial and error will dictate the ideal speed and of course the bomb will drag and bump over the bottom debris sending up little clouds of silt which is probably an added attraction to any pike lying asleep close by. Do not risk using this particular bottom-crawling rig where permanent snags, such as tree stumps or old hawsers, are lying. Obviously the method works most effectively over relatively clean bottoms of silt, rotting weeds and leaves.

As in Fig. B a small lipped, shallow-water diving

plug will work attractively behind the bomb link around 10–15 inches above bottom, whereas an out-and-out floater such as a twin propeller dying flutter (Fig. A) will dive and gurgle several inches higher in a most strange yet attractive manner.

To really drag bottom you can use a tiny lipped slow-sinking plug (as Fig. C) like a Yo Zuri jointed sinker or a Zara Gossa. But you do need to keep the rig moving along some, or the plug will snag bottom and continually pick up rotting vegetation which stifles its action. Incidentally, to achieve exactly the action you're looking for, work the rig along the bottom of clear water close into the margins so you can actually observe how each particular lure works, in conjunction with varying rates of retrieve. It's a fascinating method of working diving plugs to have crunch them right off; simply reduce to leave a ridge which will stop them from falling out. And to aid penetration further, sharpen the points of each treble regularly. They easily become blunt or even burred over if worked across the gravel bottom of pits and brick or stone slab-built reservoirs. I keep a small flat hand file in my fishing coat pocket for this very reason.

Summer pike will no doubt treat you to some tail-walking antics even if the plug was taken well below the surface, so be sure to adjust the reel's slipping clutch carefully in order that line is given instantly to a running fish and keep the anti-reverse lever engaged at all times. Play pike hard on artificials always giving the line on demand, but begrudgingly, and you'll land a large proportion.

UNHOOKING

For landing predators hooked on lures, you require just two items: an 8–10-inch pair of long-nosed artery forceps (it doesn't matter whether they are straight or curved) and a protective glove for your left hand assuming you are right-handed. A heavy gauge latex cotton-lined industrial glove will suffice provided it's tight fitting but in my opinion there is nothing on the market to beat Normark's fish-n-fillet glove. This extremely supple glove (which incidentally fits either hand) is actually made from microfine chainmail across which a sharp knife can be drawn without fear of an accident. So for the simple routine of unhooking pike in particular it is perfect.

Unless the bankside is comfortably carpeted in sphagnum moss or long grass upon which to gently lay the pike (or zander), invest in a foam-filled unhooking

For both perch and pike in depths down to 6 or 7 feet, the floating/diving Ryobi Mugger is a renowned 'predator producer'.

mat to protect its scales and body mucus once it is lowered down for unhooking. Regular boat anglers like myself find that a roll of dense (camping) foam or even an oblong of carpet underlay is just the job for protecting the pike from flapping about on bare ground or boards and hurting itself. Start by turning the pike on its back (kneeling astride really large fish to keep them still) and insert the fingers of your left (gloved) hand into its left gill opening making sure that the sensitive and extremely delicate gill rakers (through which it extrudes dissolved oxygen) are not disturbed. When fully inside, clamp down upon your

forefinger with your thumb (still on the outside) in a firm vice-like grip. This does not hurt the pike and is the safest way of handling it. To facilitate hook removal, gently curl your hand towards you and, hey presto, the pike has no option but to open its lower jaw. Its upper jaw cannot move of course, being a continuation of its skull, and once you have appreciated that it is the lower jaw which in fact hinges open, unhooking suddenly becomes a formality, not something to dread or be afraid of. With zander insert just two fingers (a glove is not really necessary) and then clamp down on the outside with your thumb.

Frankly I think perch are the most tricky of all predators to unhook because they suddenly jump and, if you are not careful or lose your grip, the point of a treble hook could easily penetrate a finger beyond the barb. So hold them firmly around the shoulders using just thumb and forefinger or, better still, bend down and remove the hooks with forceps whilst the perch is still in the water. You can unhook pike and zander in exactly the same way if the hooks are not inside the jaws.

Before returning your catch, now is most certainly the best time for taking a trophy photograph while it's still knackered. Don't be tempted to retain it in a tube or sack for photographing later (unless absolutely necessary) because once it livens up again after a short rest, trying to hold it still for the camera can prove extremely difficult. So get used to this set routine.

SINKING DIVERS

Lastly we come to plugs that sink and therefore can be counted down to the desired depth before starting the retrieve. This means that predators lying virtually at any depth can be offered the chance of grabbing an artificial meal. Most sinking plugs are also equipped with (albeit small) diving vanes so that they dive whilst being wound upwards, which in reality means they maintain a horizontal plane at the level to which they were counted down throughout the entire retrieve.

Some patterns are extremely versatile like ABU's jointed Hi-Lo which is fitted with an adjustable six-position diving vane, so it can be wiggled quickly just beneath the surface film for summer predators, or wobbled slowly along (after counting it down) at any depth you choose when exploring winter haunts.

Being an experienced lure angler Angling Times *photographer, Mick Rouse, knows full well that removing the hooks with forceps while the pike is still in the water makes life easier.*

Models which sink really slowly, like the famous (single- and double-jointed) Creek Chub Pikie can be wobbled in quite fast just a couple of feet down with that tantalizing side-to-side swaying motion or counted down deep for a slow and thorough search of the bottom layers.

Because they sink quickly and head first, I rate Normark's saltwater sinking magnums amongst the most effective in their field. Even the three smallest sizes, 2½, 4½ and 5½ inches, are extremely durable and, being fitted with top quality trebles, they can be used for any sized freshwater predator anywhere in the world from tooth-laden tiger fish to the legendary mahseer and the Nile perch. In fact whilst boat fishing in Lake Nasser in Egypt during the past few years for both tiger fish and the giant Nile perch, sinking magnams have allowed me to over come all kinds of situations. Take those almost sheer rocky faces (the tops of cliffs before the lake was flooded) along the marginal drop-off for instance, where gaps between huge rocks form underwater caves and Nile

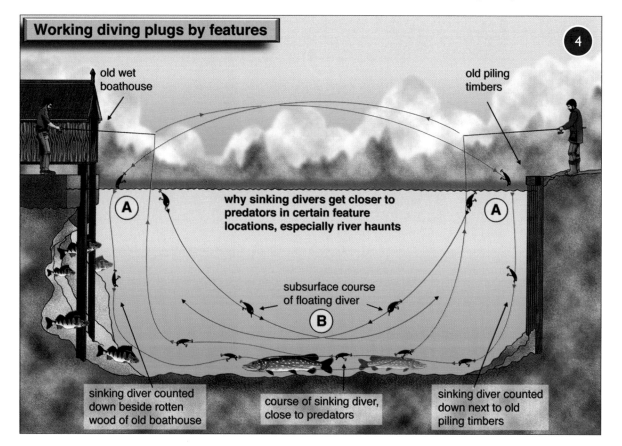

Working diving plugs by features

4

old wet boathouse

old piling timbers

why sinking divers get closer to predators in certain feature locations, especially river haunts

(A)

(A)

subsurface course of floating diver

(B)

sinking diver counted down beside rotten wood of old boathouse

course of sinking diver, close to predators

sinking diver counted down next to old piling timbers

perch lie in wait ready to ambush unsuspecting shoals of tilapia which are their staple diet.

Trolling close enough to present your artificial is not always possible due to the danger of breaking the prop or running aground on an unseen peak and possibly holing the boat. But by drifting or motoring along 50 feet out, away from the cliffs, and casting a sinking magnam within inches of the sheer rock face numbers of bonus perch came my way. My technique was to count the magnam down as it sunk head first and commence the retrieve at a different level each cast until a perch darted out and grabbed it, usually within a split second of starting to wind. Talk about explosive sport! And of course this technique works just as effectively at home with perch, pike and zander holed up beside obstructions like wide bridge supports, deeply piled banking, or alongside wet boathouses and weir sills, where there is little chance of working most other artificials close enough.

Consider the situation in Diag. 2, for instance, of cast D where due to prolonged cold weather pike are hugging the bottom of an extremely deep steep-sided bay in a gravel pit fishery. Only counting down a sinking magnam-type artificial (that dives head first) will put you in pole position for exploring the lowest depth ban across the entire bay from near to far bank and actually being able to work in a horizontal plane just above bottom throughout the entire retrieve. Alternatively see how in Diag. 4, depicting river haunts where predators hug the rotting woodwork of old boathouses or deep piling, a sinking diver counted down head first (as Fig. A) gets much closer than a big lipped floating diver (Fig. B) which is only really effective at the lowest point of its course.

Using a plug incorporated within a cold-water bottom-crawling rig (note the bomb link above) John displays the beautiful markings of a River Test pike.

WORKING SPINNERS AND SPOONS

RODS

Before we delve into the techniques involved in this fascinating subject, I think a rundown on tackle is in order. And if I were given the task of choosing just one rod for working lures all day (spinners, spoons and plugs incidentally) a lightweight carbon model of around 9 feet with a correctly positioned reel fitting and a responsive, snappy action with enough flick in the tip for effortless, accurate casting would be ideal. Such a rod should of course also be able to take on a good bend under the severe pressure of a large fish without feeling spongy. You then have the benefit of both worlds: enjoyment of all sized fish through a forgiving tip, plus the capacity for long double-handled casting and power in reserve for subduing the occasional whopper.

I mentioned reel position purposely here because many rods straight off the shelf have the screw reel fitting too far up the rod, which interrupts the enjoyment of playing fish because the butt cap scrapes against your stomach every time you bring the rod over to change angle. It also reduces the effective length of the rod. So in the tackle shop make sure that when your hand comes to rest around the reel fitting (with two fingers situated on each side of the reel stem ensuring your forefinger is perfectly placed for feathering the line down at the end of each cast and for putting pressure against the rim of the spool) no more than 2 or 3 inches of rod butt

protrudes beyond your elbow. This is just enough for double-handed casting. If the handle is too long, select another model or simply make your own customized rod.

With lure fishing you are casting continually all day, and consequently comfort is more important than in any other branch of fishing (except fly fishing). This for instance is why a 9-foot rod is preferable to one of 12 feet. The extra length and subsequent weight would take all the fun out of the method and your arm would be dropping off after just an hour or so.

In general terms it is possible to purchase just the one lightweight, narrow-profile rod to cover a multitude of species and situations, though lure enthusiasts will no doubt prefer to have a less powerful rod to obtain maximum fun from smaller species like perch and chub. And some would even go a step further in pursuit of enjoyment by flipping lures using a short American-style bait casting rod (see Method 3, 'Working Top-Water Lures').

REELS

I regularly use two types of reel for working spinners and spoons: a baby left-hand wind multiplier which has a thumb-click spool release for fast, easy casting of weighty artificials, and a smooth-running fixed spool for all general work. As casting is continual, to invest in free-running good quality reels is something you will not regret. With the overall weight of an

outfit in mind I tend to use smaller format rather than larger reels. So, providing the spools can accommodate 150 yards of 10–12lb test monofilament for pike and zander, or 100 yards of 6lb test at the lighter end of the scale for chub and perch, any quality reel should suffice. Beware however of models with narrow-diameter spools which restrict casting potential because the line comes off in tight coils.

I would suggest fixed spools in the 2000, 2500 and 3000 size range with fairly wide spools as being ideal if fitted with a deep spool and the line filled to the lip of the rim for smooth, effortless casting.

LINES AND TRACES

Super-soft, over stretchy monofilament lines are not recommended for the arduous task of repetitive casting and working spinners or spoons, often through abrasive weeds. Opt for a reasonably low-stretch (not an ultra-narrow diameter line) abrasion-resistant brand in a neutral green, grey or sorrel colour and attach a 10–12 inch, 15lb test alasticum wire trace with a good quality snap lok swivel at the business end to facilitate quick lure changing. Go for smaller swivels rather than large because they pick up far less weed.

Here's one last piece of advice about end tackle. Remember to discard the last two or three yards of reel line following every session which will have deteriorated noticeably due to the rigours of constant casting. Such a weakness might cost you dearly on your very next trip.

SPOONS

Now if I were to choose a single lure for bridging that awkward and sometimes difficult gap between summer and winter or, put another way, between dense weedy shallows and clear, deep, open water, it would be the simple spoon. Don't forget, anyway, that several companies offer spoons whose hooks are guarded, like ABU's Atom Giller which is most effectively protected from fouling weed by two long wire guards while the treble fits neatly against the spoon out of harm's way.

Actually I think I would even choose a large 4–5-inch spoon as my one lure for predator fishing anywhere in freshwater – worldwide. I've caught tiger fish and Nile perch on spoons in Lake Nasser and giant lake trout plus truly monstrous grayling from the rivers and lakes in Manitoba and the Northwest Territories in Canada. Many of my spoons are severely scratched and even dented from the crunching power of barracudas' teeth, fish caught and lost in tropical blue waters. Even the mighty mahseer inhabiting the swift-flowing and rocky Indian rivers will grab spoons and, of course, wherever you seek old 'Esox lucius' you could not be in with a better chance than when working a big spoon.

So what is it about the plain old spoon that makes predatory species chase and grab hold? Is it the attractive flash, the vibratory pulses, the speed or the erratic manner in which spoons can be retrieved, or the lifelike way in which spoons flutter backwards down to the bottom if the retrieve is suddenly stopped? Is it that sudden lifelike burst and massive displacement of water (which the predator picks up via the sensory ducts of its lateral line) when the retrieve starts again? Is it the noisy impact of the spoon hitting the surface and instant unpredictable movements? Only predators can really provide

For predator fishing anywhere in the world spoons rule OK! An ABU weedless Atom accounted for this mean machine amongst the surface greenery of a Norfolk mere.

accurate answers of course though I'll wager it's a mixture of all of these things and more.

What many anglers, even keen predator hunters, do not seem to take into account about certain makes of spoon (and I say this as an ex-tackle dealer of 25 years' standing) is that you can buy them in varying weights and thicknesses of steel or brass to suit a variety of circumstances and situations. One of my favourite spoons, for instance, is the Landa 'Pikko', a truly superb 5-inch pike getter that is available in no fewer than three thicknesses, weighing 20g, 28g and a heavy 35g respectively. It is also available in five coloured finishes from brown trout to pikelet on one side and plain finely polished brass on the other.

For many years now I have also been successful with pike when fishing plain silver, brass or copper spoons, the last especially. But you do need to keep them burnished – or that all-important flash soon goes. Restore their brilliance regularly by cleaning with a soft cloth and a paste cleaner such as Peek. It makes all the difference, believe me.

But right now we are considering the actual weight of large spoons like the Pikko. For wobbling slowly over bottom-weeds, or smartly over weed beds that reach almost to the surface, the 20g model provides me with a large but, more importantly, a lightweight spoon. For more general work the 28g suffices and for really long casting or during the cold winter months when fishing deep, by counting it down to the bottom at roughly one second for every foot of descent, I much prefer the heavy 35g model.

Other makes of heavy spoons decidedly worth a cast are Lucky Strike's Half Wave (35g) and the Lizard (28g) which has a great action and comes in several colours. The Kuusamo Professor (27g) in silver or copper has a really strange (it can be attached at either end for varying actions) yet highly effective action, and also consider ABU's 35g Atom which comes in several colours and is perhaps overequipped with a treble at both ends. Now this feature sometimes works but mostly I think it is not a good idea; it only takes but a few tangled casts before I detach the top treble (which, frankly, does not make the spoon work any less effectively). The Kilty Lure Co. also makes some terrific spoons. At 32g, being short but thick in cross section, the Miki spoon casts like a bullet and is great for both long-range situations and working deep down close to the bottom of rivers. For those who desire a really big spoon Kilty make the Heron which is available in four sizes from 30g to 100g and in six colours.

ABU's Toby range and Toby Salmo (another great big spoon) also come in a variety of coloured finishes and varying weights from 7g up to 30g, as do the almost identical Landa Lukki range from 7g up to 35g. The offset counter-balanced fin arrangement of the latter range make these lures work slightly differently from the Toby spoons. I think they flutter more.

Though all these Toby-like lures were originally designed to imitate the sand eel, and thus catch salmonoids, pike, perch and zander, all find them irresistible. Each spoon, regardless of manufacture, should be worked on the countdown principle to ensure it is retrieved purposefully through that hitting zone. For instance, consider the typical cross section of a large deep gravel pit shown in Diag. 5. Now for the purpose of understanding where pike might be lying in such a water during the coldest part of the winter, think of the water in cross section divided up just like a layer cake. Obviously the spoon needs to be worked just a couple of feet above where the pike are lying which is close to the bottom, as in Fig. A and not as Fig. B. In low winter temperatures there is no way a pike will zoom up through 10 feet of water from the bottom to grab a spoon cranked in fast just beneath the surface, not the ones I catch anyway. Yet that same pike can be caught within the shallow depth band just above the weed as in Fig. C

Working a big spoon across the surface during the autumn from a slowly drifting or anchored boat maximizes the pike potential.

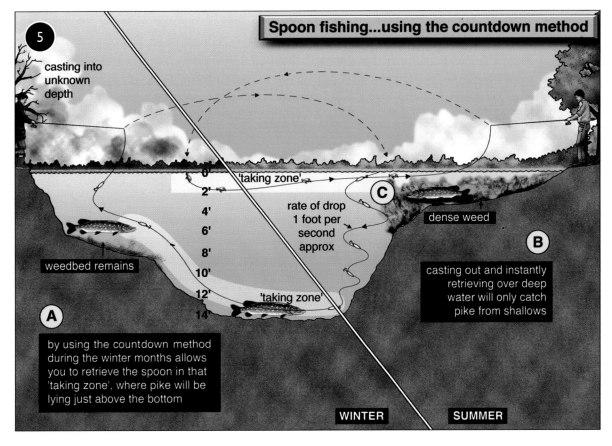

Spoon fishing...using the countdown method

5

casting into unknown depth

0'
'taking zone'

2'

4'

rate of drop 1 foot per second approx

C

dense weed

6'

8'

weedbed remains

10'

12'

'taking zone'

14'

B

casting out and instantly retrieving over deep water will only catch pike from shallows

A

by using the countdown method during the winter months allows you to retrieve the spoon in that 'taking zone', where pike will be lying just above the bottom

WINTER   SUMMER

It is imperative to keep those hook points razor sharp, so keep a small hand file in your waistcoat or tackle bag for regular honing.

during the summer months when water temperatures have increased and they are more active near the top. The trouble is so many anglers do not have any preconceived idea about depths when casting artificials and simply lob the lure out and commence retrieving straight away, as in Fig. B.

This is why learning to use the countdown method is so important. Your first cast (in unknown territory) is to ascertain the depth, so that every cast thereafter works the spoon within that taking zone which, we have already established, is around 2 feet above bottom. And it goes like this. When the spoon hits the surface allow it to free fall down to the bottom (using only slight forefinger control against the rim of the spool with the bale arm open) whilst counting it down. Should it take, for argument's sake, ten seconds before hitting bottom and the line

falling slack then, on the next cast, start retrieving on the count of eight. If the spoon picks up weed then start retrieving earlier – on the count of seven and so on. Don't simply retrieve in a monotonous, even-paced, winding action. Crank it fast, pause, give a twitch, let it free fall for a couple of feet, crank it fast again so it rises abruptly, pause to allow one or two downward flutters, crank it – and so on.

Now this countdown method really does work and it is the only sure way of maintaining presentation of sinking lures within a certain depth band. Obviously as the lure is wound towards the rod it rises and this you have to allow for either by retrieving slowly so it works parallel to the bottom, as in Fig. A, or by allowing it to free fall down again every so often to stay within the taking zone. The latter method often accounts for a pike actually on

the drop, as a following fish grabs hold while the spoon is fluttering downwards. Make a point of studying how your spoon works through clear water and you'll see that when fluttering backwards, spoons do look tantalizingly appealing.

Be ready to crank the reel like mad when this happens (there is a rather strange sensation like a gentle knocking at the rod end) and tighten up to the fish really firmly before attempting an upwards sweep of the rod. Even then the hooks often fall out because there is an enormous amount (up to 25 per cent) of stretch to be taken up in monofilament line on the strike. And the reality is that pike usually help in setting the hooks themselves by swimming away from the rod once they have grabbed the lure. So when the spoon is grabbed on the drop there is usually too much loose line out for a successful hook-up, but it is always worth trying. Incidentally, keep the reel's anti-reverse lever on at all times.

Whilst on the subject of setting the hooks, there is of course only one generally quite large treble on spoons which has to be at least as wide as the lure or the pike's jaws may miss getting pricked as they slide off the spoon. So remember to keep each hook point well sharpened (keep a small flat hand file handy in your jacket pocket) and, to help penetration, gently flatten each barb with a pair of pliers. Don't crunch them off; simply flatten them. And change the treble whenever it becomes misshapen or one of the points becomes impossible to sharpen. The cost is peanuts compared to the disappointment of a lost monster.

A little ruse worth trying when pike are repeatedly shying away is to take the treble off and replace with a baited single. Use a medium shank 2/0 (uptide extra hooks work well) to which has been added a slither of mackerel or the end half of a sand eel. It is a technique widely used abroad which also works with British pike (perch and zander too). Don't be afraid to experiment when fish are fickle. This trick gives them just that little something extra to hang on to that's real and has aroma.

As when working any lure I endeavour at all times, except when momentarily jerking the rod tip from side to side in order to impact maximum movement, to point the rod tip at the spoon. This is to ensure there is maximum torque on the line when a pike grabs hold so I can continue winding and striking all in one movement – and get those hooks to bite home. When working big spoons, hook penetration – as I have already intimated – is more crucial than with plugs and spinners. As a general rule plugs are equipped with more trebles, two or possibly three, while spinners are fitted with much smaller treble hooks than spoons, so there is less effort required in putting the hook points home.

Moreover in most cases I am certain the hook actually penetrates (if it's going to) on that initial slam as a pike attacks the spoon, so it is a case of keeping the line fully stretched and the rod well bent to ensure they are not shaken out. On a loose or slack line pike can effectively use the weight of the spoon as a disgorger when flaring their gills and shaking their head violently from side to side. This is why when a fish is lost all you feel on the rod tip is a couple of heavy thumps (head shaking) before the line goes slack. But never give up when this happens. Keep on casting over the same area and retrieving and, if anything, speed up the spoon's retrieve. Very often that same pike will have another go. It is nothing unusual to see a pike make several grabs during the retrieve until it either becomes successfully hooked or swims off in disgust when you lift the lure from the water. Even then it could snap hold on the very next cast so don't give up on a fish that is continually willing to follow. As I mentioned previously, try a sliver of fish on the hook, or quickly change over to a different colour or different actioned spoon.

The mood the predator is in, its hunting requirements at that time, the light intensity, barometric pressure, water temperature, water depth and weed density – all these things can make a difference, so it's always wise to experiment with different colours and sizes of spoons and then to fish them at varying depths until you come up with a winning formula for the day. But don't think this will work next time; always be prepared to experiment.

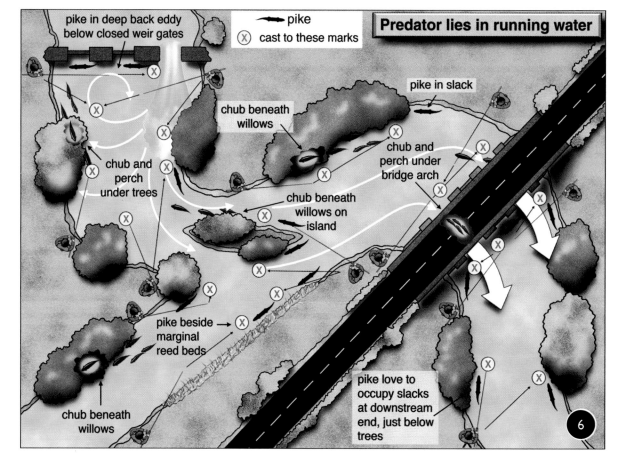

The principles of where to cast are not so different for still and running water. Consider Diag. 6, for instance, of a habitat-rich river, where most pike-lying areas or hotspots are easy to read. Very often perch, chub and pike will all be situated in close proximity to each other due to large features such as bridge arches, confluences, weir pools, sunken willows and reed lines. Learn to read the water carefully and study each part of the river before making a cast. Don't simply plonk the lure into the middle of the river and retrieve; think about where predators might be lying up in wait and, after creeping up stealthily, make accurate casts to specific features. Pike, in particular, often lie within mere feet of the bank, close up into the margins, and a clumsy lure fisherman will put his quarry on guard even before a cast is made. It makes sense therefore always to explore marginal lies first and then work progressively further out.

LIGHTER ARTIFICIALS

Much of what I have already said in relation to the way in which spoons are retrieved (using the countdown method), how the rod should be held, and casting to features, also applies to working lighter artificials such as spinners, spinning jigs and spinnerbaits. However there is a distinct difference between these lures. There is no doubt about it, the high-speed whirring action and accompanying vibratory pulses of spinners as opposed, say, to the lumbering wobble of a large spoon, is what really turns certain species on – small pike, chub and perch in particular. This is perhaps because the greater part of their natural diet consists of small fish which are continually darting about. Small revolving blade spinners such as the Mepps or Rublex range, together with other favourites like ABU's Droppen or Landa's Flipz X, all work wonderfully even when retrieved really slowly, which is often the preferred presentation for perch.

Being light, small spinners can easily be counted down like spoons and sinking plugs and worked immediately above bottom weed beds or snags, or in that really narrow, shallow layer of water between the surface film and surface-reaching weed beds. The only downside with most spinners (some like the Voblex have built-in anti-kink vanes) is that they encourage severe line twist, so remember to incorporate a plastic anti-kink vane in your wire trace. Pinching a swan shot on the line immediately above the trace swivel will also help to reduce kinking and add weight to gain extra distance when working tiny spinners, but it is fair to say that most work best without any additional weight.

If expecting only chub, perch or the migratory shad, then simply dispense with the wire trace in preference for monofilament straight through. In crystal-clear water you'll experience more hits, believe me. Another way of increasing the number of hits, especially from perch, is to bait the treble hook with a couple of small redworms, or a sliver of skin from a small silvery fish. Alternatively, and this works especially well for pike and zander, replace the treble hook of say a Mepps-type spinner of size 3 upwards with a large single, and bait with a lobworm, rubber worm, fish strip or a tiny fish. Predators hang on just that bit longer to baited spinners. Just you try it and see.

LANDING

Lastly perhaps a few words about landing predators hooked on spoons and spinners are needed, because terrible tangles detrimental to both the fish and the mesh of an expensive landing net can result.

Where possible, and especially with pike, I much prefer to hand a fish out wearing a flexible micro chainmail filleting glove on my left hand, by slipping four fingers into its left gill slit whilst pressing down firmly upon them with my thumb on the outside. Only with a real whopper would I bother netting it. In fact on most occasions I simply flip the hooks out using forceps whilst the fish is still in the water.

There are, however, one or two specialist predator landing nets on the market with treble-friendly meshes. These are worth seeking out if you cannot get used to handing out pike. They may also be useful if the type of waters you fish – steep-sided banks, or wide reed margins into deep water for instance – make the practice impossible.

Using the chinning method, rely on a micro chainmail (filleting) glove inserted into the pike's left gill opening for protecting your left hand whilst unhooking.

WORKING TOP-WATER LURES

As Autumn approaches many fisheries, particularly shallow rivers and lakes, meres, broads, ponds and pits, will still be nicely carpeted in surface plants – whether the ribbon weed and long flowing beds of rununculus of fast rivers, or amphibious bistort, broad-leaved potomotgeton and lilies of still waters, canals and sluggish river systems. Moreover many venues will be habitat rich in the form of overhanging alders, chestnut, beech and several different types of willow trees, whose branches actually lap the surface. In short, with a variety of features to cast to and with dense fry shoals taking refuge amongst this greenery to provide a regular food source for species like perch, chub and pike, there is no better time than throughout the months of summer, possibly even well into October if temperatures don't plummet drastically, for enjoying superlative action with artificial lures. Top-water lure fishing is probably the most exciting method of all, because working imitation mice, frogs, plugs and buzz baits actually across the surface or maybe just a foot beneath encourages the most spectacularly aggressive lunges, especially from pike which, from the moment they feel cold steel, provide some wonderful acrobatic action.

As long as water temperatures stay in the high 50s and 60-degree Fahrenheit range, the pike's metabolic rate remains high resulting in repeated leaps, crashes and tail-walks in an effort to rid itself of the hooks – provided you keep the pressure on.

Personally I just love to watch pike cavort and tail-walk, not really caring if they fling the hooks out as long as the action is hectic. OK, so I'll slow down when an obvious biggy grabs hold in order to obtain a trophy shot, but in most cases I purposely hold fish tight at the end of a run across the top, knowing full well that their powerful tail lashing will make them airborne. I guess this is what really turns me on and what I most like about top-water lure fishing; not so much the quality or size of fish expected, but rather their antics and the quality of technique used to capture them. This is one reason why I even use a 9½-foot fly rod to zoom large furry things across lilies or beside reed lines. Providing a 6-inch wire trace is joined to a 4–5-foot cast of 10lb monofilament, toothy predators like pike are easily catered for. (See also Method 15, 'Fly Rodding for Perch and Pike'.)

POPPERS

Many of the modern, large, ultrabuoyant deerhair fly creations with wonderful names like frog fly popper, fluffy mouse, floating frog, big-eyed marabou muddler, bullet frog, marabous mouse, sculpin, bass popper, bumble bee and so on, are quite heavy enough to be freelined short distances using an Avon rod/6lb line and fixed-spool reel combo for chub and small pike. A light carp rod (1½–1¾lb test curve) or spinning rod coupled with a 10lb test line is ideal where larger pike can be expected. Again simply add a 6-inch wire trace of around 15lb test and you can have some great fun wandering around a lily-clad lake or beside an overgrown river, casting close beside feature lies. If required, a BB or AA shot may be pinched on to the trace close up to really large extremely buoyant deerhair poppers, to obtain that extra casting distance. But, generally speaking, once they have been cast a few times and are wet (though still very buoyant) distance is not a problem.

Take time to experiment and endeavour, through rod-tip manipulation, to work life into each pattern by twitching, popping and gurgling it through the surface. Winding it in slowly with a momentous rhythm won't fool too many pike or chub. Quite simply top-water lure fishing can be as exciting or as humdrum as you choose to make it. It is restricted only by your level of adventure, opportunism and enthusiasm. Try not to think 'I'd better not cast into that awkward spot in case I loose a £2.99 popper' because, believe me, it's no coincidence that the largest predators choose to occupy the most inaccessible haunts – that's why they get so big. And don't say to yourself 'I'd better take a few livebaits along just in case they are not taking lures', or 'really big chub won't fall for lures so I'd better have a few natural baits like worms or slugs at the ready'. Please, please don't think in the negative. You are going to catch on lures and on the surface and that's it.

In fast-flowing rivers there is no need to fish at close range and possibly scare the inhabitants or limit your chances by catching just a single chub before moving on from prime feature swims where dense willows or alders hang well out over the water. Use the current to drift your floating popper downstream

Super-buoyant deerhair poppers like this fluffy mouse not only attract big chub up to the surface but pike too – so use a wire trace.

To cover all situations whilst working top-water lures during the summer months, you require a comprehensive collection of surface churners.

beneath overhanging branches 20–40 yards away to spots where it could possibly be cast, by allowing the current to peel off line from an open spool from a position well upstream. Straighten the line periodically to eradicate the shakiness created by current patterns and, when the popper is finally in position a little below the intended target area, commence the retrieve in short, jerky, erratic bursts, activated by the rod tip.

BAITCASTING OUTFITS

Whilst I just love working deerhair poppers on an Avon outfit amongst the snags and ever-changing habitat of running water there is a new challenge around every bend, and my absolute favourite top-water outfit comprises a one-piece 6-foot, American-style, trigger-grip-handle bait caster and baby multiplier reel loaded with 10lb test. For single-handed efficiency there is, in my opinion, nothing to touch these lovely little tools in both accuracy and the way in which their rigid action can impart lifelike movement to surface-popping lures.

Obviously light deerhair cannot be cast on such a multiplier and rod combo, but everything else designed for top-water action can. And because you cast, retrieve and play everything (except real monsters) using just one hand, everything – even modest 4–8lb pike – provides truly exciting sport. Small wonder that over on the other side of the Atlantic these little bait-casting sticks dominate freshwater predator fishing, particularly with species like black bass, walleyes and northerns, which are our own zander and pike. The trouble is, most free-

running baby multipliers are manufactured for the American lure enthusiast who unfortunately is actually rather cockhanded because he insists on using right-handed multipliers. That is to say he casts with his right hand but then (totally illogically) swaps the rod over to his left for the simple task of winding in. For all their skill and the level of expertise the Americans have brought to this exciting branch of lure fishing, I cannot for the life of me

work out why in basic terms they are so inept and with bait casting possess this weird mental blockage.

Fortunately there are a few left-handed baby multipliers around, some in current manufacture and some which are now collector's items. Tracking down a good one and paying through the nose for it is money well spent. I have several models, including the ABU Ambassador XLT2 and Shimano Bantams, but in practical terms I prefer the Ryobi T One (not a current model unfortunately) which suits me just fine because its press-and-flick thumb bar operated by the heel of the thumb instantly puts the reel into casting mode while the top of the thumb clamps firmly down upon the spool. I can find no more comfortable grip for hours of single-handed casting. This particular model also features magnetic brake control which ensures that only very rarely do overruns happen – perhaps once or twice only in a day's casting, that's all.

Unfortunately there are few baitcasting rods currently available on the British market designed to be specifically used with baby multipliers which is why I talked Ryobi Masterline into producing the Six Shooter, a 6-foot trigger-handled one-piece baitcaster that is positive enough in the tip to work even large lures but has an overall action that permits enjoyment from the smallest predators.

Incidentally don't try to make excessively long casts with a baitcasting outfit: 25–40 yards is the ideal range. Bringing your left hand over and wrapping it tightly around your right and over the very bottom end of the trigger-grip handle will provide a few extra yards, but this makes for tiring fishing – believe me. Concentrate on consistently accurate overhead single-handed casts along reed lines, beside and through patches of lilies, or tight alongside and even beneath overhanging branches, aiming to drop the lure into an imaginary 2-foot-square box by braking the spool with the thumb as the lure descends to the surface with a resounding splash. Then from this moment on think predator. The lure's arrival should have aroused any fish lurking close by so build on this by working the lure in an erratic, wounded-fish-come-crippled-mouse

mode. Move it a little, let it pause, twitch it, crank it fast, plop it, make it gurgle, pause again, and so on. Get used to working that rod tip like the extension of your arm it should now have become. And get ready to slam the tip backwards and up high in order to set the hooks when a head appears from nowhere to engulf the lure.

Unless the fish dives, and in the process pulls the hook home itself, the job is yours. So strike and crank fast keeping yours arms high up above your head to alleviate any chance of slack line until you are certain those hooks are well in. Then enjoy the fight. Those who repeatedly suffer lost fish on a monofilament reel line due to the stretch factor might like to try a low-diameter, non-stretch braid. Though expensive, braid is incredibly responsive and the lack of any cushioning does take some getting used to, but those hooks do go in and instantly – or they miss altogether. Something well worth mentioning here is to use braid with a breaking strain of at least twice what you would use in monofilament. This provides a margin of safety due to lack of elasticity and you won't find the fish fight any less for it.

For those who do not fancy shelling out on a baitcasting combo, an 8–9-foot crisp-action, two-piece carbon spinning rod and fixed-spool reel holding 10–11lb test monofilament will do nicely. But avoid using all-through action or soft-tipped spinning rods because it is difficult to make top-water lures come alive with them. Far too much of your arm movement will be cushioned instead of being transmitted to the lure. This is a most important point when the artificial is sitting there on the surface connected to the rod tip by 40 yards of stretchy monofilament. Then again, although braided line partners wonderfully with multipliers there is nothing to stop you enjoying the qualities on a fixed-spool reel.

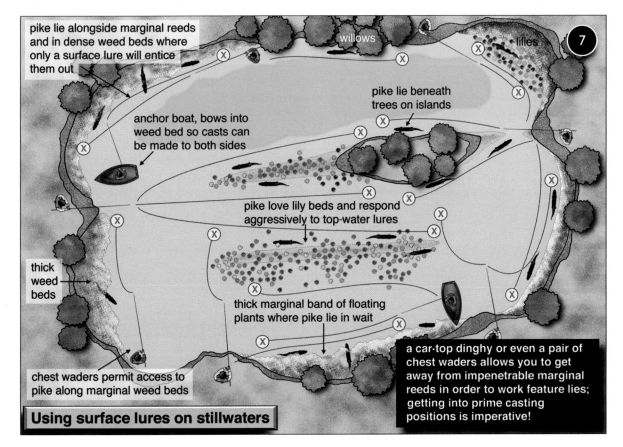

pike lie alongside marginal reeds and in dense weed beds where only a surface lure will entice them out

willows

lilies

7

pike lie beneath trees on islands

anchor boat, bows into weed bed so casts can be made to both sides

pike love lily beds and respond aggressively to top-water lures

thick weed beds

pike lie beneath trees on islands

thick marginal band of floating plants where pike lie in wait

chest waders permit access to pike along marginal weed beds

a car-top dinghy or even a pair of chest waders allows you to get away from impenetrable marginal reeds in order to work feature lies; getting into prime casting positions is imperative!

Using surface lures on stillwaters

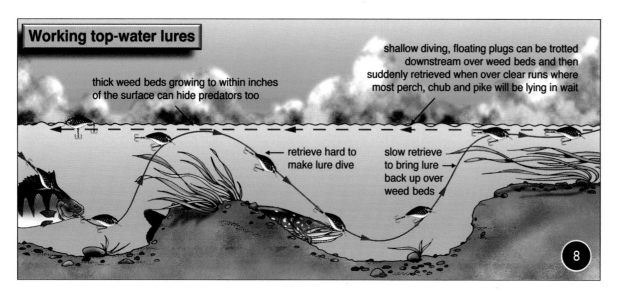

Working top-water lures

thick weed beds growing to within inches of the surface can hide predators too

shallow diving, floating plugs can be trotted downstream over weed beds and then suddenly retrieved when over clear runs where most perch, chub and pike will be lying in wait

retrieve hard to make lure dive

slow retrieve to bring lure back up over weed beds

8

(Opposite): *John caught this 70lb perch from Lake Nasser on a Rapala Magnum.*

Make a point of using these specialist surface poppers and you'll be amazed at the density of weed and reed beds through which pike can attack and be extracted. So don't be scared of casting for want of losing a lure. Nothing ventured is indeed nothing gained.

GET OUT AFLOAT

To obtain the most fun and realize the greatest potential from all still-water endeavours, get out afloat where possible. A cartop dinghy, for instance, puts you within casting distance of so many pike-holding features that are simply not workable from the bank. Consider Diag. 7 of a summer's lake; it could even be one of my local Norfolk Broads. You'll see that even a pair of chest-high waders (about the cost of a medium-priced fixed-spool reel) can get you into prime casting positions several feet out from the shoreline so that artificials can be worked beside and parallel to marginal weed beds in which pike hide up ready to ambush shoals of small fish that swim by.

USING THE FLOW

In the same way that the current can be used to drift deerhair poppers downstream to feature lies when river fishing, plugs may be presented similarly, particularly out-and-out floaters which are not likely to get hung up around subsurface weed on the retrieve. However, floaters which also dive shallow (just 1–2 feet), like Heddon's Meadow Mouse,

Ryobi's Mugger or Manns' 1-Minus, can be used most effectively for exploring holes in the river bed between weedy shallows by using the flow to work them into position before retrieving (see Diag. 8). In other words you simply trot them downstream like a float until over the desired spot, then commence the retrieve. Simple, isn't it, and it's fun too!

WEED-FREE LURES

Buzz baits, whose churning propeller and plastic skirt create massive top-water disturbance, also work favourably in rivers but are more effective in still water amongst lily pads and along reed lines or beds of surface weeds (see Diag. 7). Weed-free models equipped with fine wire hook guards are particularly recommended. So find a specialist tackle dealer who stocks a comprehensive range and who uses them himself. Amongst other surface churners the Buzz 'n' Frog is a good puller as is the Thundertoad which can virtually be wound through anything, just like Manns' Ghost. Both possess soft plastic bodies that conceal hooks, the barbs of which only come into play when the jaws of a pike clamp down hard. It's all clever stuff.

The colourful, churning propeller and pulsating plastic skirts which adorn surface-working buzz baits are not only weed free, they drive pike wild.

BOAT FISHING

A pike hooked on Rockland Broad in Norfolk portrays the excitement and tranquillity of boat fishing.

A FLOATING PLATFORM

It's not until I start sorting through a multitude of pike fishing colour transparencies on the light box, taken over close on thirty years of exploring the Norfolk Broads, that I realize fully the extent to which boat fishing has played a part. The bank fishing shots are outnumbered by at least ten to one by those taken afloat. But then in truth most of the large pike to over 30lb that have come my way from Broads completely fringed in dense reed beds and unapproachable marshlands could only have been caught through boat fishing. Much the same could be related to Scottish lochs and Irish loughs, the Lake District waters and in particular our enormous man-made reservoir fisheries where fishing from the shore could only be described as scratching the surface.

Being drawn naturally to water and after spending a couple of years in the merchant navy some while back, I would always prefer to boat fish large expanses of water if only for the option of covering a greater area. But then as I also enjoy fisheries of just a few acres from the platform of a boat, I guess I simply love being on the water. Quite apart from the fact that my largest pike, bream, trout and roach/rudd hybrid have all been taken from a boat, plus my best bream haul ever which included no fewer than nine over 10lb plus a 2¼lb perch and a 4lb roach/bream hybrid, I think I am actually more at harmony with water when sitting quietly upon it. At peace with the world, you might say.

Boat fishing also allows you to get away from other more noisy anglers (so don't go afloat with someone who is either accident prone or a natural klonker) and to explore areas where the fish are rarely bothered. Unlike with bank fishing where everything has to be packed away each time before moving to a new spot, if like me you are the wandering, opportunist type, boat fishing is brilliant because you simply lift up the mudweights and either drift silently downwind to a new area or get the oars out with not the slightest detackling of gear.

However, you do need to be quite disciplined and reasonably well organized to enjoy boat fishing fully, especially when sharing with a friend. So before we become involved in some methods of approach dedicated to boat fishing, let's chew over the pros and cons of various crafts.

THE BOAT

If you are considering a cartop dinghy for your personal use, as opposed to sharing it with others, then the choice lies between a traditional V-shaped and a twin hull. In practical terms, a simple V-hull dinghy will usually be lighter and considerably easier to row in a straight line than the twin hull. However it will be nowhere near as stable, so be careful when selecting your fishing platform. There are many other considerations to take into account.

First, I would suggest a length of no less than 10 feet (boats always look more roomy on land, but wait until you get them in the water) even if it is only going to be occupied by just yourself. A glass-fibre dinghy even with buoyancy chambers weighs considerably less than a traditional clinker-built equivalent, so don't go all sentimental and purchase a waterlogged monster which you cannot manoeuvre single handed on to a pair of luggage bars tightly fitted to your estate car's guttering.

Larger, roomier, rowing dinghies not suitable for rooftop transportation can of course be accommodated nicely on a trailer. If you shop around the boat yards at sale time, there are always good deals on boat and trailer combos of all kinds on offer. Make sure you will be able to manhandle the boat off the trailer into the water and back on again single handed even down an overgrown sloping bankside if necessary without a slipway. This is most important, because you will no doubt want to fish remote areas of water where the convenience of a slipway doesn't exist.

Aluminium boats, though expensive, are worth considering as well as glass models. Many are based on designer American fishing boats and are exceptionally well laid out with little in the way of maintenance to worry about.

Seating

What I like most about top-notch American-style boats is the seating arrangements. You won't find many Americans squatting low down on hard wooden seats with their knees wrapped around their necks, suffering an aching back and stiff legs for hour upon hour in the freezing cold. Reasons

John hands over the rods to be carefully stored by DJ Bruno Brooks, at the start of a day's pike fishing on Bruno's beautiful lake in Southern Ireland.

enough for Wilson, when I had a boat-building friend knock me up a 13-foot glass boat specifically for fishing many years back, to incorporate a comfortable, pedestal-type office chair within the centre seat. Actually all he needed to do was drill a 1½-inch diameter hole through the centre seat to accommodate the pedestal chair's stem and a second hole of the same diameter in a block which fitted on to the deck. The chair (you can pick one up cheap from second-hand office supply companies) which due to the telescopic stem can be adjusted for height, is easily slipped into both holes when required and does not stay on the boat. Simple but

unbelievably effective. If you boat fish regularly from your own craft it is an extra comfort I can thoroughly recommend which, in addition, allows you to fish more efficiently – in a full circle – on account of sitting higher up.

You must have noticed when sitting on standard seats low down to the water, especially in boats with high gunnels, that it is virtually impossible to hold the rod tip down to sink the line when float fishing or keep the rod tip low whilst spinning. Well, you can if you are sitting higher up on an office chair. Try it and see. You'll then find out over short distances you can even row from this raised position.

Oars and Engine

Whilst talking rowing, it is well worthwhile investing in a good pair of oars and installing a pair of rowlocks which actually fit the protective rubber collar on the oars. There is nothing worse than continually pulling the oars from oversize rowlocks whilst trying to get a move on, particularly against a headwind. Remember not to keep them on the boat if it is tied to a permanent mooring. Get into the habit of taking them home, along with your oars, engine and petrol tank.

With regard to outboard engines, you really do need to put some thought into what your particular requirements might be. If, for instance, you are not

Notice how in his own specially designed boat, John sits comfortably on a pedestal chair and not the middle seat. This is most important for tackle control and comfort.

likely to venture further afield than smallish local lakes or short stretches of river my advice would be simply to stick with a pair of oars; purchasing an outboard for motoring just a few hundred yards will prove to be more trouble than it's worth.

If, on the other hand, you fancy trailing your boat further afield or even abroad, to explore the wild, exciting loughs of Ireland or Scottish lochs for instance, a reliable petrol-driven outboard motor of around 5 horse power will do the business. You'll need a life jacket too. Should the major use of your outboard be float trailing for pike (see Method 27) however, on large gravel pit complexes and man-made trout reservoirs which allow pike fishing during the winter months, I would immediately recommend that you invest in an electric outboard. The American-made Minn Kota range which includes a variable (ten settings) throttle facility (to work at really slow speeds) are simply tailor made for slow-mode trailing, plus for getting from A to B silently. These electric outboards will run all day on a fully charged heavy-duty car battery. Enough said – except that they are not cheap.

OTHER EQUIPMENT

You can load your boat with as much or as little paraphernalia as you wish for a fishing trip, but remember that a boat seems to fill up in no time. Think carefully about the kind of expedition you are planning and what you will really need for a successful outing. Here are a few tips from yours truly, based on years of experience.

Fish Finders

Having used these marvels of electronic wizardry for many many years now, I would feel decidedly at a disadvantage if I set out upon open water without one. I rely on mine, not, surprisingly, as you might assume, for its fish-finding qualities but for the continual read-out of bottom contours it gives for whichever direction you point the boat.

Companies famous for the quality of high-resolution fish finders they produce are Humminbird and Eagle, both of which have large outlets in the UK. Fish finders operate by sonar and the reception comes from a device called the transducer which, via a rubber suction cap, is quickly installed just below the waterline on the transom or side of vertically sided boats such as punts. The transducer sends out ultrasonic pulses which, upon hitting the bottom (and fish), bounce back to provide a read-out upon the display screen. It instantly provides you with exact depth, bottom density and topography, weed beds and, of course, the existence of fish – and at what depth. Most models suitable for freshwater are portable and battery run, either rechargeable or dry cell. They are well worth the outlay.

Mudweights

A common denominator with most hire craft unfortunately, particularly fishing dinghies, is that the mudweights supplied are rarely heavy enough or the ropes long enough. There is nothing more frustrating than being blown away from a hotspot which is really producing, when a reasonably steady wind gets up, due to both or either of these two inadequacies.

How to make your own mudweights

1/4" mild steel bent to form securing lug

A

use 2-gallon tub for general situations
use 3-gallon tub to really anchor boat down in strong wind conditions

1/4" diameter holes 2 or 3 inches apart

fill with concrete mix to within 1/4" of rim

finished mudweight

C

2- or 3-gallon plastic bucket

9

B

lug drops down into soft earth or sand

bend steel rod to secure in concrete mix

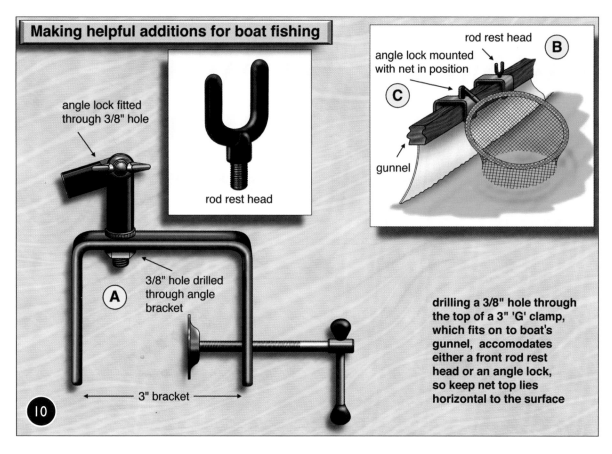

Making helpful additions for boat fishing

angle lock fitted through 3/8" hole

rod rest head

3/8" hole drilled through angle bracket

(A)

3" bracket

10

rod rest head

(B)

angle lock mounted with net in position

(C)

gunnel

drilling a 3/8" hole through the top of a 3" 'G' clamp, which fits on to boat's gunnel, accomodates either a front rod rest head or an angle lock, so keep net top lies horizontal to the surface

In a dinghy hired from Whispering Reeds boatyard at Hickling Broad, note how John has arranged and organized everything prior to setting off for a comfortable bream session.

To remedy this I have for many years now always taken my own pair of mudweights shackled to 30-feet-long ½-inch-diameter soft nylon ropes (thin ropes really bite into your hands, especially in cold weather). My mudweights are actually home made by filling 2- and 3-gallon (I have two sets of varying weights) plastic tubs with cement. Prior to filling, two ¼-inch-diameter holes are made in the centre of the bottom of each plastic bucket so that an exaggerated U of ¼-inch steel rod (see Diag. 9, Fig. A) can be threaded through to form a lug around which the end of the rope is fixed. The bucket is then upended upon soft earth or sand so the steel lug drops down into its correct position (Fig. B) and filled with a good cement mix.

Once set, you have a fabulous designer mudweight covered in plastic (the bucket) which

helps protect the side of your boat when hoisted overboard (Fig. C). But for goodness sake don't forget to swish the weight around before lifting over the gunnel, or you'll deposit a foul-smelling mixture of sticky bottom silt all over the boat.

Another source of really excellent mudweights is to keep your eyes open in old junk shops or at car boot sales for the old-fashioned steel weights, which are now fashionably used by some as doorstops. If you can buy a pair weighing around 25–35lb apiece at a reasonable price, don't hesitate. Being relatively small for their weight, they make splendid mudweights and really bite deeply into bottom silt.

Helpful Additions

Rod rests suitable for trailing and trolling for pike are mentioned in Methods 27 and 29 respectively. You

can however quite easily produce home-made front rod rests and a special keep net angle lock for gunwale fixing. To make a gunwale bracket (see Diag. 10), drill a ⅜-inch hole through the top of a small G clamp (Fig. A). (These are available from any good hardware shop.) This accommodates either the front rod rest head of your choice (Fig. B) or the special angle top tilt built into top-of-the-range keep nets, allowing the net ring to lie horizontal to the surface (Fig. C). For keep nets not fitted with this device, simply screw a commercially made angle lock into the G clamp and secure as for the rod top with a ⅜-inch BSF thread nut.

In case of torrential, or even consistently heavy rain it is wise to pack a couple of plastic bin liners in your tackle bag so that items likes your camera and spare clothing can be kept perfectly dry. Just in case darkness looms over the water before you can get the motor started or work out which boat dyke (from dozens that look exactly the same) your craft was tied up in, a small tool kit and powerful torch are indispensable additions.

For unhooking fish whilst boat fishing, so they are returned in as pristine a condition as they came out,

I take along a 6-foot by 3-foot roll of ½-inch-thick dense camping foam to go over the boat's duckboards. Not only does it protect the flanks from loss of mucus and disturbed scales should it flap about, but a soft protective flooring also cushions your own movements. This is important, especially when trying to catch spooky specimens inhabiting shallow and clear-water fisheries.

As far as food is concerned, I believe in keeping warm and always go out in a boat with two large Thermos flasks – one containing black coffee and the other filled with boiling hot water for adding to instant meals such as Pot Noodles. It's amazing how

THE ART OF SILENCE

Many anglers seem to forget that sound waves carry miraculously through water. The fish hear every little tap and bang on the side of the boat, most of which are totally unnecessary. So practise the art of being quiet and reduce shuffling about to an absolute minimum.

Another cardinal sin is not storing or laying everything out in an organized manner within the boat before pushing off. A quick getaway by dumping everything in haphazardly and instantly pulling the starter cord will cost you dearly later on when the accompanying noise of repositioning tackle bags, seats, bait boxes and setting up rods is quite liable to scare anything within 50 yards. So take time, while the boat is still tied up, to store everything where it won't slide of bang about. Set the landing net up, put bait boxes at the ready and ensure the mudweights are positioned for lowering at both bows and stern. Finally, make up the rods and rigs required, storing them lengthways inside the boat so that as you approach the intended area (from an upwind direction) the boat can be positioned side-on to the wind and the mudweights lowered simultaneously with the absolute minimum of noise thereafter.

After all, if you were creeping up on a crafty, spooky chub living in a clear flowing stream, you wouldn't walk right up to the swim, crunch your tackle bag down, rig the rod up and then expect to catch it – would you? Well, boat fishing is no different.

This massive 13¾lb bream was part of a boat-caught haul that included nine double-figure bream, all taken on lobtails beneath a slider float rig.

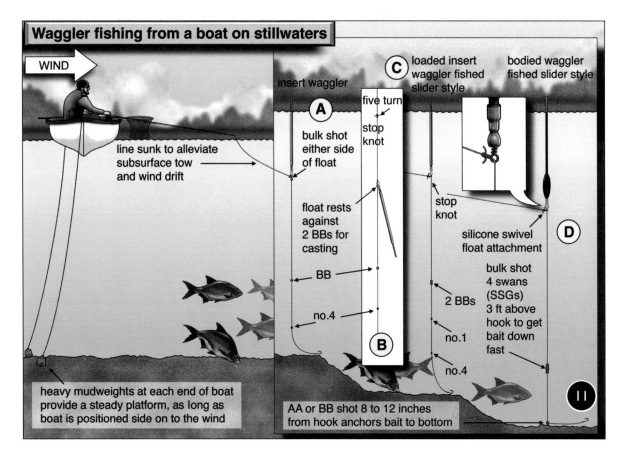

Waggler fishing from a boat on stillwaters

WIND

line sunk to alleviate subsurface tow and wind drift

heavy mudweights at each end of boat provide a steady platform, as long as boat is positioned side on to the wind

insert waggler

loaded insert waggler fished slider style

bodied waggler fished slider style

five turn stop knot

bulk shot either side of float

float rests against 2 BBs for casting

BB

no.4

stop knot

silicone swivel float attachment

bulk shot 4 swans (SSGs) 3 ft above hook to get bait down fast

2 BBs

no.1

no.4

AA or BB shot 8 to 12 inches from hook anchors bait to bottom

---

good they taste when you are out in the freezing cold, especially if you stir in a spoonful of curry powder and take along some crispy bread rolls for dunking! They are far more warming than cheese sandwiches anyway.

Clothing

Regardless of what the weather is like when you set off, always take along a set of waterproofs in the shape of a three-quarter-length coat and overtrousers, even in the summer months. It is downright dangerous erecting a brolly within the confines of a small fishing dinghy as many have found to their cost including, I am sorry to say, this writer – so be warned. During the winter months, being both dry and warm is of course imperative so you need to be kitted up with good quality waterproofs in the shape of three-quarter-length coat and overtrousers, or an all-in-one

waterproof suit with a fleecy, one-piece body warmer underneath. Better still in my view is a bib and brace which incorporates overtrousers, covered with a three-quarter-length jacket with a built-in hood. Then if our variable winter weather suddenly starts to improve halfway through the day with a drastic rise in air temperature, you don't have to sit there sweating uncomfortably; you simply remove your top coat.

As an enormous amount of body heat is lost via the head, I recommend a warm hat, preferably one with a peak, thus eradicating the need to be constantly squinting against reflective glare. I always take a pair of Polaroid sunglasses along when boat fishing, not necessarily to see through clear water, although they are handy for watching the reactions of predators following the bait or lure, but more for visual comfort. To enjoy bird-watching, a pair of

binoculars is also always taken along. Indeed, when exploring vast, remote areas of water I probably spend as much time watching the antics of our feathered friends as I do actually fishing.

As cold feet can be an acute and sometimes painful problem, I suggest a good pair of thermally insulated, waterproof boots, often referred to as moon boots because to allow for the extra thick bottom insert plus foam and synthetic lined inners, these boots end up looking two or three sizes larger. But really – who cares?

Gloves are a handy option too if only to wear after hooking on baits and unhooking pike, which leaves your hands sopping wet and freezing cold. Obviously a dry piece of old towelling is worth taking along too. Neoprene gloves without or with the tips of the fingers removed (for extra sensitivity) are a most worthwhile investment for boat fishing and as back-up for extra warmth during long hours of inactivity and for rowing in cold winds. I also own a pair of thermal, fleece-lined mittens. Well, why get cold if you don't really have to? I prefer to leave the macho image to the likes of Clint Eastwood.

Waggler Fishing

I have covered working lures from a boat and fly rodding afloat elsewhere in the book. In addition, all those methods concerning working wobbled deadbaits, float trailing, downrigger trolling, basic trolling, drift fishing and presenting float-fished roaming livebaits from a boat have also all been given exhaustive coverage, so see those respective methods which all relate to catching predators whilst afloat. What I have not covered, however, is waggler fishing in still waters from a boat and, in particular, slider float fishing for our non-predatory species.

Let's start with some basic rules. The first is being able to control the float rig by sinking the line to counteract subsurface tow and wind drift. You need

A superb 2lb-plus perch which also shared a liking for lobtails presented beneath a slider float on the lake bed in 13 feet of water.

to be sitting comfortably and up reasonably high to achieve this (not low down on the seats) so take along a high folding chair, or doctor the middle seat to accept an old pedestal office chair as I suggested earlier. Then cast beyond the baited area and quickly dunk the rod tip a foot beneath the surface and speedily crank the reel handle a few turns in order to get all the line sunk immediately. Keep the rod tip low to the water (see Method 13, 'Waggler Fishing'). Good float control is imperative when sitting in a rocking boat. However, do remember that if you keep too tight a line between float and rod, when the

boat swings gently from side to side on the mudweight ropes, the float tip is liable to be pulled under, registering a false bite, and the bait dragged unnaturally through bottom debris.

This is why for general fishing in depths of up to say 10–11 feet (within the fixed float capabilities of a 13- or 14-foot waggler rod) the best rig is a tipped or insert waggler set up (as shown in Diag. 11, Fig. A) with most of the shot bulked around the bottom ring and just a couple of small shots down the line so the bait is presented just off bottom. To lay the bait hard on, especially effective when after bream, fish a foot

over depth and fix the lowest shot within 10–12 inches of the hook.

Slider Float Fishing

For depths beyond the capabilities of the fixed float, say 12 feet plus, a sliding waggler is recommended – particularly a loaded, insert waggler which, due to its loaded base, requires only minimal shots down the line, so that bites both on the drop and on the bottom are registered (as Fig. B). See how the float rests against the top shot for casting, with a monofilament (same as reel line) five-turn sliding stop knot tied on at swim depth (Fig. C). When species like rudd occupy the warmer upper water layers during the summer months, start with the float set just a few feet deep and slowly increase depth in increments of a foot or so, until bites indicate the level at which the shoal is hanging. Remember to wet the sliding stop knot and reel line with saliva before gently moving because heat produced through friction could weaken it.

Once you have dunked the rod tip beneath the surface to sink the line after casting, remember to open the bale arm immediately in order that the line peels from the reel as the shots take the bait down. Shaking the rod gently often expedites this. Remember also that once the stop knot comes up against the float's end ring, bites on the drop will be indicated if the tip fails to settle at its lowest position on time. So strike at once in a sweeping sideways motion – just as you would if fishing from the shore.

When clear water conditions dictate that you need to fish at distance into deep water from the boat for bream which really want the bait nailed to the bottom, use the heavier slider rig shown in Fig. D. This illustrates a long-bodied peacock waggler with a shotting capacity of, say, four swan shots which are pinched on just 3 feet above the hook, with a BB or an AA only 8–12 inches from the hook. The stop

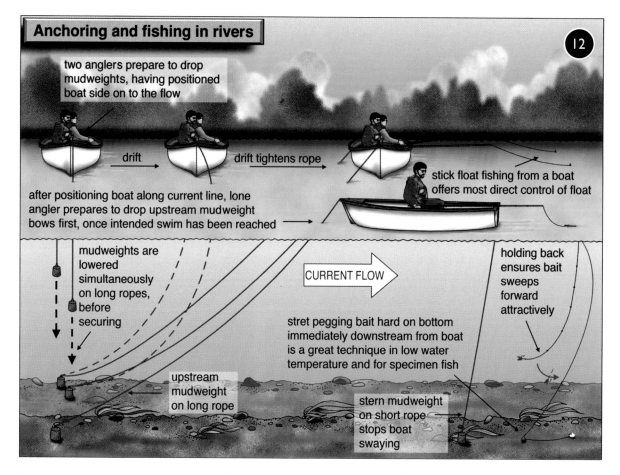

Anchoring and fishing in rivers

two anglers prepare to drop mudweights, having positioned boat side on to the flow

drift

drift tightens rope

after positioning boat along current line, lone angler prepares to drop upstream mudweight bows first, once intended swim has been reached

stick float fishing from a boat offers most direct control of float

mudweights are lowered simultaneously on long ropes, before securing

CURRENT FLOW

holding back ensures bait sweeps forward attractively

stret pegging bait hard on bottom immediately downstream from boat is a great technique in low water temperature and for specimen fish

upstream mudweight on long rope

stern mudweight on short rope stops boat swaying

knot is set so that the lowest shot actually rests on the bottom and thus anchors the bait down. This is most important if seeking specimen bream that refuse to inhale a dragging bait.

Due to the enormous angle of line between rod tip and bait, and this is only accentuated the further and deeper you fish, I recommend you crank the reel handle like a maniac for several turns when the float tip disappears before leaning the rod back into a sweeping strike. It makes all the difference, believe me, and picks up sufficient line for the hook to be driven home. This is particularly important when presenting large baits like a lobtail or breadflake on a size 8–6 hook, whereas only minimal force is required for setting a size 16 hook holding two maggots.

Stret Pegging and Stick Float Fishing in Rivers

Catching dace, roach, hybrids, bream, chub, barbel, even the occasional sea trout, tench and carp from a river whilst anchored in a boat immediately upstream of the swim is an absolute delight. You can enjoy holding back a stick float with ultra sensitivity, being directly upstream and not sitting across the flow of the bank, or you can lay baits both large or small hard on the bottom using the deadly stret pegging method. See Method 10, 'Stick Float Fishing', and Method 11, 'Stret Pegging', for technique and tackle details because I have covered both in detail. What is most important though is actually anchoring the boat in a strong flow.

If you are alone, set the boat bows into the current well above the run you intend fishing and stop rowing

or cut the motor. Quietly walk to the bows and lower a mudweight gently down to the bottom once the boat has drifted to the desired position. Pay out extra rope to encourage an angle between bows and mudweight. If tied on a short vertical rope the mudweight will quickly lift up or bounce free and you will have drifted over the very spot you intended fishing. Get it right first time. With a length of rope out equivalent to around twice swim depth (more in really fast water) secure the bow's mudweight and lower the stern mudweight directly down to the bottom on a short, more or less vertical rope and secure.

When sharing a boat so that two can fish immediately downstream, follow the procedure for approaching the swim with the boat positioned sideways on to the flow. If the anglers then stand one at each end with mudweights at the ready, both can be lowered down to the bottom simultaneously. Due to the extra current pressure with the boat anchored side on, each must pay out plenty of line (at least twice swim depth) for the boat to hold position. It sounds a bit of a rigmarole but in practice becomes second nature after a while. When you want to move position further down the run, simply lift the weights simultaneously and use the current to drift quietly down river (see Diag. 12).

Boat fishing in this way on my local tidal rivers is not only effective for catching roach and bream but pike also. My favourite routine is to stret peg a half or whole deadbait quite close to the boat (see Diag. 38, page 91) on one outfit, presented a little to one side, and on the second outfit trot a livebait beneath a sliding float rig (see Diag. 97, Fig. B, page 188) set to fish the bait a foot or so above bottom.

While shooting 'Go Fishing' from a punt anchored in the Hampshire Avon at Christchurch in search of sea trout, John found that precise anchoring was critical.

FLOAT FISHING

FLOATER FISHING

There are, in all probability, more diversions, tricks and ruses to try when floater fishing than in most freshwater techniques. In high summer when water temperatures peak, there is no better time for luring chub, carp and, to a much lesser extent, oddities like golden orfe up to the surface where they can be caught on floaters. You can add dace, and occasionally roach, to the species already mentioned though tackle and rigs must of course be drastically scaled down. Everything else nevertheless applies.

FREELINING

If you enjoy stalking fish at close range in overgrown waters, carp in particular, then try freelining. Whilst it may be old hat to some anglers and obviously cannot be practised on heavily fished lakes and pits where everyone has two or three rods spread out over the margins and spends the day walking from one bivi to another chatting with neighbours, it remains amongst the deadliest of techniques. But it requires quietness. What you soon learn from observation whilst floater fishing is that carp quickly become spooked by line coming from the floater whether it is on the surface or sunk beneath. So marginal freelining in particular, where you can lower a floater vertically on to the surface from above, minus the accompanying floating line and a weighted controller, creates a large proportion of immediate and exceptionally confident bites (see Diag. 13, Fig. A).

What takes time, of course, is working yourself stealthily into a marginal position without scaring feeding carp and then ensuring that only a few inches of the rod tip extend beyond the shrubbery (unless there is a thick sedge or reed line amongst which to hide its stark outline – fish are looking up into brightness remember, while we peer down into much lower light values) and the bait can literally be gently lowered on to the surface as a carp comes slurping along sucking down your free offerings. Indeed it is often possible to refrain from lowering the bait until a particular large specimen comes into view. There is really no need for continual casting around and retrieving. You simply lower the floater gently on to the surface as the fish approaches. To reach fish that will not come within dunking range, flick the bait over a broken rush or reed stem (which acts like a built-in swing tip) so the line hangs down vertically (Diag. 1, Fig. B). When carp are working through

Freelining...surface baits for carp

13

always keep low down behind the marginal screen of reeds, sedges or rushes

A — bait hangs directly below rod tip

B

when carp won't come within lowering range, flick bait over a broken reed stem so the line hangs down vertically

C

line rests unseen across lily pads with floating bait eased into small gap or wound back to rest against a lily pad

In a carp lake covered in lilies there's little to beat the suspense, anticipation and excitement of freelining floating baits amongst the pads – but concealment is vital.

lilies, the same ruse applies except that the line rests unseen across the pads with the bait eased into a tiny gap or wound back so it rests up against a pad (as in Fig. C).

Stalking

Close-range freelining is real nail-biting stuff where absolute stealth and camouflage are essential and where even a sudden arm or body movement, or a snapping twig, will result in the carp slowly doing a disappearing trick. So be warned. Dress appropriately in drab colours and wear an old pair of trainers instead of wellies or waders which clump along. Shooting rats around my own two overgrown and well-stocked carp lakes with my old 410 constantly keeps me in touch with just how sensitive to vibrations and sudden movements wildlife can be, both fish and rodents. I can, for instance, take several minutes to cover a 10-yard span from one tree to another along the lake margins without scaring carp slurping merrily away in mere inches of water, but somehow a certain body movement will give the game away to the rats.

My goal is to pretend my life depends on achieving a one-to-one ratio: a dead rat for every cartridge fired. This is how it would be in a perfect world if I were to become totally engrossed in shooting rats. Now don't get the wrong idea here. It's not the price of cartridges, merely that a careless footfall or hurried movement instantly has the rat scurrying for cover without chance of a shot. But it's all good fun and a great learning curve for anyone who also loves to stalk carp. In addition, when stalking there is no place for rod rests, stool and bedchairs. You creep and crawl and when settled, kneel throughout, use your unhooking mat, holding the rod with the bale arm closed (adjust the reel's clutch accordingly) and a loop of line in your free hand which permits the carp to take a little loose line whilst getting its head down. Only then is the strike made. And hang on!

There are few carp variants equal in beauty to this double-figure silver metallic common, which sucked in Nick Fletcher's floating cat treats.

On days when you have much of the water to yourself it pays to introduce floaters into the margins of numerous (a couple of dozen say) swims and then rotate each throughout the session, moving on to another in order to allow the commotion of landing or losing a fish to subside and the carp to resume feeding with confidence again before perhaps returning when all is calm. All of this applies of course to golden orfe and to still-water chub, arguably the wiliest adversary of them all.

RODS AND REELS

A quick reference about tackle is perhaps in order here because close-range fishing demands a rod that will arch over quickly into a full bend and thus suppress the lunges of a fish panicking away. For species like chub and small carp an 11-foot Avon-actioned rod coupled to a small fixed-spool reel and 6lb test is absolutely ideal. However, for carp which reach into double figures and larger you need the backbone of a 1¾–2lb test curve rod and lines in the 10–12lb bracket. I prefer 11-foot models for overgrown spots and a 12-footer for picking up line across lily patches or distances beyond 30 yards. Reels in the 2500–3000 size format which have wide spools to ensure line evaporates in loose coils are the perfect partner, as long as the slipping clutch mechanism is super smooth.

RUNNING WATER

In rivers chub are most willing risers to baits such as breadcrust and wasp cake, particularly during warm sunny conditions and, apart from the odd spot from which a bait can be dunked (off a high bank, through the branches of a tree, or beside a raft of rubbish or cut weeds), more success is achieved by purposely keeping them at a distance using the current to drift down freelined offerings of loose feed plus the hook bait. As long as the line is treated with mucilin and permits the bait to float naturally with the surface currents, river chub are nowhere near so spooky as their still-water counterparts. Incidentally, try an air-injected lobworm or two on the same hook (for casting weight) when chub are hitting on the surface. You'll be amazed at the response. There is of course nothing to stop you weaning river chub on to smaller floaters once breadcrust wanes such as mixer biscuits, or floating sweetcorn (hair rigged for super-wary specimens) or casters. Dace especially really respond to the latter in warm weather and for both casting and ultimate control particularly of small offerings, some sort of floating controller positioned 2 to 4 feet up the line from the bait is imperative. It is in fact the next stage from simple freelining tactics.

FLAT FLOAT CONTROLLERS

As can be seen from Diag. 14 a controller fished flat on the surface made from either plain sections of peacock quill, common reed or the much heavier stained hardwood dowel of ⅓-inch diameter and attached to the line with a wide band of silicone rubber at each end, is the ideal close-range float. Whether after dace in a fast river or flicking small floaters out to chub or carp in still waters further out and beyond freelining distances, the flat float provides an incredibly sensitive and unobtrusive controller,

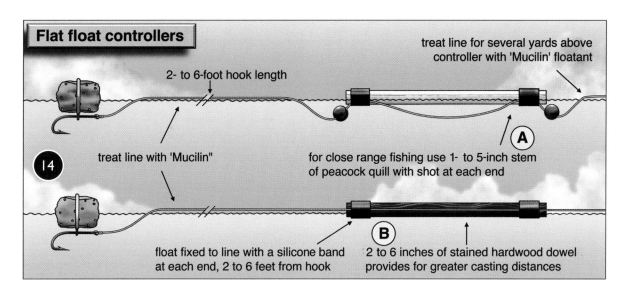

Flat float controllers

2- to 6-foot hook length

treat line for several yards above controller with 'Mucilin' floatant

14

treat line with 'Mucilin'

for close range fishing use 1- to 5-inch stem of peacock quill with shot at each end

Ⓐ

float fixed to line with a silicone band at each end, 2 to 6 feet from hook

Ⓑ 2 to 6 inches of stained hardwood dowel provides for greater casting distances

which simply glides across the surface following the fish. And of course only the minimum resistance is felt. You can easily pull even a large boat across the surface on a rope, but just you try pulling it under! And this is the secret of the flat float controller.

For short distances and with dace and chub in mind a 1–5-inch stem of peacock quill with a shot at each end is attached 2–6 feet above the hook with the line given a treatment of mucilin to a point at least several yards above the float (Fig. A). For greater casting range, stems of hardwood are ideal (Fig. B). Possessing inherent weight they do not require the addition of shot and may be painted black or coloured dark green or brown using a wood stain/preservative which makes them look like a piece of drifting wood. Their presence is thus most unlikely to spook the wariest of carp. Plain peacock quill may also be painted, yet in truth there can be nothing more natural drifting on the surface of still water than the white quill from a bird's feather.

SURFACE CONTROLLERS AND END RIGS

Beyond distances of say 10 yards specialized weighted self-cocking controllers which are available

in various sizes, such as my own Tenpin shown in Diag. 15 (and there are numerous lookalikes on the market), are the answer whether making a powerful overhead cast or a gentle underarm flick. Actually it was to reach carp working along a line of sunken willows on the opposite side of one of my own small lakes, perhaps a cast of 35 yards, that first prompted me to design a specialized weighted controller. Thus the Tenpin was born which creates the very minimum surface displacement whilst accurately placing the tiniest of floaters. As can be seen from Diag. 15 the controller can be stopped 2–6 feet above the hook in three different ways. The first, as in Fig. A, employs a small (size 12) swivel and tiny bead as a stop and joins a separate (lighter than reel line) hook link to the other end of the swivel. Alternatively simply use a five-turn sliding stop knot the desired distance from the hook, as in Fig. B, against which bead and controller come to rest. Or finally, simply join a lighter, finer-diameter hook length to the reel line using a four-turn water knot which, provided controller and bead are first threaded on to the reel line, effectively becomes the stop once the ends are trimmed (as in Fig. C). I do in fact use this last method of presenting a lighter hook

Summer chub are absolute suckers for floating crust. This 5-pounder came from Hampshire's River Test to the rod of John's wife, Jo Wilson.

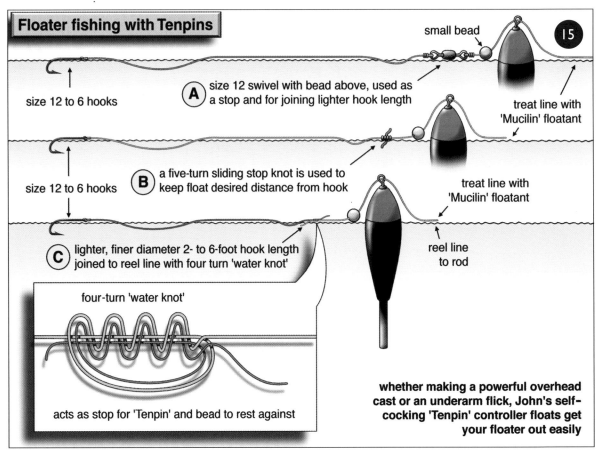

Floater fishing with Tenpins

15

size 12 to 6 hooks

A size 12 swivel with bead above, used as a stop and for joining lighter hook length

small bead

treat line with 'Mucilin' floatant

B a five-turn sliding stop knot is used to keep float desired distance from hook

size 12 to 6 hooks

treat line with 'Mucilin' floatant

C lighter, finer diameter 2- to 6-foot hook length joined to reel line with four turn 'water knot'

reel line to rod

four-turn 'water knot'

acts as stop for 'Tenpin' and bead to rest against

whether making a powerful overhead cast or an underarm flick, John's self-cocking 'Tenpin' controller floats get your floater out easily

length for the majority of my carp fishing.

Once carp are rising freely to loose floaters, the controller rig should be cast beyond the area and wound back over it so as not to spook confident feeders. Alternatively it can be cast well upwind and allowed, on a free line with bale arm open, to drift slowly around together with a group of free floaters catapulted around the hook bait. Every so often it helps, particularly when distance fishing, to mend the line and move the controller slightly in order to identify which floater is in fact the hook bait. It goes

without saying, I hope, that at no point should the rod be rested when floater fishing. It should be held – in expectation of a bite at all times. As the reel line passes through the swivel in the top of the controller, which merely nods and wavers when a carp sucks the bait in, keeping your eyes glued to the hook bait is of paramount importance. But try not to hurry the strike. Always allow the carp to close its lips and get its head down before slamming the hook home in a long sweeping strike. Due to panic and feeling last-second resistance, a per centage of fish will always forget the bait in their mouths and do a runner virtually hooking themselves in the process. Many however merely approach the floater close up and swirl away at the last second which gives the impression that it has been sucked down. So get used

to watching the line on the surface, and if it doesn't tighten don't be tempted into striking. The carp will probably come again anyway, whereas a pricked fish could be put down for hours.

When consistent refusals occur, try reducing the diameter of the hook link by using prestretched mono or a lighter hook length – within reason. Alternatively go down in hook size, or rig the floater on a short hair (as in Diag. 16, Fig. A). Or ensure the hook floats horizontally beside it in the surface film by gluing a strip of buoyant foam along the shank (Fig. B). The permutations of bait presentation are endless and there are numerous specialist aids marketed specifically for floater fishing, such as the John Roberts' bait bands (Diag. 17, Fig. A). These expanding rings made from clear silicone slide along the hook shank and hold baits

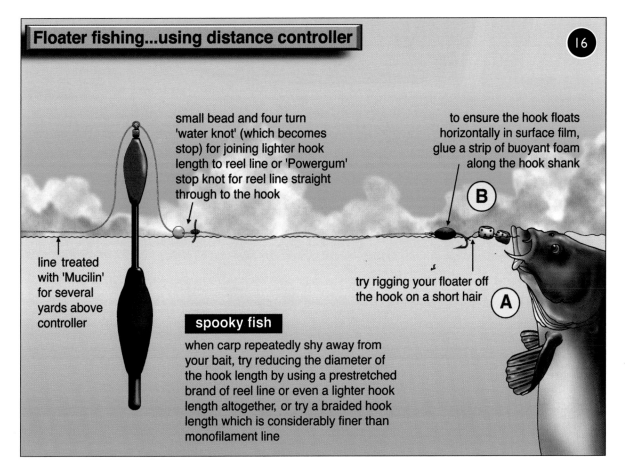

Floater fishing...using distance controller 16

small bead and four turn 'water knot' (which becomes stop) for joining lighter hook length to reel line or 'Powergum' stop knot for reel line straight through to the hook

to ensure the hook floats horizontally in surface film, glue a strip of buoyant foam along the hook shank

B

line treated with 'Mucilin' for several yards above controller

try rigging your floater off the hook on a short hair

A

spooky fish

when carp repeatedly shy away from your bait, try reducing the diameter of the hook length by using a prestretched brand of reel line or even a lighter hook length altogether, or try a braided hook length which is considerably finer than monofilament line

like chum mixer biscuits and large trout pellets securely with the hook situated immediately beneath. With two bands, two mixers can be superglued together (Fig. B). Smaller, stretchier bait bands are also available for presenting trout and carp pellets.

To achieve a similar result, simply make a tiny groove in a mixer, floating sweetcorn or in a floating trout or carp pellet (using a fine-toothed junior hacksaw blade) and secure the top of the hook shank using a little superglue (Fig. C).

SUSPENDERS

Quite frankly almost any ruse and different method of presentation is worth a try until the carp respond by sucking down the hook-bait floater instead of just the loose ones around it. As I said in the freelining section, floaters dangled straight down from the rod tip without any line touching the surface are invariably sucked in unhesitatingly. And there are two specialized controllers which actually achieve this: namely the Gardner suspender and the Revolution surface float from D & S Angling Products. Both tend to drift about and twist round in a wind and the latter does make one hell of a splash when it hits the surface but both, via a long arm and a little adjustment, present small floaters without any line on the surface and so consequently encourage hittable takes from spooky fish. And strangely once a carp is hooked the enjoyment of the ensuing fight is not ruined by the encumbrance of the controller arm just up the line as one might imagine.

FLOATING BAITS

I have purposely left baits until last because it is such an enormous subject. Whilst I have already mentioned breadcrust which always seems to work with river chub and in carp fisheries that receive next to little attention, in most popular fisheries the effectiveness of crust has in all probability long worn off and should you require a fair-sized floater of a rubbery consistency to ward off the attentions of kamikaze roach and rudd, baking your own coloured and flavoured floater cake from which triangles, tiny cubes, oblongs, or even rough-edged pieces can be taken, opens up an exciting field of possibilities.

(Recipes are given in many bait supply catalogues, but dare I suggest here that you obtain a copy of my *Improve Your Coarse Fishing* bait book which lists several recipes for baking a superb floating cake plus how to colour and bake your own bread should you wish to stay with varying colours and ways of catching on crust).

It may seem strange but marshmallows, yes marshmallows, can prove an extremely effective large floater. They don't work in all waters but they

Peacock quill and hardwood flat float controllers are superb for presenting small floating baits to dace, chub, rudd and carp at close range.

In the clear water of summer lakes baits, like casters, presented on a controller/greased-line combination, can tempt the wariest of specimen rudd like this 3lb-plus beauty.

Floating baits and summer carp go hand in hand. Note John's organizer bucket, purposely designed to contain both bait and tackle sundries for this highly mobile technique.

are worth a try. You can use marshmallows whole on the hook on a hair and either halve or quarter them to be hair rigged. The Brown Bear Bait Co. of Pittsburgh in the US is obviously aware of marshmallow baits and their highly visible products which are available in UK tackle shops come prepacked in screw-top plastic jars. Available in three sizes and several colours with pungent flavours these mini marshmallows are worth a try presented either singly, or as a cocktail, using their buoyancy to help float not so buoyant baits such as any small particle. Their use also goes beyond the surface. A single mini yellow marshmallow, for instance, will pop up two grains of sweetcorn enticingly above dense bottom weed when ledgering. Try them and see.

Still the most widely used floater by far is the old faithful chum mixer dog biscuit. It can be coloured and/or flavoured as required and continues to work because it is just the right size. As with all small cat and dog biscuits (spend an hour in your local pet centre for the complete range of possibilities) mixers can be fished straight on the hook, secured with a bait band, glued on as I have already mentioned, or you can make a hole through the middle with a nut drill and hair rig them one or two up.

For putting straight on the hook, mixers and most other larger biscuits such as Febo, should be thoroughly splashed with water and left in a polybag for 20 minutes (tie a knot in the top) so that all the moisture is absorbed. This turns the biscuit decidedly rubbery. The hook may then even be pushed into the bait and completely hidden or it can

be side hooked. Floating boilies, whether using mini's or gobstoppers, are a deadly option in all waters where carp have learnt to associate little round balls with succulent food. Premade floaters are available from most tackle shops should you not fancy making your own and they are best hair rigged and, I find, used in conjunction with a different surface loose feed, such as mixers or small cat biscuits. Carp then seem to home in on the hook bait much quicker.

Generally speaking seeds and grains are not a practical surface bait except, that is, for sunflower seeds and expanded maize – which is none other than popcorn. Both should be hair rigged and the sunflower seeds need to be soaked in hot water for half an hour in order for the needle to go through easily.

Last but certainly not least, because the types of baits that can be presented on the surface is endless, I suggest that you also give floating trout and carp pellets a try. In practical terms those from around 5–12mm in diameter are ideal and should be hair rigged using a nut drill. Try a few handfuls of sinking pellets or, better still, salmon fry crumbs to get carp working through a particular area down below and then catapult in some floating baits. They'll soon get the message.

Like chub and rudd, golden orfe eagerly respond to small floaters. This beauty came from John's own two-lake Norfolk fishery.

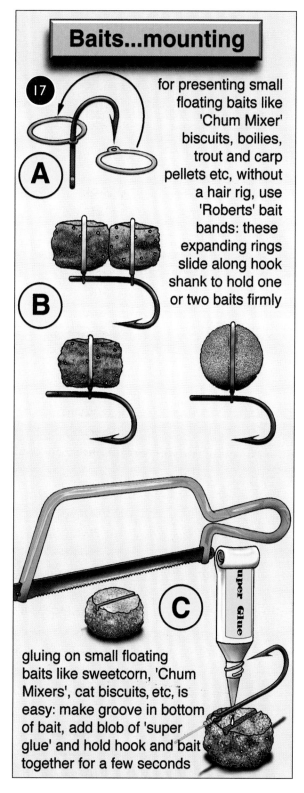

Baits...mounting

17

A

B

for presenting small floating baits like 'Chum Mixer' biscuits, boilies, trout and carp pellets etc, without a hair rig, use 'Roberts' bait bands: these expanding rings slide along hook shank to hold one or two baits firmly

C super glue

gluing on small floating baits like sweetcorn, 'Chum Mixers', cat biscuits, etc, is easy: make groove in bottom of bait, add blob of 'super glue' and hold hook and bait together for a few seconds

FLOAT LEDGERING

There are numerous occasions in both still and slow-moving rivers when, to induce bites from species like roach, bream and their hybrids plus tench and carp, the bait must be presented completely static on the bottom, or resting gently upon dense beds of bottom weed. Because it combines the visual pleasure of watching a float tip together with the distance casting of ledgering, float ledgering is a method I just love using.

END RIGS

Weight in the form of swan shots, bomb or feeder may be added to the reel line via a fixed paternoster link (tied with a four-turn water knot) at 6–30 inches above the hook (as in Diag. 18, Fig. A), or by way of a running ledger stopped above the hook with a ledger stop. Personally I prefer the fixed paternoster end rig because by the time a fish has run far enough away with the bait causing bomb or feeder to drag (and therefore drops the bait because it feels resistance) the float tip will have long since disappeared. And should it swim towards the rod, the float will rise exaggeratedly above the surface (just like the lift method) when the bomb or feeder is dislodged. After this the float tip will still dip down enough to register a hittable bite. So strike immediately at the first positive bite indication.

I also prefer a fixed paternoster because buoyant baits like breadflake or crust, or crust/corn cocktails, can so easily be made to lie naturally on top of dense bottom weed. You simply use a bomb/feeder link even longer than the hook length if necessary. Consider Diag. 18, Fig. B for instance where a 2-foot ledger link comfortably permits the hook bait (on a shorter length) to rest delicately on top of the weed whilst bomb or feeder goes through it to settle on the lake bed. I have found this set-up particularly effective when seeking rudd from the distant areas of relatively shallow but extremely weedy bottomed lakes.

There is another specific occasion when I employ a noticeably longer weight link and that is when fishing over and actually amongst the soft green lettuce-like subsurface leaves of the common yellow lily (Nuphar lutea) often referred to as cabbages. In many slow-moving river systems, sometimes because boat traffic chops them off and sometimes because a persistent algae bloom retards their growth, most of the actual surface pads and flower stalks of this particular plant do not reach the surface beyond a thin marginal covering. But down below on the bottom in depths of up to 12 feet a 2-foot bottom carpet of cabbages exist. It

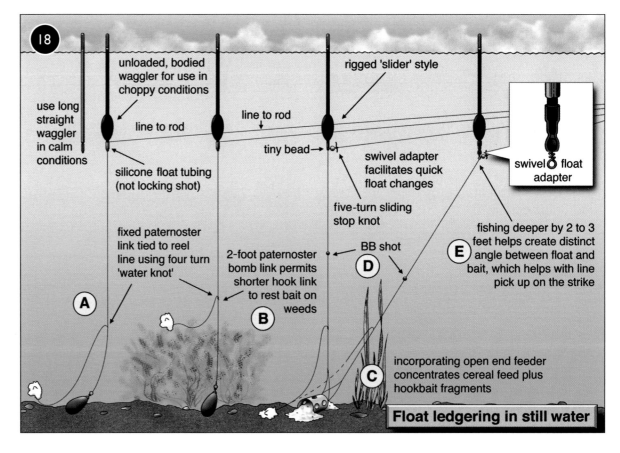

18

use long straight waggler in calm conditions

unloaded, bodied waggler for use in choppy conditions

line to rod

line to rod

rigged 'slider' style

line to rod

tiny bead→

silicone float tubing (not locking shot)

swivel adapter facilitates quick float changes

swivel ⦵ float adapter

five-turn sliding stop knot

fixed paternoster link tied to reel line using four turn 'water knot'

2-foot paternoster bomb link permits shorter hook link to rest bait on weeds

BB shot

fishing deeper by 2 to 3 feet helps create distinct angle between float and bait, which helps with line pick up on the strike

A

B

D

E

C

incorporating open end feeder concentrates cereal feed plus hookbait fragments

Float ledgering in still water

makes trotting extremely difficult. It makes straight ledgering even more difficult because the bait often becomes hidden amongst the greenery and I find the only way of presenting a bait on top of the cabbages, where roach and bream plus the occasional tench can easily locate it, is by float ledgering.

The rig I adopt here (shown in Diag. 19) can be used in a gentle flow and by far the best float (due to its buoyancy) is a really long, straight peacock waggler, fixed bottom end only with a length of silicone tubing (as Fig. A). You can economize here simply by using a slim 12–15-inch length of plain peacock quill, painted with a ½-inch band of fire orange paint at one end. At the other it is secured directly to the line with a thick band of silicone tubing. I actually prefer cutting a stem with scissors from a long peacock quill to get exactly the length and, more importantly, the amount of buoyancy required. A small bomb or two or three swan shots (Fig. B) are fixed to the end of the 2–3-foot link leaving a 20–24-inch hook link resting gently on top of the cabbage leaves, presenting buoyant baits most attractively (as in Fig. C).

Crust, breadflake, or crust/corn, crust/maggot or even crust/stewed-wheat cocktails are the baits best suited to this rig which in a flow can only be fished at close range, say up to a rod length out. So loose feeding by hand is no problem, although you can use a small feeder as part of the set-up. To ensure the float is not dragged under by the flow, set up a 13–14-foot float rod on two rests with the tip angled upwards to keep as much line off the surface

Big fish specialist, Chris Turnbull, puts the float ledgering method to good effect in capturing this superb 3¼lb crucian carp from a Norfolk lake.

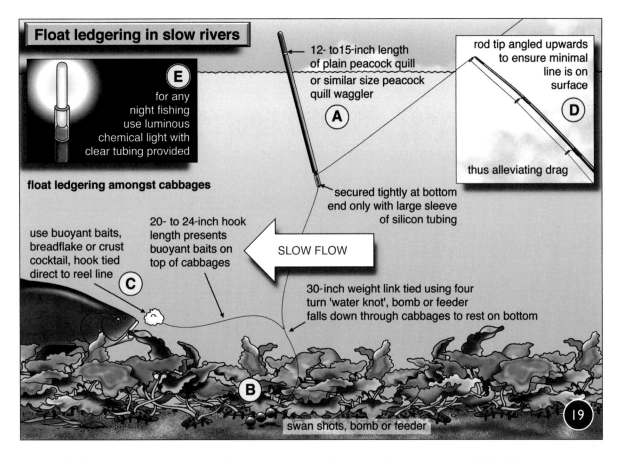

Float ledgering in slow rivers

E
for any night fishing use luminous chemical light with clear tubing provided

float ledgering amongst cabbages

12- to15-inch length of plain peacock quill or similar size peacock quill waggler
A

rod tip angled upwards to ensure minimal line is on surface
D

thus alleviating drag

use buoyant baits, breadflake or crust cocktail, hook tied direct to reel line
C

20- to 24-inch hook length presents buoyant baits on top of cabbages

SLOW FLOW

secured tightly at bottom end only with large sleeve of silicon tubing

30-inch weight link tied using four turn 'water knot', bomb or feeder falls down through cabbages to rest on bottom

B

swan shots, bomb or feeder

19

as possible (Fig. D). Because you are fishing at such close range, swims up to the length of your rod can be managed with ease.

If you want to fish on into darkness, simply sleeve on a luminous chemical element to the float tip with the clear tubing provided (as Fig. E). Nothing could be easier. As with all other variations of the float ledgering theme, bites will register by the float tip simply disappearing, or rising (lift style) often in a jerky manner because the bomb or shots literally bump amongst the subsurface shrubbery as a fish moves upstream with the bait.

Returning to still waters you can see from Diag. 18 that in calm conditions it is best to use a long, straight peacock waggler and a bodied peacock waggler whenever the surface is choppy. Both should be fixed to the line with a ⅜-inch length of

silicone tubing and not with locking shot. Don't worry about the float's actual shotting capacity when float ledgering because all the weight is going to be concentrated on the bottom anyway. Simply choose a float with a tip that you can see easily, especially for fishing at long range. Distances of between 30 and 40 yards are not only quite manageable, but by incorporating an open-end or cage-type feeder into the terminal rig, concentrating cereal feed plus bait fragments all around the hook bait whilst simultaneously accurately baiting up a chosen area, this is as effective as when straight ledgering (see Fig. C). Close to medium-range swims can of course be loose fed or ground baited by catapult.

To counter strong wind resistance and surface tow once the rig has settled on the bottom, sink the rod

tip (waggler style) and gently wind down to the float, which should be set 1 foot over depth until just enough of the tip remains easily visible above the surface.

In choppy conditions don't attempt to fish ultra sensitively. Even with 2 inches of the float tip showing, bites using this method are invariably registered in a most positive manner. The tip disappears or lifts.

Casting a fixed float rig is generally only practicable in swims up to 10 feet deep, even when using a 13–14-foot rod. The problem of overcoming really deep water can in fact be solved in two ways: either by using a self-locking float such as the specialized Polaris or Locslide models, or by using a large (unloaded) peacock bodied slider. Look at Diag. 18, Fig. D and you will see that a BB shot is pinched on the line 4–5 feet above the hook. The float rests against this for casting, using a tiny bead and five-turn sliding stop knot above the float set at 2–3 feet deeper than the swim. This helps create a distinct angle between float and the bottom rig which aids line pick-up on the strike in extreme depths (as Fig. E).

To put the hook firmly home in any water deeper than 12 feet when slider float fishing I always try to remember to crank the reel handle like mad (to pick up that great angle of line) before sweeping the rod firmly upwards and back into a powerful strike and then continue winding until the tip stays hard over. In deep and distant swims there is, of course, absolutely no chance whatsoever of breaking off due to the inherent stretch in monofilament which can be as much as 25% per cent. Give it a try. It is most effective and will put many more fish in the net which would have otherwise come adrift within seconds simply because the hook point was not driven home on the strike.

SELF-LOCKING FLOATS

Now let's consider the new breed of sliding floats which first made an impression in 1995, and which, through ingenious bottom-end devices, utomatically lock the float at swim depth once the weighted end rig lands on the lake bed. This of course, like all float-ledgering rigs, means that you benefit from having a built-in plummet which is extremely useful for ascertaining swim depth wherever you are fishing. Both the well-proven Polaris and Locslide range of self-locking sliders actually include heavier predator floats which, for exploring previously unfished water through careful plummeting, are unrivalled. (See also Method 24, 'Float Fishing Static Deadbaits for Pike and Zander', and Method 26, 'Float Paternostering for Predators'.)

To set these floats up, thread the reel line through the specialized locking device at the bottom and make up a fixed paternoster end rig incorporating either bomb or feeder of at least the suggested weight for the particular float being used. Then pinch on a No. 1 shot 3 feet up the line (just like Diag. 20, Fig. C).

It is imperative when using these specialized floats not to use less weight on the terminal rig (whether bomb or feeder) than is recommended. Otherwise the float's buoyancy will drag the end rig along the bottom when you attempt to tighten up. Numerous models are available, from canal specials to bodied wagglers for those deep and distant areas taking G ounce up to 2 ounces. When casting remember not to close the reel's bale arm until the end rig hits bottom and the self-locking float pops up to the surface and lies flat. Then put your rod tip beneath the surface and tighten up by winding in gently.

The small, black tubular frixon device of the Polaris floats is an extension of the float's base and was created by Terry Smith and Martin Founds of Anglers World Holidays. It has two holes both in the top and bottom offering a choice of lines (see Diag. 20, Fig. A). The small hole accommodates lines in the 3–6lb range and the larger 8–20lb line which means that even the carp angler can put this brilliant float design to good use when fishing either at distance or into really deep water swims or both.

The Locslide device created by ex-World Champion, Dave Thomas, is slightly different in that it fits horizontally at the base of the float but works on the same principle (as Diag. 20, Fig. B) illustrates. Remember that the float automatically locks to the line and will remain at that depth whilst playing fish right up until it touches the tip ring. You then wind through the automatic locking device until the float is at a suitable depth for netting the fish.

When recasting simply wind through the locking device so the float eventually comes to rest immediately above the small shot pinched on 3 feet above the terminal rig. It's as simple as that – honestly!

Though after bream, John was understandably delighted when this massive roach/rudd hybrid weighing only an ounce short of 4lb, sucked up his float-ledgered breadflake.

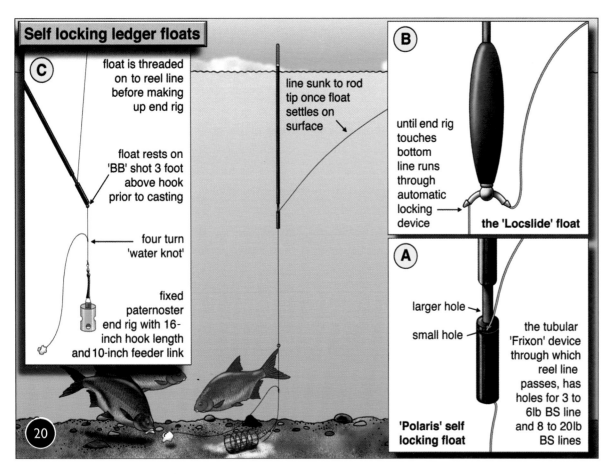

Self locking ledger floats

C float is threaded on to reel line before making up end rig

float rests on 'BB' shot 3 foot above hook prior to casting

four turn 'water knot'

fixed paternoster end rig with 16-inch hook length and 10-inch feeder link

line sunk to rod tip once float settles on surface

B until end rig touches bottom line runs through automatic locking device

the 'Locslide' float

A larger hole

small hole

the tubular 'Frixon' device through which reel line passes, has holes for 3 to 6lb BS line and 8 to 20lb BS lines

'Polaris' self locking float

20

Float ledgering sorts out the specimens, as this brace of 11lb-plus gravel pit bream proves. The lower fish is a male, easily identified by its spawning tubercles.

Line Pick-up

This comparatively new breed of floats has revolutionized float fishing in deep water particularly for species like roach, rudd, tench and bream inhabiting gravel pits, reservoirs and especially Irish loughs. Anglers are now enjoying catching hauls of fish on the float from large, wild open waters where once upon a time feeder fishing using a quivertip would have seemed the only option open. However you do need to be constantly aware of that enormous right angle of line which exists between rod tip and bait. Over distances in deep water beyond 10 yards for instance, trying to pull the hook from a large piece of paste into a fish is almost impossible using a normal strike, unless the fish is belting off in the opposite direction.

When using small hooks and just two or three maggots, much less force is obviously required to set the hook. With large hooks and baits I find it advisable to sit well back from the rod and to wind in fast for several seconds (which greatly reduces the angle and takes up most of the slack) before whacking the rod back into a really firm, sweeping strike and continuing to wind until the tip buckles over. With carp and, to a lesser degree, tench, exaggerated striking is not necessary due to the aggressive way in which they motor off with your bait. But should you repeatedly miss bites inexplicably then I'll wager that line pick-up is the problem.

Quite apart from that extra enjoyment gained from using light tackle and watching a float top, float ledgering is also the best way of beating that eternal problem experienced when ledgering for bream, namely line bites. Because the line angles vertically upwards as opposed to a horizontal ledgered line, even when bream are packed tightly into the swim and in a feeding frenzy, only the occasional liner is experienced. Try float ledgering for yourself and experience the difference.

(Opposite): *The frixon device, built into a polaris self-locking waggler, allowed John to float ledger for carp in depths down to 18 feet in a Norfolk gravel pit.*

LONG TROTTING

Of all the wonderful techniques we anglers use, I rate the ability to catch species such as dace, roach, chub, barbel, grayling and even sea trout by long trotting the most challenging and certainly the most skilful of all. Indeed, what sets this technique apart from the rest is that so many factors need to be taken into account when working a float downstream to explore those tempting lies 20, 30 and even up to 40 yards away. Variables include current speed, the presence of weed beds and snags and, of course, surface-flow deviations which greatly affect float control, as does wind direction. And what about actual bottom topography? Because depth is constantly changing, both down and across, let alone from swim to swim, the trotting enthusiast must be forever altering his terminal set-up to suit. This method is certainly not for the lazy fisherman; it is for the explorer, the wanderer, the opportunist and the angler who says 'I want to know what lies at the end of each run'. Long trotting is the ultimate searching-exploring method.

WHICH REEL?

The biggest decision of all, and one which each newcomer to the art of this fascinating method must make, is whether to invest no small amount of dosh on a quality, really free-running centre-pin reel that ensures the float will trot the bait smoothly downstream at current speed or slightly slower (if held back gently) or to stick with a fixed spool or closed-face reel, neither of which can compete with the centre pin. Or perhaps you could buy a cheap centre pin?

The last suggestion, in my opinion, is a complete waste of time and money ill spent. This is something you will quickly find out, in fact during the very first trot down, because if the float's passage is in any way impaired due to the line not peeling off freely and smoothly from the spinning drum, the bait can only behave unnaturally and most fish will refuse to suck it in – hence few bites.

Frankly those not willing to part with say £80.00 upwards (which let's face it is no more than most specialist anglers pay for designer carp and pike fixed-spool reels) would, I think, be better off sticking with a fixed spool or closed-face reel rather than purchasing an unworkable centre pin.

The trouble is, despite the most sensitive and gentlest of pressure applied to the rim of a fixed-spool reel, with the forefinger controlling line as it peels off to the pull of the current, any kind of direct contact is just not there. And this invariably also results in extra loose line to pick up on the strike. Nothing can match that immediate contact when the float goes under from thumb pressure upon the rim of the centre pin which instantly connects you to the fish. There is no slipping clutch to worry about or back winding when a big fish hooked on light tackle belts off downstream. The centre pin's drum revolves easily, controlled by thumb pressure alone – and there are few more sensitive parts of the anatomy than the skin beneath your thumb.

It is all so simple yet so devastatingly effective. This prompts me to recall that in over 40 years of trotting with centre-pin reels I have yet to experience a break-off due to an excess of pressure being accidentally applied at the reel.

TERMINAL TACKLE

As for line, I generally use 2½lb test where small- to medium-sized fish are expected, going up to 3lb, and certainly 4lb test in rivers where barbel are likely. And here's a tip. Don't fill your centre-pin reel up with several hundred yards of line, or you could experience problems on the next cast after playing a big fish, due to the line bedding in deeply. Wind on just 200 yards of fresh line and be prepared to replace it regularly, discarding the first 20 yards or so after every trip that has included several hours of trotting. When you come to think about it, compared with the heartbreak of a lost monster due to negligence, the cost of 200 yards of line is not worth bothering about. Is it!

I much prefer the safety of tying hooks direct to the reel line but as there is often a case for delicate presentation, say of a single maggot or caster when seeking chub, dace or roach in clear water, a lighter 1¼–1½lb hook link of around 24 inches is joined to the reel line using a four-turn water knot. In the smaller sizes, say 14–20s, I prefer the neatness of

Master wildlife photographer, Hugh Miles, who made the highly acclaimed series 'A Passion for Angling', long trots for roach using a centre-pin reel on the Hampshire Avon.

spade ends but from size 12 upwards I use eyed hooks.

A point worth remembering here, particularly if repeatedly dragging a bunch of maggots over clean gravel, as when grayling fishing for instance, is to be aware that hooks easily blunt and therefore need to be changed several times during an all-day session or you risk bumping out of fish on the strike.

One of the problems experienced by many anglers using the centre-pin reel is loose line flapping around and becoming caught around the back plate. This is particularly common during windy weather and can only be overcome by fitting a line guard. As modern centre pins do not come with workable line guards already fitted, the only option is to make you own from 18-gauge stainless-steel sprung wire, the kind that tackle shops sell in coils for making up sea leads. I have previously gone into this in great detail in at least two of my previous books and anyone interested might like to examine the diagram on page 49 of *Catch Barbel* or page 87 of *Coarse Fishing*. This particular guard does not become obtrusive in use and will fit all modern slimline centre pins such as the excellent Stanton Adcock range, match aerials and the Youngs Purist which I have been using for several reasons now when long trotting and which I cannot fault. It spins forever and even works relentlessly in the rain due to a double ball race when other reels start to grit up and loose their smoothness.

RODS

Let's now consider trotting rods which today means a reasonably robust 13-foot carbon float cum match rod. Even budget priced models are now so well made I am tempted to say that virtually any model with a snappy, waggler-style will suffice, as long as it doesn't fold up easily at the butt end or you'll never hit those bites at 20–30 yards plus. Top-of-the-range float rods are of course noticeably slimmer in profile which means they cut through wind resistance more easily than thicker, cheaper models and being lighter are of course more desirable to the angler who literally holds the rod all day through. I guess it all depends on how much you value the enjoyment gained from a particular technique, doesn't it. Models to avoid are those known as stick-float rods with super-fine spliced-in tips. These are designed specifically for close-range, light-line work (see Method 10, 'Stick Float Fishing') and not for trying to bang the hook home at 25 yards.

Taken on long-trotted maggots in Berkshire's River Kennet, John displays every river angler's dream: a 1lb-plus dace.

(Opposite): *Andy Davison makes an annual winter pilgrimage from Norfolk to Hampshire to long trot its marvellous chalk streams for dace, roach and grayling.*

TACKLE SUNDRIES

As long trotting is by nature a roaming, probing, searching method of obtaining the richest rewards that a particular stretch of water has to offer (and only in really large rivers are you likely to want to remain in just one swim all day through), the most valuable addition to your kit is a bait pouch. Continually opening and closing plastic snap-on bait-box lids, especially when finger tips are painfully cold, is just not on. Invest in a pouch which belts snugly around the waist and is divided into two sections, one for maggots and one for worms say. Or one for sliced bread hook bait and the other for mashed bread feed. And so on.

Extra tackle requirements depend totally upon how much of the river you then want to explore. When long trotting specifically for grayling, for instance, I personally take neither stool not tackle bag preferring the delight of roaming completely unhindered, save for a collapsible net clipped on to a large D ring sewn on to the back of my waistcoat so it is always at the ready but well out of the way. All small tackle sundries such as floats, hooks and shots, plus forceps, disgorger and a bait dropper (for those deep fast runs) are contained in my waistcoat pockets. My one cheat is the camera bag, because photographing beautiful river scenes which are ever changing, seemingly with more tempting glides, or challenging pools always just around the next bend, is very much part of the enjoyment, particularly on those sunny, crisp winter days when there is frost or snow on the ground.

Should my trotting travels take in swims, which for roach or chub really need to be carefully worked up by regularly introducing loose feed in order to encourage that first bite, I find a two-section keep-net bag makes a great carryall. Inside mine for instance is a lightweight stool, keep nets, scales and bait selection for the day – and that's it. I am all too aware that extra weight gained from including any unnecessary items

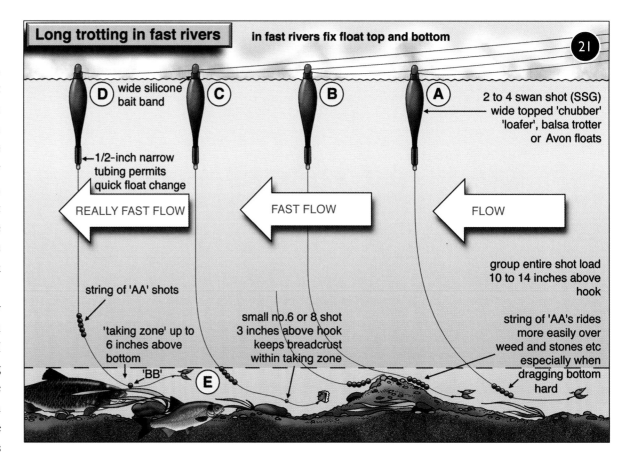

is bound to inhibit my urge to move on and thus dull my enthusiasm for searching out new areas which could very well demand a lengthy walk. And I won't really want to end up spending half the day in the first comfortable or productive spot.

SHOTTING CAPACITIES

Now let's get down to the art of long trotting and sending the bait a long way downstream beneath a float so it tumbles slowly along, no faster than current speed, just above bottom as would items of natural food. To achieve this fish, if anything, on the heavier side rather than the lighter. If for instance current speed would seem to indicate a shotting load of say four or five BBs then settle for extra stability given to the bait by employing a float taking six BB

and so on. It is wrong to imagine that a more sensitive approach can be achieved (as you would if stick-float fishing) by presenting the lightest shotting pattern you can get away with, because trying to control such a rig at long range will repeatedly jerk and pull the bait either away from the loose feed line, or make it behave unnaturally, or both. These problems get worse the further downstream you send the float, especially in strong currents which demand upwards of two or three swan shot.

FLOAT SET-UPS DOUBLE RUBBER

One reason why I choose to use chunky wide-topped floats, like loafers, chubbers and balsas, is that they can also be easily seen at long distances without

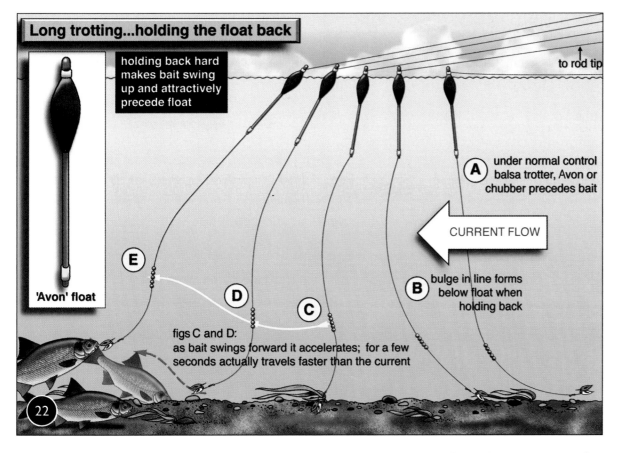

Long trotting...holding the float back

holding back hard makes bait swing up and attractively precede float

'Avon' float

to rod tip

(A) under normal control balsa trotter, Avon or chubber precedes bait

CURRENT FLOW

(B) bulge in line forms below float when holding back

figs C and D: as bait swings forward it accelerates; for a few seconds actually travels faster than the current

22

Terry Houseago displays a superb 2lb-plus grayling caught 30 yards downstream from a shallow glide on maggots. Bulk shot close to the hook aided presentation in the strong flow.

having to squint. Moreover, I invariably bulk the entire shotting load in a string between 10–14 inches above the hook. Something which may well look crude but which is actually the most effective way of ensuring the bait remains in and works steadily through that all-important taking zone just above the river bed and does so throughout the entire trot, not just now and again (see Diag. 21, Figs A and C).

If the float takes say three swan shots, rather than use these large shots which tend to hang up more easily in weed and behind large stones, a string or a line of six AA shots (the equivalent weight) are pinched on. Such a string rides easily over clean sandy and stony bottoms allowing the bait to be fished well over depth and even dragged hard along the bottom if required (see Diag. 21, Fig. B) without the float tip totally disappearing.

Obviously we are talking about trotting in fast currents here during the cold winter months, generally in extremely low temperatures. This is when most species keep their heads down within mere inches of the bottom, moving only from side to side in order to suck in food items brought down by the current which are at their own level and not swimming upwards to intercept them. Should the float keep sinking at a particular spot down the swim, denoting a snag, bed of weed or a hump on the river bed, don't be tempted to push the float down a few inches to compensate, because the bait might then be presented too high throughout the rest of the trot through. Simply hold back hard on the float just before it reaches the shallow spot (as in Diag. 2, Fig. D) to raise the bait up and over, before restarting a controlled trot again. On some really

long glides you may need to raise the bait by holding back in this manner several times to overcome shallow areas but you eventually get so used to the technique it becomes second nature. There is one small alteration I make to the basic fast-water rig in the way of a tiny shot (6–8) nipped on 3 inches above the hook (Diag. 21, Fig. C) which ensures buoyant baits like a cube of breadcrust (deadly for dace, chub and roach if used in conjunction with mashed bread loose feed) remain in that all-important taking zone (Fig. E) throughout the trot. In exceptionally fast runs I pinch on a BB shot between the line of AA shots and the hook (as in Fig. D).

A devastatingly effective ploy for use in mild conditions, whenever fish can be encouraged to intercept baits well off bottom above their heads, is

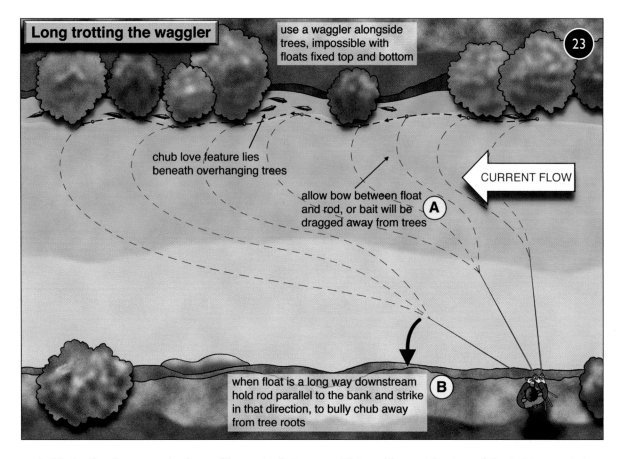

Long trotting the waggler

use a waggler alongside trees, impossible with floats fixed top and bottom

23

chub love feature lies beneath overhanging trees

allow bow between float and rod, or bait will be dragged away from trees

A

CURRENT FLOW

when float is a long way downstream hold rod parallel to the bank and strike in that direction, to bully chub away from tree roots

B

to hold the float's passage back steadily so the bait swings forward and upwards ahead of the shots (as in Diag. 22, Figs C, D and E). Hold back too hard in a strong pull and the bait could end up literally hanging in the flow at mid depth (as in Fig. E). Only experience by long trotting can suggest the correct degree of control but an excellent idea of what happens to the bait down below when the float is controlled and held hard back can be gained simply by watching the rig trot through in clear water just a few feet out from the bank. You'll be surprised just how far behind the float the bait is situated during an unchecked trot through (as in Fig. A). And you'll also notice how it instantly speeds up the very second the float is held back and how it seductively sways up off the bottom in an arc (during Figs C and D) to precede the shots.

This sudden quickening of the bait's pace (when the float is held back hard), as unnatural as it would seem to be, is often what triggers species like dace, chub and especially grayling into grabbing hold, lest it gets away. So be prepared to work your bait whenever bites do not materialize from a gentle but controlled trot through.

If using a centre-pin reel (and herein lies their true worth) you'll find that you can afford to overshoot the float slightly so that the tip almost disappears if put through unchecked. Yet as it trots steadily downstream, because the line is in direct contact from reel to float, this itself is sufficient to raise the tip a little providing enough to see even 30 yards away. This is trotting at its most sensitive and most productive, believe me.

As you will have appreciated, until now everything

I have said has been related to the float being fixed top and bottom, or double rubbered as some would call it. Remember not to thread the line through the bottom ring because you cannot then change quickly over to another float. Simply sleeve a ½-inch length of narrow-gauge tubing over the bottom (eye) end and a nice wide piece just below the coloured tip. Then virtually all types of balsa trotters, chubbers, loafers and Avons may be used without derigging – simply by the addition or subtraction of shots.

WAGGLER FISHING

There will be times (as shown in Diag. 23) when because fish are hugging feature lies along the opposite bank, such as overhanging or submerged bushes and willows (typical chub haunts), it is imperative to trot the bait close up to the trailing foliage. Now in all but the narrowest of rivers the very second you try to control a float attached top and bottom that is being worked along the opposite bank, you will immediately pull it and the bait off course, away from the features and the fish.

The answer, of course, is to swap over to a bottom-only float such as a waggler and to allow the current to pull the line from the reel and to allow a definite bow to form in the line from rod tip (helped by a gentle lifting of the wrist every so often) without altering the float's course (as in Diag. 23, Fig. A). I much prefer thick-stemmed peacock quill wagglers for this kind of trotting which take a good shotting load and do not subsequently dip under when the bait is dragging over a relatively clean river bed.

Once the float has travelled a good distance downstream you might well find that angling the rod tip parallel to your own bank (as in Fig. B) actually picks up more line on the strike and thus sets the hook more easily. In addition, the bent rod is now at a perfect angle for keeping fish away from submerged tree roots or branches. If held at A, for instance, fish can easily reach the sanctuary of the trees. Ensure the line above the float actually floats on the surface by applying a light coat of mucilin for at least several feet above it, because trying to strike upwards and pull the hook home via a sunken line is impractical and will cost you many a fish. Only in really strong winds would I consider trying to sink most of the line from rod tip to float and then striking sideways as though still-water fishing. River fishing is a different ball game.

As can be seen from Diag. 24, Fig. A, in really powerful currents most of the bulk shot is fixed in a line 20 inches above the hook with a small shot between and only minimal shot used to lock the float, whereas in Fig. B and for trotting in gentle currents the bulk shot is used to lock the float with just a couple of No. 1s and a tiny shot down the line. In both cases small baits such as a single caster or maggot can be dragged along clean river beds without the tip dipping under, due to the wonderful, inherent buoyancy of peacock quill. If you want to drag bottom really hard by fishing well over depth, ensure there is a fair length of tip (at least ¾ inch) above the surface. It's as simple as that!

Once weed has been removed by Jack Frost, winter long trotting for dace and roach becomes a joy to the wandering river fisherman.

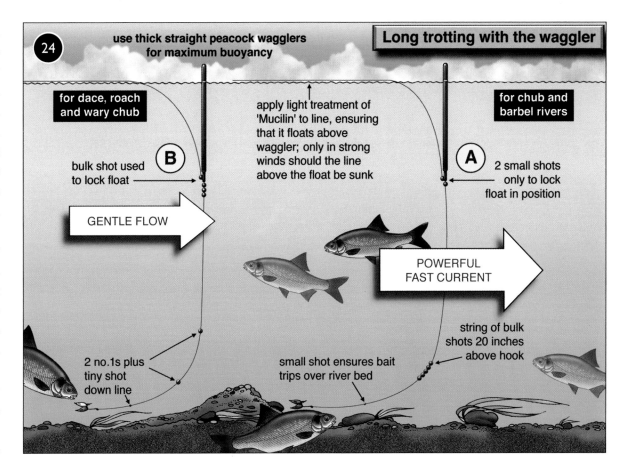

Long trotting with the waggler

24   use thick straight peacock wagglers for maximum buoyancy

for dace, roach and wary chub

apply light treatment of 'Mucilin' to line, ensuring that it floats above waggler; only in strong winds should the line above the float be sunk

for chub and barbel rivers

bulk shot used to lock float   B

A   2 small shots only to lock float in position

GENTLE FLOW

POWERFUL FAST CURRENT

string of bulk shots 20 inches above hook

2 no.1s plus tiny shot down line

small shot ensures bait trips over river bed

POLE FISHING
IN RIVERS

Having starting pole fishing on the Rivers Lea and Thames, using stewed hempseed to catch roach back in the 1950s, it will come as no surprise that one of my most prized angling possessions is indeed an old pole made by the famous firm of Sowerbutts. It was given to me by an old and dear friend, the late Ernie Bond, who for many years was the LAA bailiff at the Lakes in Lenwade, Norfolk. In those early precarbon days roach poles were made by craftsmen from carefully tempered and straightened bamboo, adorned with decorative, varnish-covered black whippings from tip to butt, and fitted with precision-turned brass ferrules which made that delicious plop as you unshipped each section. Mine is just 19 feet long, weighs a ton, and comprises just five sections, the top three of which fit into the 48-inch-long bottom two. The tip is of spliced in built cane and has a ring to which the float rig is attached.

While poles have become longer, lighter and infinitely more effective compared to the bamboo heavyweights of yesteryear, the actual technique of presenting a light float rig directly beneath the pole tip on just a few feet of line for maximum control has changed little and is of course as valid today as it was to our forefathers 100 years ago. This, compared to all other methods of float fishing in both still and running water where an angle exists between float and rod tip, is what sets pole fishing apart. Almost regardless of wind velocity and direction, pole fishing provides unrivalled control of the lightest rigs,

smallest hooks and tiniest baits, all of which can be gently eased out (as opposed to casting) and lowered slowly into the swim with the utmost accuracy. What's more, unlike any other method, they can be lifted up and allowed to free-fall attractively time and time again to induce bites on the drop.

You can even land quite sizeable specimens on light tackle provided your pole is fitted with internal elastic to absorb the lunges and runs which would otherwise cause an immediate break-off.

WHICH POLE?

Before we go any further let's look at the kind of pole that is suitable for general river fishing and doesn't involve forking out the price of a quality second-hand car. In terms of dosh, we are talking in the low hundreds as a starting point and not thousands. What you gain, of course, when purchasing top-of-the-range poles, apart from state-of-the-art technology and space-age materials used in the construction of these carbon-fibre thoroughbreds, is maximum length coupled to a firm action at the very lightest weight. This is what it's all about, because for optimum results the pole has to be held throughout an entire session whether it is for two or ten hours. Remember that.

Because the entire advancement in modern pole technology started on the Continent, pole lengths and distances being fished are referred to in metres

and not yards or feet. In fact everything about modern pole fishing has that Continental jargon: we talk of line strengths not in pounds test but in diameter and fractions of a millimetre such as 0.08 (which is 1¼lb) and shotting capacities in grams instead of so many BBs or AAs. But you soon get the hang of it.

The longest tournament poles currently on the market measure a staggering 16m and comprise no less than thirteen to fourteen separate sections. But we are talking big time here and I suggest that a good starting point is with a pole in the 9.5–11-metre range. If there comes a stage in the future when extra length would seem a good investment, you will by then at least have a valid reason for forking out more on a new pole, or buying an extension butt for your existing pole to increase its effective length. Many manufacturers produce extensions of up to 1.5m as optional extras.

Poles usually come with a maker's recommendation as to the size (or strength) of elastic they can safely handle. General poles usually take up to size 10, whereas those suitable for carp crunching go as high as size 18. (See Method 9, 'Pole Fishing in Still Waters'). Most have put-over, non-stick joints, except for the top two or three sections which tend to be telescopic. Quality models come with one, two or even three spare top three kits, which permit different elasticated rigs to be made up at the ready. These are imperative for enthusiastic and competition pole anglers. So shop around carefully before choosing a model to meet your personal requirements.

I would suggest that to increase the effective depth range of the extra top three kits supplied, you

Presenting a light float rig directly below or downwind of the pole tip, with only minimal line between, is what sets pole fishing apart from all other methods.

Kevin Wilmot, editor of Angling-Plus *magazine, demonstrates the importance of a back roller while shipping and unshipping using the long-pole-short-line technique.*

For catching small fish just beyond the marginal greenery, say 2–4m out, you can use the top three to five sections of your long pole, fitted with internal elastic, or the plain flick tip, or invest in a 6m glass or carbon-fibre telescopic whip to which the float rig is attached via a quick-release Stonfo-stlye connector glued on to the tip end using superglue. This plastic connector has a hook over which the loop on your rig line goes, held in place by a small sleeve that pushes over the hook. This is called flick-tip fishing which, without the cushioning of internal elastic, relies upon the flexibility of the telescopic whip to subdue fish up to a medium size only – roach, small tench, bream and crucian carp. By purchasing a 6m whip (although shorter models are available) any distance up to 6m can be covered. Being extremely slim and light in weight, whips should be held supported below the forearm just like a traditional rod.

POLE CONTROL

Whilst you can use a whip like a conventional rod, in the standing position, crouching, even from a reclining stool (should you so wish), a long pole, unless it is supported butt beneath your crotch and in front with your strongest hand whilst standing up, can only effectively be used from a comfortable and level sitting position. Ten-metre-plus poles are top heavy and unwieldy objects likely to produce acute backache, arm ache and shoulder ache if you are not positioned correctly. Sit on a rigid box when pole fishing and invest in an adjustable platform for banksides which are anything but level. It takes time, it's more gear to lug around and, in the winter, your hands get freezing cold just erecting and adjusting the telescopic legs of a platform – but there are no short cuts, believe me. Besides, you can then arrange groundbait trays, bait boxes, catapult and small tackle items all within easy reach around the

also purchase at least one extra fourth section, if not an extra fifth section as well. Note also that while some poles come already cut back at the tip section to accommodate a PTFE bush through which the internal elastic runs, others will need cutting back up to 6 inches with a fine-toothed hacksaw, a little at a time until it fits, unless you decide to use the tip as a flick tip. There are in fact two kinds of bushes (as if all this isn't complicated enough), one fitting over the cut-back pole tip, the other inside. Now because the elastic has no chance of rubbing against the carbon on the inside, the internal PTFE

bush is much the preferred option. However, because less of the pole tip needs to be removed with overfit bushes and thus thicker elastics can be used, the latter are more popular with the carp crunching fraternity. It's horses for courses. If in doubt, fit an internal bush, but don't glue it in. Incidentally some manufacturers now offer their top-of-the-range poles with the tips cut back and bushes already fitted but you still need to rig up the internal elastic and bung yourself (as in Diag. 27), although most specialist tackle dealers will do this for you.

platform, and optional side trays to facilitate quick one-handed use whilst supporting the pole with the other.

This brings me to how the pole should be held or, rather, what is the most comfortable way for you. Being of the old school, although it does reduce the pole's effective length by 2 feet (big deal), I much prefer to cradle the pole, resting it across my right knee supported in front by my cupped left hand with my right hand gripping the butt firmly. To strike (or lift, remember only inches are required here to set a tiny hook), you simply twist the right hand quickly and the entire pole instantly lifts across the thigh whilst being steadied with the left hand. It's an old-time technique geared to steadying the heavyweight bamboo poles of yesteryear – but one which also can be adopted for contemporary pole fishing.

The most common technique today, however, is the side-on grip whereby the pole rests along the top of your thigh with the elbow of your strongest arm forcing the butt down and therefore taking most of the weight, while the other hand is cupped beneath the pole 6 inches in front of the knee. To strike, you simply lift the pole – no more. It is imperative that the upper (strongest) arm is in a vertical line down to the butt with the forearm at right angles resting along the length of the pole's butt section, otherwise pains could develop, particularly if you are prone to rheumatism or arthritis. The side-on technique permits quick and efficient use of the catapult. You simply use the (strongest) hand supporting the pole to grip the pouch tab whilst filling, and fire with the frame pushed forward by the other hand. It doesn't take much practice.

Serious pole fishermen also introduce groundbait, liquidized bread and loose feed in the way of chopped worms, maggots and jokers, with a pole pot fitted a little way back from the tip of a spare top three kit. You can purchase ready-made commercial pole pots of various sizes or adapt your own from various-sized plastic tops of aerosol cans. Simply glue a mini plastic-coated Terry clip on to the bottom. Loose feed such as maggots and casters can also be deposited straight down to form a carpet on the bottom, using a small, frying-pan type bait dropper.

Another option for pole control (just like supporting the butt under your crotch when standing) is literally to sit on the butt end which alleviates most of the strain against your arms. It is a particularly good technique for fishing a long way out, which subsequently leaves your hands free for loose feeding, and specialized pole seats which have a gap down the middle to accommodate the butt are now incorporated into certain seat box designs.

When unshipping the pole (taking it down to the top three or four sections) for unhooking fish or rebaiting, a four-legged pole roller positioned a few yards behind and to the side is an indispensable addition. You simply feed the pole back quickly and evenly with your right hand (assuming you are right-handed), running it over your left hand, after first lifting the butt on to the roller.

Obviously unshipping is required only when the depth you are fishing is considerably less than the length of pole being used – also taking into account the extra 3–5 feet of line between float and pole tip. It is known as the long-pole-short-line technique where the comparatively short length of rig is equivalent to the top three, or four, pole sections. So the entire lower half of the pole is slid back to the third or fourth section and unshipped for baiting up or unhooking, and then shipped out again in reverse. It's surprising just how quickly you can accomplish this with the aid of a rear roller set-up.

For deep-water situations, fishing to hand is the answer, where the terminal rig actually matches pole length, regardless of how many sections are being used.

SUNDRIES

Before we become involved in various rigs and set-ups for river fishing however, let me say a few words on floats, winders and the weights used for pole fishing. First, as a general rule, most floats used for running water have heart-shaped or round bodies with maximum buoyancy at the top (as in Diag. 25) compared to the reverse heart shape used in floats for still-water fishing (see Method 9, 'Pole fishing in Still Waters'). There is bound to be a crossover situation here, because while a canal might well be classed as running water, in terms of actual presentation, a more powerful subsurface tow which develops across a huge windswept still water (an Irish lough for example) will demand a far more buoyant bodied pole float. Don't loose sight of the fact that pole fishing demands a horse for a course, no more, no less. Some of the floats I am going to suggest you use later on, for instance to combat strongly flowing water over 20 feet deep, are more like pike bungs taking over 10g in weight. But it is all relative.

Along at your specialist tackle centre you'll find all kinds, lengths and sizes of plastic pole winders so that every conceivable rig can be made up and ready to go. You can also purchase ready-made rigs, but it is always best to prepare your own designer float set-ups tailored specifically to your personal fishing requirements. Therefore you can have at the ready a selection of say 3m and 4m rigs for short-line situations for instance, or much longer, 7–9m to-hand rigs. Anyway it's one way of passing away those long winter evenings isn't it? One of the main considerations of pole rig making is deciding whether you are going to incorporate the hook length or not. If you do, then like as not you'll need the same rig duplicated several times over fitted with say size 18, 20, 22, 24 and 26 hooks respectively. Whereas if the rig is made up preshotted with an overhand loop at

Not only is the pole more comfortable to control when seated squarely on an adjustable platform, but look how close to hand everything is on the side tray.

It's more fun and more economical by far to prepare your own float set-ups on winders, tailored specifically to your needs.

the end, you can then simply add a hook to nylon which suits the bait and situation at hand. It saves an enormous amount of work, believe me, and you have immediate choice not only of hook size but the strength (or diameter) of monofilament to which it is tied. Consult the following list which gives a diameter or breaking strain of Pro-Micron, one of the most accurate of the so-called hi-tech monofilaments.

Lastly, (ugh) comes the contentious subject of pole fishing weights. The choice consists of Styl weights, which are attached to the line by using specialist Styl pinchers; olivettes, which are best used as a streamlined bulk weight to ensure the hook bait goes swiftly down to the desired length; and lead microshot, which are available from size 18 down to size 14, would you believe.

With Styl weights which, due to their long, flattened shape, are fabulous for shotting up specifically to fish on the drop, tangles are unfortunately rather difficult to unravel. In addition, Styl's are far from easy to remove, although sliding them up and down even superfine monofilament is easy. So I guess that microshots are an overall better choice for use as small balancing weights.

With regard to bulk shotting, nothing compares with the single olivette. These brass, tungsten or alloy weights have a centre pole through which the line passes and are plugged to the line with a piece of bristle from a pole float or, as with lock-and-slide type, are fixed to the line with a sleeve of microbore silicone tubing over the peg at each end. All these are available in sizes from 0.1g (really tiny) to size 8.5g.

RIGS FOR RUNNING WATER

Let's consider a few rigs suitable for moving the bait along with the flow, or lying perfectly static on the bottom of rivers. As I am not a competition angler, far be it from me to illustrate 1,001 different set-ups using the most complicated of shotting patterns. If you really get the bug for pole fishing, within no time at all you will develop your own ideas. So the following are merely starting points and not yardsticks.

Let's begin therefore with Diag. 25, Fig. A which shows a superlight rig for canal fishing with only the slightest draw on the water. The float, like all pole floats, has the line threaded through the tiny ring at the top of the slim body and is secured at the bottom of the wire stem with a sleeve of microfine-diameter silicone tubing. Because the tip is made from a wire bristle, and therefore requires only minimal pull to sink and register a bite, it is smeared with silicone mucilin to aid buoyancy. This rig is ideal for presenting bloodworm, punched bread, squatts or casters. Adding a few inches of depth so the lowest shot actually rests on the bottom, which raises the wire bristle so bites are easily seen, often produces better quality fish which prefer a static bait. Remember to loose feed on the little-and-often principle using a pole pot to deposit free bait directly over where the rig is being presented. When bites are coming on the drop, spread the group of No. 10s out

PRO-MICRON HI-TECH MONOFILAMENT

Diameter (mm)	Breaking Strain (lb)
0.05	10oz
0.055	12oz
0.06	14oz
0.065	1.03
0.07	1.16
0.075	1.27
0.08	1.45
0.085	1.67
0.09	1.96
0.1	2.27
0.11	2.49
0.12	3.04
0.13	3.57
0.15	4.87
0.16	5.6
0.18	6.94
0.2	8.24

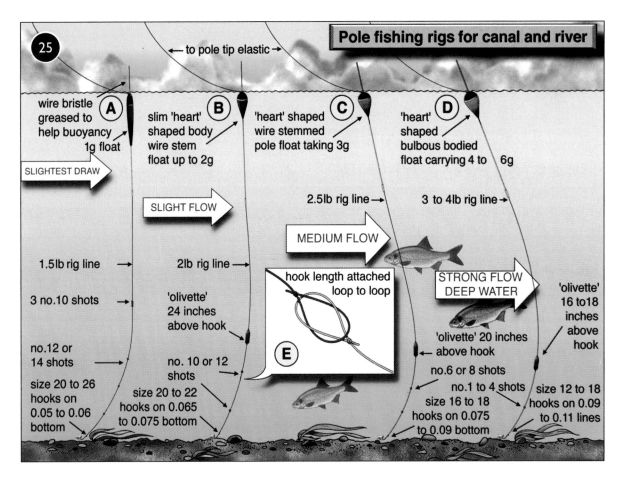

evenly further up the line. Plummet the swim carefully so the hook initially just touches bottom, and every so often lift the rig up to either side so the bait free falls naturally.

Fig. B shows a slightly more buoyant but slim heart-shaped bodied float with a wire stem for trotting in a slight flow taking a shotting load of up to 2g. Most of this is concentrated in a single olivette 24 inches above the hook with two or three No. 10 or 12 shot between it and hook. Presentation is of course far superior using the long-pole-short-line technique in depths of say 8 feet and below. In depth of 10 feet plus, fishing to hand will prove more effective by far, being much quicker than unshipping the pole after each cast to unhook or rebait, although remember that with an excess of line between float and pole tip

(beyond 3–5 feet) presentation is often impaired.

The strength of pole fishing in rivers is that you can hold back gently on the bulbous-bodied floats to slow the bait down dramatically so it trundles through the swim close to the bottom in a natural manner just like all the loose feed around it. Select the size of float necessary for the speed of current being fished, always erring on the heavy side rather than the lighter.

To introduce groundbait or loose feed accurately, dip the pole tip so it touches the surface and aim for that exact spot. For deep water lock the maggots or casters up in a ball of stiff groundbait or use a mini bait dropper to lay a carpet along the river bed.

Concentrate on holding the pole tip directly above and a little upstream of the float for maximum control, ensuring it is not repeatedly jerked or lifted. When strong winds prove troublesome, use a small back shot pinched on the line 10–12 inches above the float. In absolute howlers you may need as much as a swan shot which is far better than the float being repeatedly pulled off course by the wavering pole tip. Try it and see.

In Fig. C, a heart-shaped bodied float carrying up to 3g should be sufficient for presenting the bait trotting along just above bottom in medium-paced currents. This is the equivalent, for argument's sake, of around 5–6 BB if you were waggler fishing the same swim.

To take the bait straight down, an olivette is fixed around 20 inches above the hook with a couple of No. 6–8 shots between it and the hook. Remember that occasionally it pays to dispense with the control yardstick of always having the pole tip directly above or upstream of the float. In smallish rivers, especially where overhanging trees line the far bank with shoals of roach or chub beneath, don't be afraid to trot down several feet beyond the pole tip.

For still faster, and especially deeper, swims, use the rig in Fig. D which sports a bulbous-bodied, wire-stemmed pole float with a shotting capacity of 4–6g (depending upon flow) and concentrate the bulk shot closer still with a single olivette – say 16–18 inches above the hook. To ensure the bait actually trundles along the river bed, a No. 1–4 shot is pinched on midway between hook and olivette to complete the rig. Note how in all set-ups the hook is attached to nylon (as in Fig. E) loop to loop by tying a double overhand loop at the end of the rig line.

For combating the flow of exceedingly deep rivers (12–20 foot plus) and fishing to hand whilst presenting a static bait for bream or hybrids, which is imperative when water temperatures are low and the fishes' metabolism has slowed right down, consider the three completely different rigs in Diag. 26 which

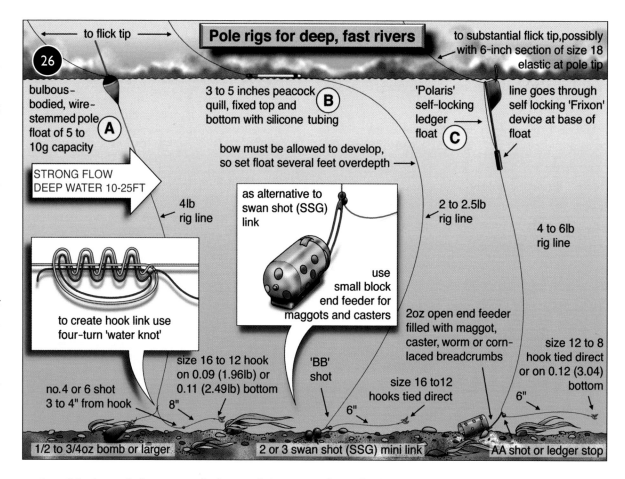

are best fished on a flick tip instead of internal elastic. Fig. A has a conventional bulbous-bodied wire-stemmed float with a capacity of 5–10g fixed 2 feet over depth (to allow for the subsurface bow formed by the current) with a mini fixed paternoster on the river bed to ensure the bait remains static, comprising a ½–¾-oz bomb on the link and an 8-inch hook length (tied to the rig line using a four-turn water knot) with a No. 4–6 shot 3–4 inches from the bait.

Or how about the lighter flat float rig in Fig. B with a 3–5-inch section of plain peacock quill fixed several feet over depth (to allow for a subsurface bow to form) with silicone bands at each end? Down below, you simply stop a mini ledger link of 2–3 swan shots, or a block-end feeder around 6 inches

from the hook with a BB shot. It may seem crude and you may wonder why the float needs to be flat, but the truth is, unless you set the float far enough over depth so it lies flat, current force will pull it under. Bites are registered as distinctive shakes or twitches of the flat float, or in the case of a big fish grabbing hold, the float zooms straight under. Indications where it suddenly half cocks also merit striking. To appreciate the mechanics of this particular rig, consult Method 11, 'Stret Pegging'.

Now we come to Fig. C and a rig developed relatively recently by my old mate, Terry Smith of the Anglers' World Holidays team, for combating the fast and deep water of Ireland's bream-bagging rivers – rivers like the Shannon, for instance, where you could have anything up to 25 feet of strongly flowing water beneath the pole tip or just beyond the marginal drop-off.

The float is one of the new breed of Polaris self-locking ledger floats which through a frixon device at the bottom automatically locks on the line at swim depth once the 2oz feeder has settled on the bottom. It works an absolute treat when fishing a long pole to hand in deep water for big roach or hybrids and bream. The feeder is stopped by a shot or ledger stop 6–8 inches above the hook which is either tied direct to a 4lb rig line or to a 3–4lb hook length when increasing the rig line to 5–6lb. Much depends on the size of fish expected and upon prevailing snags. Now usually this rig is best used on a fairly substantial flick tip and, as an extra safeguard, just 6 inches of size 18 (carp crunching) elastic can be incorporated between rig loop and tip.

Being wafer thin with an offset indicator tip, the float will hold out in the strongest currents without lifting the feeder. And by really tightening up to the 2oz feeder, only a minimal subsurface bow will form in the current regardless of depth. This float will also indicate lift bites, should a big old bream dislodge the feeder. Although the Polaris ledger float automatically locks on the line when the feeder settles, once depth has been established (unless the bottom is particularly uneven) pinch a small shot just below the float to speed up the process of tightening up.

There's much more to pole fishing than amassing a bag full of tiny roach, or bites in the field of competition angling. Through expanding various techniques numerous problems can be overcome.

Heavy float rigs taking 4–8g are the order of the day for catching jumbo-sized hybrids in Ireland's River Bann where depths over 20 feet accompany fast currents.

POLE FISHING IN STILL WATERS

Much of what I have said in relation to various pole types, their purchase and sundries in the preceding method also applies to wielding a pole in still water. Indeed there are numerous crossover points. For instance, pole fishing in a narrow drain or canal which, because they sometimes flow, are technically classed as rivers, often requires more delicate float rigs, compared say to fishing heavy in a gravel pit complex for carp where rig lines up to 6lb are used in conjunction with elastic up to size 18.

Indeed as the majority of pole-caught carp come from still waters, I think a few words are called for in this method about the new breed of super poles now produced by several companies for the sole purpose of subduing sizeable carp on thick elastic – carp-crunching poles, as the terminology goes. Using stronger elastics and getting really stuck in with an extremely thin-walled pole that simply wasn't designed for heaving up carp could cost you an arm and a leg – so read on.

Carp poles are designed with a through action, increased wall strength, strengthened stress points and real lifting power which is displaced throughout their entire length. This enables dead weights of up to 4lb to be lifted off the floor with some models. But rarely will you need this kind of animalism because, thankfully, a fish's specific gravity is considerably less when swimming. In other words it actually weighs far less in water. So you can hang on without worry and watch as the thickest, strongest elastics do their job.

ELASTICS

On the subject of elastics, while there is unfortunately no common colour-for-size yardstick used by the various manufacturers, I hope the table of elastic sizes and their uses (shown opposite) provides a helpful guide to both still water and river fishing.

Most serious pole anglers not only match the size of their elastic to their hook length and to the size of fish expected, but also to the strength of rig line (main line) and the hook being used. For instance, using a large size (thick) elastic in conjunction with a size 22–26 hook will result in bumping off both small and large fish, simply because the set-up is unbalanced. Conversely if using a large hook on a rig coupled to a small size (fine) elastic, you are then decidedly underpowered for hook setting. Again, the set-up is unbalanced. When marrying a small hook to fine elastic, however, you do stand a chance of eventually landing an unexpected whopper should one happen along. But obviously when seriously seeking larger fish only, the perfect partners are large size (thick and stronger) elastics and medium to large hooks. It is worth inspecting your fitted elastics regularly for abrasion or any nicks and unevenness which could suddenly fracture and cost you the entire rig, not to mention a fish towing it about. So look too at the knots at both the connector and bung ends.

ELASTIC SIZES

1–2	Suitable for hi-tech hook lengths down to 0.05 (10oz) in shallow still waters and canals for small fish to 8oz or thereabouts
3–4	Ideal for depths of 6-8 feet and hi-tech hook lengths up to 0.08 (1.45lb) for roach and skimmers up to 1½lb
5–6	Used with slightly beefier rigs incorporating hi-tech hook lengths to 0.11 (2.49lb) for big roach, hybrids, small- to medium-sized tench and bream.
8–10	Ideal for quality chub, tench, bagging up on big bream and for small- to medium-sized carp up to 5–6lb. Hi-tech lengths to 0.13 (3.57lb) or even higher
12–18	Purposely designed for carp crunching and landing specimens to over 10lb using hi-tech hook lengths up to 0.18 (6.94lb)

Match fisherman Richard Duke takes a firm grip of his long pole as a carp goes charging away at Gold Valley Lakes in Hampshire.

POLE CONNECTORS AND FITTING INTERNAL ELASTIC

The perfect way of telling at a glance which particular top two or top three kits is fitted with what size elastic, is simply to use coloured connectors to match that elastic. These brightly coloured connectors also allow you to see exactly where a big fish is heading and come with two sizes of cap, one for thinner and one for thicker elastic, which is extremely useful.

To secure a connector to internal elastic use two half inches, one after another (as in Diag. 27, Fig. A) each bedded down tightly. Ensure the elastic is perfectly dry and lubricate free or the knots will slip. At the other end use a double overhand loop for connecting to a mini bung (again, see Diag. 27 which shows how to rig pole elastic internally within a top two or three kit).

For fishing light, the top two sections only should be elasticated (some anglers only rig the top section), whereas for carp crunching a greater amount of stretch is provided by internally rigging the top three sections. To accommodate thicker elastic an external PTFE bush is recommended (as in Fig. C). In either case, for threading available the elastic through the top sections of your pole, use a special diamond-eye threader available at most tackle shops. Slip the end (an inch or so) of the elastic into the threader and push through from the tip section once the internal or external PTFE bush has been fitted. Once it's through, first attach the tip connector and then the bung. Incidentally the double overhand loop when

Get 'colour coded' when fitting internal elastic by using brightly coloured connectors so you can immediately differentiate between various top two and three kits.

tied at the end of your rig line is the best knot for enabling the hook length to be attached loop to loop, (as in Diag. 25, Fig. E on page 69). Don't bother with any other. After fitting the internal elastic, test it for tension and adjust at the bung end if necessary, then treat with a few drops of pole elastic lubricant through the PTFE bush to ensure that it stretches smoothly through the tip.

FLOATS

I have already stated that for river fishing floats should have bodies that are heart shaped in order to withstand current deviations. This top buoyancy is not required for fishing in still waters however and so float bodies are reversed, with the narrow part at the top. This is why floats recommended for still-water

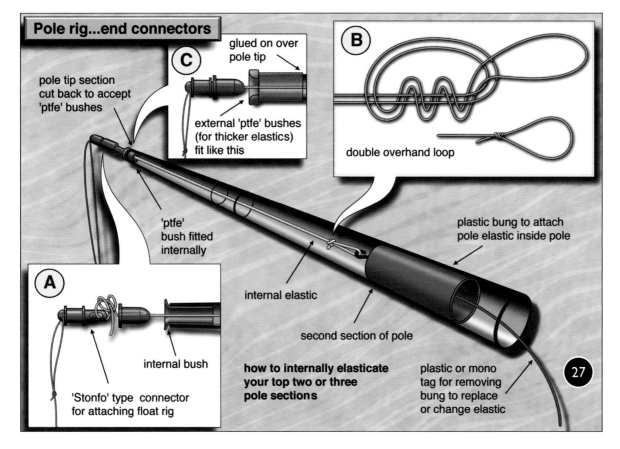

Pole rig...end connectors

pole tip section cut back to accept 'ptfe' bushes

C glued on over pole tip

external 'ptfe' bushes (for thicker elastics) fit like this

B

double overhand loop

'ptfe' bush fitted internally

A

internal bush

'Stonfo' type connector for attaching float rig

internal elastic

second section of pole

how to internally elasticate your top two or three pole sections

plastic bung to attach pole elastic inside pole

plastic or mono tag for removing bung to replace or change elastic

27

pole fishing have upside-down heart- or pear-shaped bodies (also called body-down floats) which create minimum resistance to a biting fish.

If in any doubt about the usage of a particular shaped float body, simply ask the guy who sells it to you – your tackle dealer. And while you're there, purchase a selection of plastic pole winders so you can make up an armoury of ready-made rigs (they're cheap enough) ensuring they are wider and longer than the float to prevent damage. To this end remember to put two or three sections of silicone tubing on wire-stemmed floats so they don't bend, and include some quick-drying paint and strong marker pens in your kit so you can change tip colour instantly to suit the background you are looking at.

Lastly when making up rigs at home, ensure you have two identical set-ups of each in your tackle tray so an instant replacement is at the ready in case of loss, and invest in a specialized shotting aid. These remove all the guesswork from what can be a frustrating necessity, by allowing you to put your weights in a tiny tray into which the float is slotted. Add a bucket of water and away you go. Shotting up rigs becomes easy.

Try not to become overawed by the sheer choice of Continental-style pole floats now available in the UK. No one can possibly provide a separate use for each and every slightly different model; it is quite literally product cosmetics gone completely barmy. I guess the same could be said of bristle (float tip) materials, with a choice of nylon, wire and cane, though for presenting an ultra-light rig to the shyest fish in crystal clear water, there is no doubt that wire bristles coated in a smear of mucilin (or bristle grease) not only become easier to shot, but provide the ultimate in terms of resistance to a biting fish. Just a smear of grease on the surface, and you can't beat that. But we are talking tiny, tiny bites here. For general close-range work in still waters, a range of slim-bodied floats, taking from say four to five No. 12–14 shots

should cover most situations for small roach, skimmers and crucian carp, whether presenting small baits like punched bread, bloodworm, casters or squatts on the drop or just above bottom. Consider the set-up shown in Diag. 28, Fig. A, for instance which is ideal for use with whips or the long-pole-short-line technique. It comprises a super-slim, extremely long taper body-down wire-stem float with a cane tip carrying four or five No. 14 split shot or the equivalent in Styl weights evenly spread down to a size 18–22 hook so that light or buoyant baits such as casters or punched bread are presented naturally on the drop. Watch how the float settles slowly in stages, finally coming to rest on the bottom with the merest dot of the cane tip showing. Obviously the slightest hold-up on the way down demands instant action. If, once the bait finally settles on the bottom, there is little interest shown, dragging and lifting the float gently from side to side imparts natural movement and will incite bites.

When stepping up somewhat you should also include amongst your armoury a reverse-body float range that carries a shotting capacity from say 0.10g up to 0.30g which are again suitable for both whip or long-pole short-line situations (as shown in Fig. B). It always helps to remember, if you are new to pole fishing and these suggestions seem rather light, that unlike stick or waggler fishing, pole floats do not have to be cast, simply lowered creating the absolutely minimum of disturbance. This is the real beauty of presenting a float rig directly beneath a pole tip. You can use a rig taking fewer than a quarter of the shots that would be required with running tackle. And that's a fact.

In Fig. B lock the bulk shots (sizes 10–12) 30 inches above the hook and pinch on a size 12 and 14 in between, so the bait falls really slowly before it finally touches bottom. This bite-inciting movement can be repeated at any time, of course, simply by

John took this lovely net of plump crucians on a 3m whip from the prolific waters of Willow Park Lakes in Ash, near Aldershot.

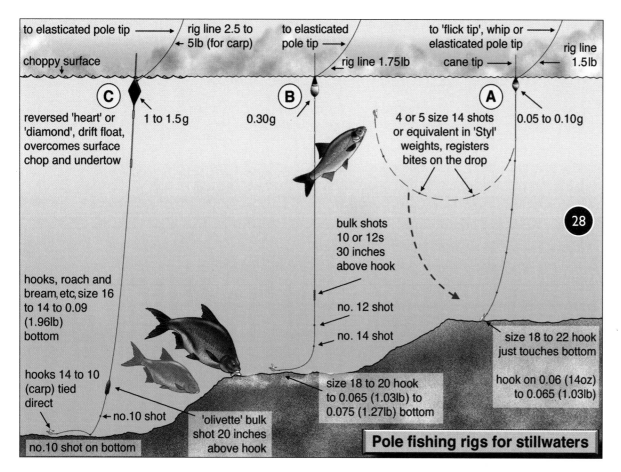

to elasticated pole tip → rig line 2.5 to
← 5lb (for carp)

choppy surface

(C)

reversed 'heart' or
'diamond', drift float,
overcomes surface
chop and undertow

1 to 1.5g

hooks, roach and
bream, etc, size 16
to 14 to 0.09
(1.96lb)
bottom

hooks 14 to 10
(carp) tied
direct

→ no.10 shot

no.10 shot on bottom

'olivette' bulk
shot 20 inches
above hook

to elasticated
pole tip →

rig line 1.75lb

(B)

0.30g

bulk shots
10 or 12s
30 inches
above hook

no. 12 shot

no. 14 shot

size 18 to 20 hook
to 0.065 (1.03lb) to
0.075 (1.27lb) bottom

to 'flick tip', whip or
elasticated pole tip

cane tip →

rig line
1.5lb

(A)

4 or 5 size 14 shots
or equivalent in 'Styl'
weights, registers
bites on the drop

0.05 to 0.10g

28

size 18 to 22 hook
just touches bottom

hook on 0.06 (14oz)
to 0.065 (1.03lb)

Pole fishing rigs for stillwaters

A) set to fish at 2–4 feet deep with several tiny shots or Styl weights evenly distributed between float and hook. Bites will register with the float failing to settle, or disappearing like greased lightning. Remember to keep the loose feed going in with each cast and endeavour to drop your hook bait right in the middle of it.

PLAYING FISH ON THE WHIP

Remember that the ultra-fine carbon tip (flick tip) of the whip acts as the cushion or buffer between you and the fish, enabling quite sizeable fish to be beaten on comparatively light rigs without elastic. Fortunately small hooks are usually pulled from the lips of oversized specimens long before damage to the fine tip occurs, or the finer hook length itself breaks.

Generally whips are used to hand with the rig line slightly shorter than pole length so that small fish may be swung out and straight into your hand – hence the terminology. When the situation occurs however, such as fishing into quite shallow water 5–6 metres out, the whip can be used in a long-pole-short-line situation, where the whip is carefully fed behind as the fish is played out. While most whips are fully telescopic, certain top-of-the-range models are telescopic in the top four sections only with take-apart, put-over lower joints. This makes them absolutely perfect for the long-whip-short-line approach. You can even purchase an optional extra 1m put-over joint for such whips increasing their to-hand function to 7m.

PLAYING FISH ON THE ELASTIC

Whether fishing a long pole to hand or a long pole and short line, it is only your elastic which allows sizeable fish eventually to be tired out and landed on a rod which hardly bends. It is in fact a complete

lifting the float up and allowing the bait to fall again. It works particularly effectively for species such as perch when used in conjunction with chopped worm loose feed – and half a brandling or a bloodworm on the hook.

Going up to much heavier rigs for greater stability in still waters, to overcome subsurface tow or wind drift, I recommend a reverse-heart, or diamond-bodied range of floats carrying 1–1.5g, which have reasonable tips that can easily be seen if fishing at, say, 11 metres to hand in rippled deep water. As Fig. C illustrates, here a single olivette concentrates the bulk shot 20 inches above the hook which takes the bait straight down to the bottom for species like bream, tench and carp when using corn, maggots, bread punch, casters or worm, and just two size 10–12 shots

between it and the hook. The lowest shot is actually lying on the bottom ensuring the hook bait is presented static, which is how bream, in particular, like it. To this end ensure you keep them grubbing about on the bottom by the regular introduction of stiff groundbait balls, well wetted. They need to go straight down to the lake bed and only break up once there, not halfway down or the fish could start moving up in the water to intercept loose particles.

For carp of large proportions, increase rig (main) line from 2½lb to 5lb and tie strongly forged hooks up to size 10 direct. When carp, rudd or roach move into the upper water layers to take maggots or casters on the drop, as they do in really warm weather, dispense with the rig in Fig. C in preference for a super-light presentation and an on-the-drop set-up (shown in Fig.

reverse to the art of landing sizeable trout or salmon on fly tackle, where the line itself has little stretch, but the rod does and arches over into a full circle to act as the consummate buffer against the lunges of powerful game fish.

So learn to use your pole elastic as the truly wonderful buffer it most certainly is, without panicking. Occasionally you might need to add an extra section or two (if you have any left) when a portly carp goes charging off towards the opposite side of the lake. If fishing long pole and short line, it may seem an eternity before the fish is tired sufficiently for you to unship the lower joints and think about getting the landing net into position, but provided your elastic, rig line, hook length and hook are all balanced, as I mentioned earlier, and perform in harmony, you stand a fair chance of tiring most adversaries. Look at those you don't tire philosophically – and tie on another hook length.

Actually, many carp-crunching enthusiasts simply

Jan Van Schendel might come from Holland but he's obviously at home bagging up on bream from the Fennes Fishery in Essex. Note his organized tackle and bait layout.

don't bother with finer, lighter hook lengths when utilizing the stronger size 16 and 18 elastics, preferring to tie the hook direct to a 5lb rig line. In hi-tech lines you can even safely go up to 0.18 which is 6.94lb test.

STICK FLOAT FISHING

This delightful technique is the lightest, most delicate, most sensitive and some would say the most rewarding method of trotting. It is especially suited to catching smaller, clear-water, shy-biting river species such as roach and dace, although quality sized chub and even the occasional barbel will most certainly also come your way. It is of paramount importance to remember that whether trotting in narrow or really wide rivers, stick float fishing is, above all, a close-range technique, suitable in depths of 4–10 feet in currents from really slow to medium fast. Currents that are fast or really moving along are better suited to larger, more buoyant floats carrying an increased shotting load.

Being secured with silicone tubing at both ends, the stick float can be trotted along with the absolute minimum of slack line between its tip and the reel, and periodically held back so the hook bait simulates the speed and natural movements of all loose-fed maggots or casters working through the swim around it (see Diag. 31). For instance, if you throw some casters, maggots or liquidized bread into a clear river and watch carefully, you will observe that while the loose feed initially gets whisked quickly along at surface speed, after a few yards it drastically slows down as it starts to sink, proving that the surface current is moving far quicker than those fish-holding layers down below close to the bottom. Consequently by the time it reaches that all-important taking zone which is invariably within 2 feet of the river bed, it might only be moving at half the speed of the surface. It is with the help of a sensitively shotted stick float rig and careful manipulation at the rod and reel end, by which this much slower presentation of the hook bait can be achieved – ensuring it is sucked in confidently.

The common mistake made by those trying stick float fishing for the first time is that they fish too far out. Indeed because you need to employ such a tight control, compared to waggler fishing for instance, the method cannot effectively be executed any further than one and a half rod lengths out. Otherwise the bait will be pulled away from the feed line every time the float is held back (see Diag. 30). So for swims beyond a distance of, say, 20 feet and in really windy weather (when it is impossible to fish the stick), concentrate on the waggler.

Calm conditions in fact are tailor made for stick float fishing, where the float can be shotted down so only the merest suggestion of its tip showing. And if

There can be few more delightful ways of seeking roach, dace and chub than putting a stick float down an even-paced run on a crisp winter's day.

Stick float fishing

line to rod tip

29

shotting load graduated down line 'shirt-button style' with smallest closest hook

bait now precedes float, clear of bottom

E holding back hard on float swings bait enticingly away from bottom

D

C float held back steadily brings bait directly in line below it

silicone tubing

CURRENT FLOW

B float under gentle control

A float trots unchecked

3/4 to 1.5lb hook length, with hook sizes 16 to 24

single maggot or caster, catches less on bottom

there is a gentle upstream wind to slow those surface layers down a shade, so much the better. The secret at all times, after careful plumbing of the swim, is to set the float a little over depth and actually to overshot so it almost disappears when running through unchecked.

The shotting load is graduated at regular intervals (often referred to as shotting up shirt-button style) providing a great stabilizing keel for holding back and slowing the float's passage down. You can see from Diag. 29 how the shots are spaced evenly between float and hook to achieve the most sensitive presentation of the bait with the smallest nearest the hook. A good yardstick to remember is always to use too much shot rather than too little, ensuring the tip

of the float is a mere blimp in the surface film so the tiniest of bites are indicated.

During the winter months, especially when water temperatures remain low, you will connect with numerous bites that barely sink the tip – bites which simply would not be seen with a full ¼ inch of the tip showing. In addition, endeavour to present the bait as far over-depth as the current strength will allow before catching bottom (see Diag. 29, Fig. A). Even big stick floats carrying a shotting load of say 5–6 BB are best fished well over-shotted to ensure the bait is presented as slowly as possible, with the absolute minimum of tip to disappear in registering a bite. This level of sensitivity can only ever be achieved when trotting at close range.

Every so often holding back hard on the float for a few seconds will swing the bait enticingly up and forwards in the way that loose feed around it is trundled along by the current, as in Diag. 29, Fig. D. So watch out for those sudden snatches when the float tip dots under momentarily prior to resettling.

RODS AND REELS

It is to accommodate the striking of these really tiny bites and the use of just 1½–2lb reel lines that specialized stick float rods with fine-diameter spliced-in tips were designed. The 20–24-inch supersensitive tip permits lightning-quick strikes yet maintains a safety margin whilst using hook lengths down to as light as just 12oz and size 20–22 fine-wire hook patterns. In short, everything, when stick float fishing, is geared to offering the bait as sensitively and naturally as possible.

Most purpose-designed stick float rods are 12½–13 feet in length and extremely light. Top-of-the-range models usually contain a higher carbon content and thus have an extremely narrow profile that cuts far quicker through air resistance, compared to thicker-diameter, heavier, sloppier, cheaper rods.

Having described the virtues of the perfect stick float rod this does not of course preclude you catching fish on a stick float using a waggler rod. Indeed most anglers make do. It is simply more enjoyable and more exact when using the correct tool for the job.

Perhaps the most important of all is reel choice. For allowing the current to pull the float along, whilst ensuring line peels smoothly from a revolving drum (which also helps to slow its passage down incidentally), I have no hesitation in suggesting that the perfect reel for stick float fishing (and most other forms of trotting) is the centre pin. Good quality centre pins come fitted with a micro drag adjustment which, by means of a knurled knob (because it puts

Having waded out to stick float a deep run along the far bank of Yorkshire's lovely River Tees,
John is rewarded with a good chub.

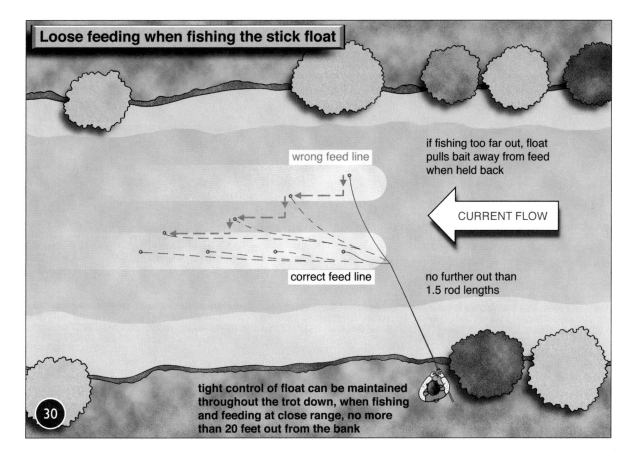

Loose feeding when fishing the stick float

wrong feed line

if fishing too far out, float
pulls bait away from feed
when held back

CURRENT FLOW

correct feed line

no further out than
1.5 rod lengths

tight control of float can be maintained
throughout the trot down, when fishing
and feeding at close range, no more
than 20 feet out from the bank

30

*Scaling down to a 22 hook and a pound
bottom beneath a 5 no. 6 stick float
produced this net of River Tees chub and
dace – all on casters.*

gentle pressure against the spindle or pin), permits extremely fine tuning of the spinning drum as the float is drawn downstream by the current. This not only creates a tight line between reel and float throughout the trot, but ensures the float will go steadily down the swim under exactly the degree of control intended.

From running through unchecked, to holding back hard, no other kind of reel can possibly give this kind of absolute control. You simply take your thumb off the rim of the drum and allow the float to do the work and pull line out steadily. I particularly love this mode of fishing when trotting a stick directly downstream in a perfectly straight line from an anchored boat. It is then possible to overshot the float completely (to the point where if run through unchecked it would sink) but send it down with just

a mere blimp visible above the surface simply by finely adjusting the micro screw so the drum revolves to give only just the right amount of line.

In my opinion the closed-face reel (because it is particularly effective in windy weather) would be second choice, with standard fixed-spool reels coming third. But neither can compare with a centre pin and if you intend doing any amount of stick float fishing I urge you to invest in a top-performance centre pin. It will last a lifetime and unlike most things in this world, save for wine and spirits, can only improve with age. The beauty of the centre pin is that it is so simple to use and because the thumb releases pressure on the drum for line instantly to be given with the minimum of torque on fine lines and tiny fine-wire hooks (compared to the roller or stainless-steel pin around which the line must travel

at right angles with both fixed-spool and closed-face reels) the centre pin is unrivalled.

Those wishing to use either fixed-spool or closed-face reels should endeavour to be miserly when allowing line to peel from the spool. Under gentle control from the forefinger against the rim (outer casing in the case of closed-face reels), permit just enough line to be taken downstream on demand from current pull. Keeping the rod tip low so that several feet of line (floating on the surface) are thus drawn by the grip of surface tension makes this far easier, tending to dampen that sudden release and burst of line each time the forefinger is momentarily lifted.

Keeping the rod tip low is also a useful tip to remember when putting the stick float downstream against an upstream wind. Any line flap will of course jerk the float tip which in turn pulls the bait unnaturally off course.

LINES

As for the correct line strength, well, overall I prefer a 2lb test reel line. Considering the amount of wear monofilament suffers from being continually pulled backwards and forwards over the metal of rod rings (modern lined rings with silicone carbide or aluminium oxide centres obviously reduce this friction) often under the severe pressure of a hard-fighting chub or roach after roach, I prefer a reasonable degree of safety. Besides it is only at the hook end where line diameter actually makes any significant difference as to whether a fish bites or not. It makes sense therefore to have at the ready a selection of hook length spools in tests from say 12oz up to 1½lb and to join a 24-inch length to the reel line using a four-turn water knot before tying the hook on. Those brands of a low diameter and of low stretch are particularly useful for inducing bites from extra spooky roach and dace. Their greatly reduced diameter compared to standard monofilament of identical strength creates minimal water resistance, enabling light baits such as a single caster or a tiny pellet of punched bread to behave as naturally as the loose feed around it.

HOOKS

If you use hooks pre-tied to nylon, don't just ask your tackle dealer for size 18 spade end hooks to nylon. Most shops nowadays stock a choice of hook length breaking strains, coupled to a wide selection of actual hook patterns. Small species can easily be handled on fire-wire hooks, whilst if a specimen chub or maybe a barbel is on the cards, a forged pattern would be advisable. And if you are using punched bread, a wide-gape, fine-wire hook is the model to go for.

Ideal patterns are the Tuberini Series 2, the Drennan Polemaster wide-gape pole hooks and the Kamasan B511. The B611 is an extra-strong version of the latter, designed for larger fish.

It is essential to remember whilst using punched bread not to blunt the hook point when lifting out the pellet. Therefore choose a punch which is chamfered below the hook slot – ensuring the point does not touch the bowl. Simply insert the hook point into the middle of the compressed pellet and carefully ease out – all in one fluent movement. To cover a variety of situations, acquire a set of bread punches with head (bowl) diameters ranging from 1.5mm up to 5mm.

Incidentally, for producing exactly the right feed to accompany punched bread on the hook, prepare some liquidized bread feed. Really fresh doughy white sliced loaf makes the best liquidized bread. You simply cut the crusts from a dozen or so slices and put one or two at a time into an electric liquidizer, and it's ready in an instant. To give the feed a lively yellow colour, which could be useful in water with a distinct grey or greeny tinge, sprinkle a little turmeric over the bread prior to switching on.

FISHING THE STICK FLOAT

To avoid tangles and to be sure the float set-up lies down nicely at the head of the swim, it is important always to cast out using a gentle underarm swing and

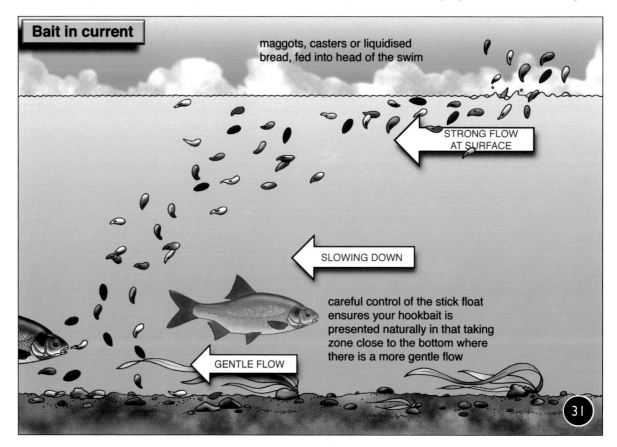

Bait in current

maggots, casters or liquidised bread, fed into head of the swim

STRONG FLOW AT SURFACE

SLOWING DOWN

careful control of the stick float ensures your hookbait is presented naturally in that taking zone close to the bottom where there is a more gentle flow

GENTLE FLOW

31

flick. Then quickly pull the float over the feed line so the bait is immediately presented correctly and beware of those instant on-the-drop bites which fail to allow the float tip to settle down on its preshotted position – when it should be struck immediately! Dace especially are renowned for snapping up a caster as it is being taken down by the lower shots – on the drop – which is something I discuss later.

For now, look carefully at the standard shotting patterns in Diag. 29, Fig. A and you will notice the small shots, Nos. 8, 6, 4, or No. 1, or even BB (depending upon the capacity of the float being used) are spread evenly with a single dust shot pinched on around 15–20 inches above the hook. Incidentally, and this is one of the benefits of using the stick float, should your choice prove wrong because you misread current strength or you need to swap over to a wider or narrower tip, as the line is not actually threaded through any part of the float, changing from one to another is accomplished in seconds.

Sometimes bites will occur when the float is left to trot along totally unchecked and preceding the bait as in Fig. A. Usually, however, though not always, I have to admit (sometimes fish simply want it dragging through) many more bites can be induced by constant and careful control of the stick float's passage, which in the case of the centre pin simply means applying thumb pressure upon the rim of the drum. This results in gentle control as in Fig. B which slows the bait down most effectively.

Holding back steadily as in Fig. C will bring the bait forward so that it almost fishes directly beneath the float. And in Fig. D and Fig. E holding back hard on the stick float cause the bait to swing enticingly up and away from the bottom so it actually precedes the float. Small fish in particular are attracted to this upward swing of light baits and so bites are naturally going to be quick. Incidentally, whenever bites from

nuisance species such as bleak, minnows or immature dace occur within the mid-water layers as a delicately shotted stick float rig is falling, loose feed may be introduced with the aid of a bait dropper instead of being loose fed by hand.

BAITS

The bait favoured by stick float enthusiasts is, of course, the single sinking caster which, due to its inherent buoyancy, is most attractively presented; with a single maggot or small pellet of punched bread following close behind. Larger baits such as bunches of maggots or casters being heavier, all too easily catch on the bottom when the float is set well over depth. A handy tip here, especially where the bottom is uneven or snaggy, is to use a really dark caster which being more advanced in the process of metamorphosis, and thus lighter, will drift easily above.

Actually the colour of a caster and which is best is a subject that always promotes discussion amongst stick float fishermen. Some say casters should all be the same even deep red colour while others, myself included, prefer a variation from the honey colour of those which have only just turned, and consequently sink the fastest, to orange, red, deep red and brown, in order that various presentations may be achieved to suit a variety of situations.

Another aspect worth considering is the colour of a caster in relation to actual water colour. For instance a yardstick followed by many top match anglers is: the more colour in the water, the lighter should be the colour of the caster on the hook.

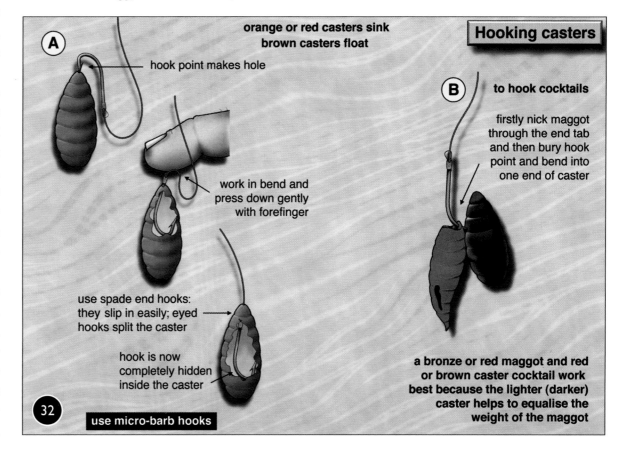

A
orange or red casters sink
brown casters float
hook point makes hole
work in bend and press down gently with forefinger
use spade end hooks: they slip in easily; eyed hooks split the caster
hook is now completely hidden inside the caster
32
use micro-barb hooks

Hooking casters

B to hook cocktails
firstly nick maggot through the end tab and then bury hook point and bend into one end of caster

a bronze or red maggot and red or brown caster cocktail work best because the lighter (darker) caster helps to equalise the weight of the maggot

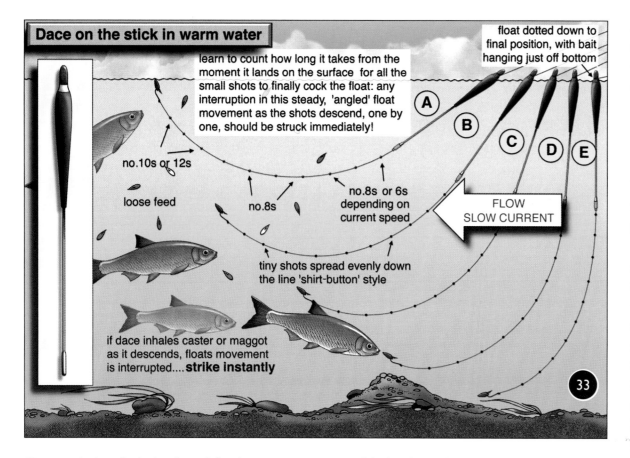

Dace on the stick in warm water

learn to count how long it takes from the moment it lands on the surface for all the small shots to finally cock the float: any interruption in this steady, 'angled' float movement as the shots descend, one by one, should be struck immediately!

float dotted down to final position, with bait hanging just off bottom

Ⓐ Ⓑ Ⓒ Ⓓ Ⓔ

no.10s or 12s

loose feed

no.8s

no.8s or 6s depending on current speed

FLOW SLOW CURRENT

tiny shots spread evenly down the line 'shirt-button' style

if dace inhales caster or maggot as it descends, floats movement is interrupted....**strike instantly**

33

However, in heavily (tea) coloured flood waters, say, a dark caster is by far the most easily seen.

Some prefer deep red casters because they are distinctly crispy and far less prone to bursting when inserting the hook. Whilst on the subject of hooking, remember it is imperative to bury and completely hide the hook inside the caster's shell as in Diag. 32, Fig. A. This can only be achieved using a size 18 hook or smaller and ensures there is nothing to catch up, even when the caster drags over bottom debris. Start by making a hole in one end of the caster with the hook point and then follow on by gently easing the bend and shank inside (pressing against the spade end with your forefinger) until the hook completely disappears inside. If using a caster-maggot cocktail, start by nicking on the maggot gently through the tab of the thick end and then bury the hook point and

part of the bend into the caster, as in Diag. 32, Fig. B.

Due to the neatness of the spade–end knot compared to the far bulkier junction of an eyed hook knot, always use fire-wire spade-end hooks for caster fishing to achieve the most natural presentation.

An elderberry on the hook can produce excellent results wherever dace and roach may become used to loose-fed hempseed, while a small cube of breadcrust can often produce those better quality fish. For both crust cubes and punched bread use liquidized bread as loose feed on the very-little-and-often basis. This also applies to fishing with maggots and casters. Feed in no more than a few, say three to six, every trot through in slow swims, or every other trot through in fast swims, and the shoal will keep competing. Overdo the loose feed and the shoal will quickly become disinterested, so

remember to gear your rate of feed accordingly. It is a case of constant thought and constant control throughout when stick float fishing – if you desire constant action!

DACE ON THE STICK IN WARM WATER

The answer here is, of course, to use as light a stick float as you can get away with and shot it down progressively with tinier shot every 6–10 inches (depending upon current strength and swim depth) so that virtually nothing of the tip remains on the surface if the float is held back when being run through. Then get used to counting down and observing how many seconds it takes for all the shots finally to dot the float tip down, from the moment the rig is flipped in (as in Diag. 33). Then instantly hit the slightest interruption of that angled movement as one by one the shots descend with the bait and eventually cock the float. To help facilitate a slow descent, remember that darker casters are more buoyant than lighter coloured ones. It's not unlike watching for the float to rise whilst presenting the lift method, except that the float tip won't lift; it simply won't continue to sink at the speed it should. This is the reason for using lots of tiny shots and spreading them evenly down the line between the float and hook shirt-button style. One big shot close to the hook would cock the float instantly; a dozen tiny shots may take several seconds, and this is your striking period for bites on the drop.

For the specimen dace enthusiast like Bruce Vaughan, stick float fishing really comes into its own during the winter months once the bottom has been scoured by floods.

STRET PEGGING

If I was asked to select just one method of float fishing for running water that's guaranteed to present the bait completely static on the bottom, exactly where you want it for contacting those larger-than-average-sized fish, it would be stret pegging every time, both summer and winter.

Though seldom used by the vast majority of freshwater anglers, this devastatingly effective technique can put whoppers on the bank inhabiting those slow or fast runs close into the margins, from both shallow and deep water alike, where ledgering is otherwise the only other viable option. So if, like me, you enjoy watching a float and fancy getting into the swing of this basically simple yet fascinating method, study Diags 34 and 35 and read on.

Stret pegging (also sometimes referred to as stret corking and cork bobbing) could well be labelled the utility method of float fishing because it is one which can be employed throughout the year in marginal swims, virtually regardless of current speed, as long as the float is set far enough over depth. It is therefore an ideal method during the winter months, especially for tackling flood waters when due to minimal visibility all species grub about along the bottom and respond wonderfully to an anchored bait.

You see, when rivers are running fast and the colour of coffee, fen fish dart about sucking in food items at all levels, as they do in normal conditions. They prefer to keep their heads down and rely more upon smell than sight.

THE SET-UP

As you can see from Diag. 34, to alleviate current pressure against the line between float and shots the float is pushed up the line from 2 feet (in gentle currents) to as far as 4 or even 6 feet (in fast swims) over depth. If this is not done, it will of course be quickly pulled under as in Diag. 35, Fig. B instead of lying flat on the surface. Ensuring the float lies flat instead of being half cocked is what allows the bait to be presented completely static on the bottom with the absolute minimum of resistance to a biting fish. Note the accentuated bow in Diag. 34.

So that the rig does not drag round across the current and collect debris or snag up, the cast must always be made directly downstream and a little

With slower water and a deep run immediately downstream of the rod tip, this mouthwatering swim is screaming out to be stret pegged.

Stret pegging...correctly — **34**

balsa trotter, plain peacock quill or float from the optional selection, fixed at both ends with silicone bands

how the rig should look beneath the surface

float should lie flat — to rod

the subsurface 'bow' formed by the line is what actually allows the float to lie flat and provide minimal resistance to a biting fish

float is set 2 to 6 feet over depth, enabling subsurface 'bow' to form in line

remember: without this 'bow' the bait will not 'hold' in position!

reel line 2 to 3lb for dace, roach, bream, etc, reel line 5 to 8lb for specimen chub, barbel and carp

CURRENT FLOW

single 'AA' or swan shot (SSG) pinched on line 8 to12 inches above the hook, tied direct

large baits ward off unwanted attention of smaller species

see diagram 37 for bottom-end options

float options

'chubber'

'Avon'

'balsa'

'stick'

across so the shots settle the bait exactly where you want it, at the end of the run without fouling, followed by the line taking on a subsurface bow from shots to float (as in Diag. 36). Allow this bow to form simply by playing out several feet of line once the shots have settled, then gently tightening up. Don't just cast out, close the bale arm and plonk the rod down. The rod must, of course, also be angled downstream preferably on two rests (unless held with just a supporting front rest) so the float lies perfectly flat and sways gently from side to side in the current. If it wants to cock due to extra-fast currents, either pay out a little more line, raise the front rod rest so less line lies on the surface or simply slide the float further up the line until it does lie flat. That's all you do.

It really is so basically simple, once you have learnt

to appreciate the necessity of that bow in the line between float and shots formed by the current. The line can never lie straight from the float to shots as in Diag. 35, Fig. A – it's an impossibility. Sea anglers who boat fish using the uptide method will appreciate stret pegging because unless they pay out a huge bow of line in the tide between lead and the boat, their bait will simply not hold its position. It will get pulled across the sea bed until it is directly down tide of the boat and even eventually lift off the bottom.

For stret pegging floats I prefer stems of plain peacock quill in lengths of 4–7 inches with a ¾-inch tip band of fire orange. However any commercial straight peacock waggler is ideal as long as it fixed to the line with a silicone band at both ends. For swims where the surface is broken

or in extremely fast water, I change the peacock quill over for a balsa trotter, which is less susceptible to subsurface vortexes and suction. Both floats can easily be converted for fishing after dark by adding a chemical night light, attached by the tube of clear silicone provided. Remember that stret pegging during the hours of darkness is a most successful way of coming to grips with ultra-shy specimen river roach, bream, chub or barbel – and especially carp.

BOTTOM RIGS

Now for the bottom end options, of which there are several. In really slow currents simply pinch on an AA or a swan shot 8–12 inches above the hook (see Diag. 37, Fig. A). For currents demanding extra weight to ensure the bait stays anchored and completely static, mini ledger links can be quickly made by folding a couple of inches of line around the reel line just above the swan shot (Fig. B) and pinching on a single swan shot, or two, or three. Being dense, 2 x SSG and 3 x SSG shots (Fig. C) are tailor-made for making these mini running ledgers. Another way is to add a small Drennan ring to an inch or two of line and pinch sufficient shots on (Fig. D) or even tie on a small bomb (Fig. E). For depositing seeds, finely chopped worms, maggots or casters accurately, in really fast water you can even add a small block-end swim feeder (Fig. F).

Alternatively stick with a swan-shot rig and simply make regular use of a bait dropper to achieve the same result. This is why stret pegging is so successful with species like barbel. Using the float rig itself for dropping down a carpet of hempseed for instance, prior to and during the session, is achieved with a degree of pinpoint accuracy that no other method can match.

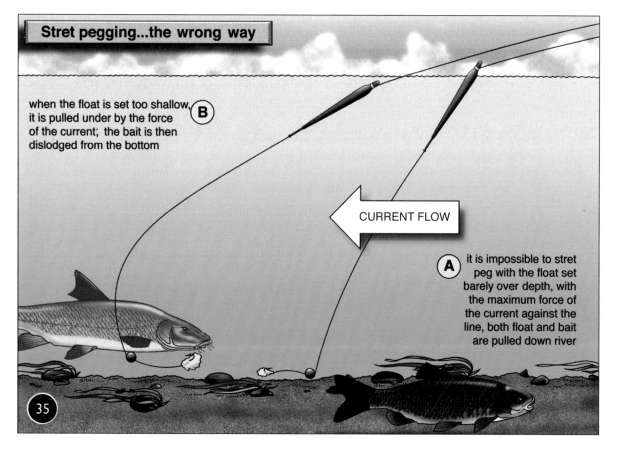

Stret pegging...the wrong way

when the float is set too shallow, **B** it is pulled under by the force of the current; the bait is then dislodged from the bottom

CURRENT FLOW

A it is impossible to stret peg with the float set barely over depth, with the maximum force of the current against the line, both float and bait are pulled down river

35

Wherever trees overhang and in deep runs where the bank has been piled, expect a perch to gobble up your stret-pegged lobworm.

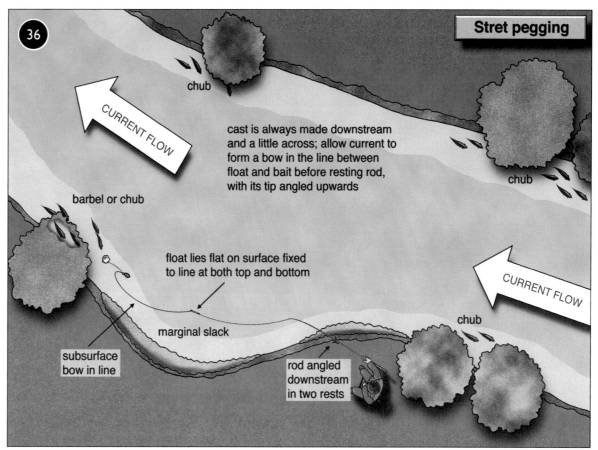

As a point of reference, I would suggest that currents demanding say more than four or five swan shot will be just too fast for employing stret pegging tactics with sensitivity – unless stret pegging for pike using much heavier tackle (see Diag. 38). And here lies the secret to obtaining consistent success from this versatile method, because it is all about observing surface currents and searching out those deep marginal runs close beside beds of sedges or bullrushes, areas of slack water immediately downstream from the inside of

a bend, lay-bys, cut-ins, and slacks behind sunken trees and bridge supports. Even a sunken bush will, in high levels of flooding for instance, provide a small area of slack water immediately behind, just downstream. And all a shoal of roach or a group of chub requires is a yard patch of quiet water where they can rest up just away from full current force. Perch tend to take up residence in such spots too.

So spend time in carefully selecting these marginal swims using the stret pegging rig like a built-in plummet (which of course it is) to locate all the suitable depth spots which can later be explored. Needless to say, because the method can only be used close in (unless fishing directly downstream from an anchored boat) treading

stealthily is of paramount importance when the fish you hope to catch are rarely more than one rod length away.

RODS AND REELS

Talking of rods, when using light lines, say in the 2–3lb test range, for dace, roach, bream and the occasional chub, I use a 13-foot carbon float rod. But when specimen chub, barbel and even carp are the target species the outfit is stepped up to an 11–12-foot carbon Avon-actioned rod coupled to line strengths of 5–8lb test. Line strength largely depends on whether the swim contains any snags or sunken branches, or is capable of throwing up a real monster requiring a degree of strength in reserve.

Even the tiniest runs between dense beds of sedge or reed are likely to contain the occasional group of big dace or roach – and stret pegging is the answer.

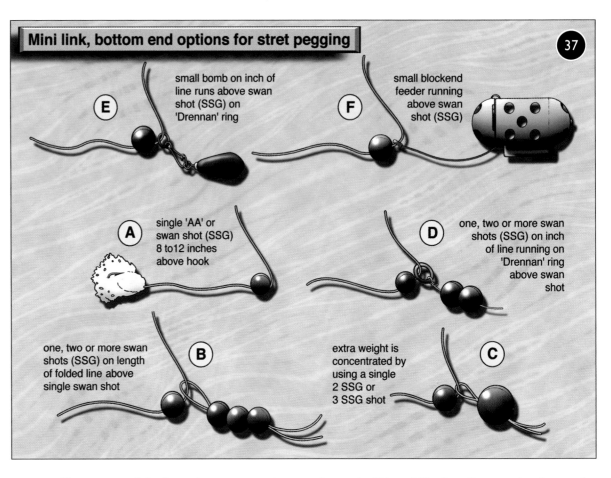

Mini link, bottom end options for stret pegging

37

E small bomb on inch of line runs above swan shot (SSG) on 'Drennan' ring

F small blockend feeder running above swan shot (SSG)

A single 'AA' or swan shot (SSG) 8 to12 inches above hook

D one, two or more swan shots (SSG) on inch of line running on 'Drennan' ring above swan shot

B one, two or more swan shots (SSG) on length of folded line above single swan shot

C extra weight is concentrated by using a single 2 SSG or 3 SSG shot

Either way the hook is always tied direct to the reel line and for stret pegging there is nothing to beat a centre-pin reel.

BAITS

As far as baits are concerned I cannot think of one I would not use whilst stret pegging. What's more for spooky chub, barbel, or carp, baits like meat cubes, seeds, nuts, beans or even boilies can be most effectively presented on a short hair rig for that extra pulling power. My favourite stret pegging baits are breadflake, a thumbnail-sized piece of covering a size 8 hook and a large, lively lobworm on a size 6 or 4. Both take you straight through to the whoppers.

STRET PEGGING FOR PIKE

I mentioned earlier that stret pegging for pike is a very effective method and indeed it is whether exploring deep holes, eddies, or runs close into the bank from amongst the marginal growth, or better still from the platform of an anchored boat which allows to you offer a static deadbait in a most natural manner anywhere across the river's width. By using a sliding float whilst stret pegging (as shown in Diag. 35) virtually any depth may be tackled.

Simply sleeve a small bead and a through-the-middle pike sliding float on to the main line, followed by a second bead, then thread on a size 10 snap swivel (to take the ledger weight) followed by a size 10 swivel. I then tie on a 20-inch length of reel line to which is added the pike trace itself. Mine is made from 20 inches of 15lb test alasticum for instance, holding a duo of semi-barbless size 8 trebles. Lastly, at around twice the swim depth (to account for that bow, remember) I tie a five-turn sliding stop knot with 7lb test power gum to the reel line above the top bead.

The cast is then made directly downstream and a little across so the deadbait is taken down to the

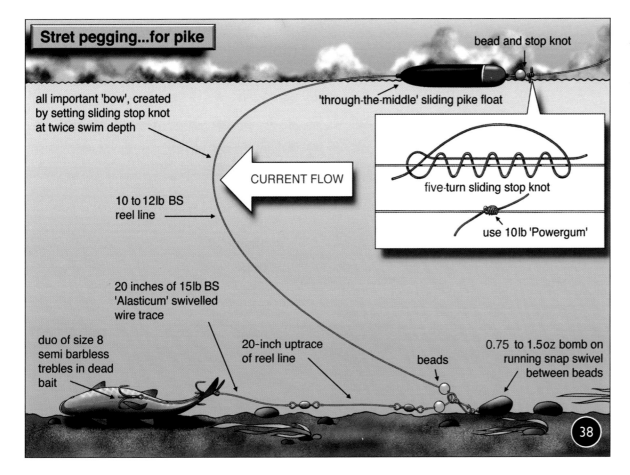

Stret pegging...for pike

bead and stop knot

'through-the-middle' sliding pike float

all important 'bow', created by setting sliding stop knot at twice swim depth

CURRENT FLOW

five-turn sliding stop knot

use 10lb 'Powergum'

10 to 12lb BS reel line

20 inches of 15lb BS 'Alasticum' swivelled wire trace

duo of size 8 semi barbless trebles in dead bait

20-inch uptrace of reel line

beads

0.75 to 1.5oz bomb on running snap swivel between beads

38

John stret pegging a cube of luncheon meat on the River Severn above Bewdley. Note how his float lies flat – until a barbel turns up.

bottom by the bomb and comes to rest attractively, whereupon extra line is played out to allow for that all-important bow to form between float and bait.

Bites whilst pike fishing vary little from stret pegging with much lighter outfits. Sometimes the float merely shakes or quivers as the bait is picked up which is the release of tension upon the set-up. Sometimes the float suddenly half cocks and sometimes it merely twitches. Whatever happens, invariably the end result is an unbelievably positive and confident registration as the float simply glides beneath the surface and away out of sight.

One last piece of advice here: remember always to strike hard. With such a lot of line out that hook really needs to be banged home forcefully.

THE LIFT METHOD

The lift method was first popularized by my old mate, Fred J. Taylor, his brother Ken and cousin, Joe, who took lots of hundredweight catches of tench during the 1950s from the lakes they fished at Wootton Underwood in Buckinghamshire.

Ever since then the method has always proved a devastatingly effective way of registering bites on the float from certain species in both still and moving water. It works especially well during the warmer months when fish metabolism is at its highest rate and when medium- to large-sized baits can be selectively used to ward off the attentions of small shoal fish.

Species which tilt their head downward like bream, tench (and sometimes carp, including crucians), often actually stand on their heads vertically to suck up the bait and so are tailormade (no pun intended here, honestly Fred) to be caught by this most fascinating of float-fishing techniques.

WHICH ROD AND REEL?

As far as rods are concerned virtually any 11–13-foot float, Avon-come-carp rod can be used for implementing the lift intended. Really stiff powerful models are to be avoided at all costs because without that 'flickability' in the top third of the rod, casting out a lift rig using a simple underarm pendulum swing followed by a flick is almost impossible. For species such as tench, bream and crucian carp, I prefer the increased line pick-up gained from a 13-foot float rod, waggler models being ideally suited to lines in the 2½–5lb category. For specimen tench and carp most Avon-style rods and carp rods up to 1¾lb test curve should suffice for lines in the 6–10lb range.

As for reels, for fishing mere yards out, a centre-pin offers superlative control using just your thumb upon the spool's rim, regardless of line breaking strain and I endeavour to enjoy using my centre pin whenever and wherever the opportunity exists. For delicate use of light tackle there is no finer reel. For most situations, however, a fixed-spool reel in the 2000 size format is probably a more versatile choice in that underarm flicks from narrow gaps amongst reeds or trees, or from awkward overgrown swims, are often necessary to position the bait.

Yes! Of course you can catch big carp on the lift, and from a boat, as long as you practise being quiet.

USING THE LIFT METHOD

Before I continue, let me state categorically that success on the lift method relies totally on the entire shotting capacity of the float being fixed really close to the hook – between just 1 and 6 inches away, depending on the species expected. I shall elaborate on this later.

For the present just get used to the fact that all shot, whether a single BB or an AAA or even one or two SSGs, are always fixed on close to the hook. They're not fixed up the line or locked around the float's base, or the rig will simply not operate as it should. Moreover, if you lock the float waggler style with two small shots – should a carp or tench go charging through lilies or a dense weedbed – the line will quickly break. Whereas if secured to the line with a silicone float band you only lose the float and do not leave a fish with the hook in it. The vast majority of anglers who dabble with the method still, unfortunately, find problems appreciating this simple fact. So I'll say it again: the float should not be locked by shot, simply attached with a sleeve of silicone tubing or, in old-fashioned lingo, a float band.

Now I know full well that club and match fishermen go to great lengths to present baits delicately beneath a stick or waggler rig, or to wield a pole in conjunction with superlight rigs where a size 12 or 14 microshot can make all the difference. But if you want to be successful with the lift method you really can forget all about being supersensitive. It's the perfect method for taking you straight through to those bigger specimens and I often add more shot than is actually required, simply to stop small nuisance fish pushing the bait along, something which has little bearing upon the bait being sucked up by a whopper. The specific gravity of shots in water is much less than out of it so one extra pinched on makes next to no difference when fishing the lift (although the reverse is true, of course, when delicately shotting all other float rigs).

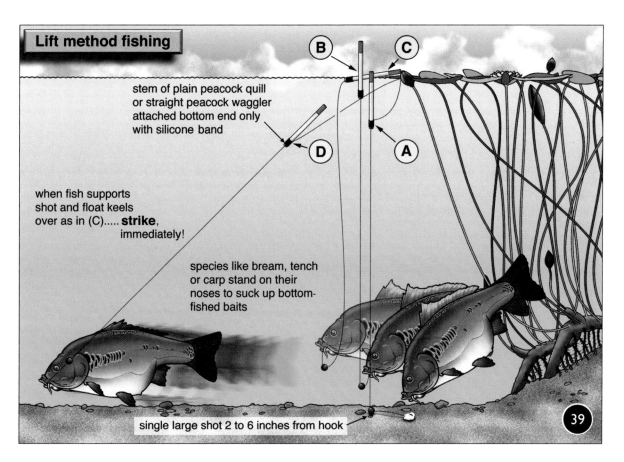

Lift method fishing

stem of plain peacock quill or straight peacock waggler attached bottom end only with silicone band

when fish supports shot and float keels over as in (C)..... **strike**, immediately!

species like bream, tench or carp stand on their noses to suck up bottom-fished baits

single large shot 2 to 6 inches from hook

39

When to Hit Bites

The word 'lift' means that the inherent buoyancy of the float (which is why a length of plain peacock quill or a straight peacock waggler works best) literally supports the shot or shots when the bait has been sucked up (see Diag. 39, Fig. A). It goes on partly supporting that weight during its upward lift (Fig. B) – hence the method's name – right to the point at which it keels over and lies flat (Fig. C). Now and only now is the fish totally supporting that same weight and thus quite likely to eject the bait. So strike at once! Fast – hard and upwards.

Advice given in many of the older angling books of subsequently waiting for the float to right itself and glide away after keeling over flat before striking has, of course, lost many an angler a fine fish. So do not wait! The lifting float is just as positive an indication as if it were gliding under and away out of sight (Fig. D). Lots of bites on the lift do this anyway because the fish has sucked the bait in and carried on moving directly away from the rod, instead of righting itself from standing on its head and sucking the bait back to its pharyngeal teeth for chewing on the spot (Fig. B). So, whatever the species, get used to striking instantly as the float starts to lift (between Figs B and C) following through and upwards with the rod. Think of such bites being similar to and equally positive as those drop backs when ledgering, when the rod or quivertip suddenly eases or springs back.

Hold the Rod

Unless a lengthy wait between bites is expected you should continually hold the rod when fishing the lift and, being right-handed, I find the most comfortable position is with my forearm on top of the rod, supported across my right knee. I then have the best possible chance of converting the vast majority of bites into hooked fish. Make no bones about it, that split second it takes to snatch the rod up from a pair of rests while the float lifts will result in numerous misses. Crucian carp especially are masters of sucking the bait in and blowing it out with remarkable speed so holding the rod is imperative for hitting crucian bites in popular fisheries, or you could repeatedly miss bite after bite. The best baits on the lift for crucians are sweetcorn and small pieces of breadflake on size 14–10 hooks. For casters and maggots step down to size 16.

One final word about rod control I think is in order before we move on and that is concerning the subject of casting. While the occasional side or overhead cast will be needed to reach distant spots, the lift method is first and foremost a close-range technique and should be considered as such. By far the most effective and easiest way to cast accurately is with an underarm pendulum swing of the bait, followed by a flick, in complete contrast to general waggler fishing where most of the shot is locked around the float, so you are in effect casting the weight of the float. With the lift you are casting the weight of the bait because the shot is always within a few inches of it. This allows you to fish in the tightest, narrowest gaps between trees and bushes, even with branches overhead and hanging out over the water. The simple underarm flick does it every time.

THE LIFT IN FLOWING WATER

The lift method is also effective when fishing in rivers of gentle flow for bream, chub or tench, providing they can be tempted along or just beyond the marginal shelf by prebaiting (Diag. 40, Fig. A). By adding a luminous chemical element to the top of the plain peacock stem or waggler fishing on into darkness becomes a fascinating way of enjoying the lift method.

Incidentally always attach the quill to the line with ¼-inch wide sleeve of silicone tubing – nothing else. And don't forget, from a single peacock quill which costs less than one ready-made waggler, you can cut five or six usable stems. Being so very positive and accentuated by the flow, bites in flowing water are immediately apparent even with the slightest lift. Again it is important to strike upwards and follow through with the rod. Bream, especially, have a habit of moving a couple of feet above bottom with the bait (away from other feeding shoal members) and unless you follow through firmly, bites will be missed for sure. Just how far over depth you need to fix the float depends entirely upon current strength and depth but by angling the rod tip upwards, set up on two rests (again hold the rod when bites are immediate) even a strong pull may be tackled with confidence as long as you strike properly. The secret is to fish directly downstream and not across the current and to keep the rod tip out as far as possible (Diag. 40, Fig. B).

If keeping the bait anchored on the bottom proves troublesome, simply add another shot or two (Fig. C). Bream, especially, will not be deterred. And remember until it lies flat the buoyant peacock quill will in part support and lessen the true weight of extra shot while it is lifting.

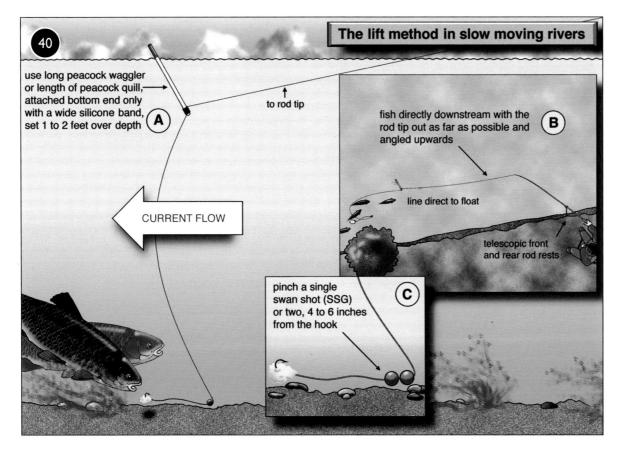

The lift method in slow moving rivers

40

use long peacock waggler or length of peacock quill, attached bottom end only with a wide silicone band, set 1 to 2 feet over depth (A)

to rod tip

CURRENT FLOW

fish directly downstream with the rod tip out as far as possible and angled upwards (B)

line direct to float

telescopic front and rear rod rests

pinch a single swan shot (SSG) or two, 4 to 6 inches from the hook (C)

FIXING YOUR SHOT

How far from the hook to fix the shot is something that confuses a lot of anglers attempting to use the lift method. I find the distance is best related to species and the size of fish expected. For instance if crucian carp are the target fish, where a reel line of 2–2½lb breaking strain is the order of the day, a distance of 1–1½ inches usually works best.

After selecting the single BB or AAA shot required for casting I use an extra-slim stem of peacock quill (painted fire orange one end) and simply cut the other end down with scissors until the single shot cocks the float nicely. That's the beauty of using just a sleeve of tubing for float attachment with the extra benefit of minimal cost and tackle loss, not to mention a lost specimen should a tench or carp go ploughing through snags. The float simply pops out from the band, allowing you a chance of landing the fish.

When specifically seeking tench and bream with a reel line of between 3lb and 6lb breaking strain, depending upon snags, weeds and the size of fish expected, be prepared to juggle around with varying distances between shot and hook. I suggest that somewhere between 2½ and 4 inches will prove ideal. However when contemplating carp, and let's say we are talking 10lb fish upwards here on lines of between 8lb and 12lb, I would plump for a distance of between 5 and 6 inches. To be truthful there is no best distance. As I said earlier, you must be prepared to experiment by moving the shot up or down until bites are registered in a clear manner.

ACCURACY

The lift is an extremely accurate method of float fishing because once the float has cocked after winding up the slack line, you can be certain the bait

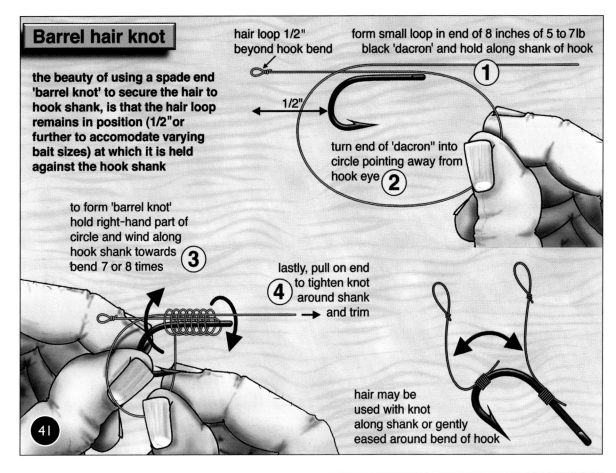

is then just a foot or so further out beyond the float. This naturally makes the method extremely effective for 'bugging the bubblers' – individual tench or carp that can be pinpointed from the stream of bubbles rising from the position at which they are feeding on the bottom.

Do not cast right on top of the fish and spook it; instead, using the underarm flick, cast several yards beyond the last patch of bubbles spewing up to the surface and quickly wind in with the bait at mid-water until the rig is approximately over the area, allowing the float to settle and then cock before slowly winding down until the float tip is a mere blimp on the surface. You must be quick when doing this or you will drag the bait along over bottom debris. So close the reel's bale arm

When fishing the lift method you use your own simple floats: stems of peacock quill painted at one end with a sleeve of silicone tubing at the other.

immediately the bait lands upon the surface and wind in smartly to the desired spot. And be ready for instant action. How I wish I had a fiver for every tench and carp I have caught over the seasons fishing in exactly this way. When you have the water to yourself it can truly be regarded as a mobile, opportunist mode of tempting bubbling fish. Bites sometimes occur within a second or two of winding down to the float tip.

Although carp of over 30lb have come my way thanks to the lift, and from really close into the margins too where ledgering would be totally impracticable, one particular 27lb 8oz leather carp immediately springs to mind here, because it sucked up a couple of black-eyed beans on a lift rig in just 4 feet of water beside a thick reed line with such lightning speed that it actually had the float lifting before I could close the reel's bale arm. I struck anyway with my finger clamped

around the spool and snapped the bale arm over afterwards and then wound down quickly.

INSTANT PLUMMET

Because the lift rig has a built-in plummet by the way in which the shots are pinched on close to the hook, not only does swim depth immediately become apparent when casting around to different areas, but

extra bites resulting in bonus fish can often be instigated simply by lifting the rod tip every so often and slowly winding the bait a few inches closer. Obviously, this only works effectively on relatively clean bottoms.

I known that baits such as breadflakes, beans or boilies are not supposed to crawl along the bottom, but no one has told tench this – and even the odd carp will make a snatch at a meal which looks like it is getting away. With animal baits like lobworms or cockles, this ruse can really produce the goods. Try it and see.

BAITS

I cannot think of a bait that cannot be presented on the lift rig, even a single caster, maggot or grain of stewed wheat, maize or sweetcorn will instigate a lift bite if presented on a light lift rig incorporating just a single BB or AAA shot. And when smaller species like roach or rudd need to tilt down among cabbages, for instance, in order to suck up their food, a lift bite will of course register on the float as long as the shots have been placed close to the hook. Generally speaking, however, presenting a good mouthful invariably does the business by producing a positive bite.

When seeking carp on the lift and general baits like meat cubes, breadflake or crust, pastes and lobworms are not producing, however, due to clear water or overfishing, it is time to hair rig an alternative bait in order to produce not only more bites but more confident bites. As can be seen from Diag. 41, hair tying can be made so simple by

(Opposite): When fishing close in beside marginal features few methods can match the lift, whether seeking crucians, tench or sizeable carp.

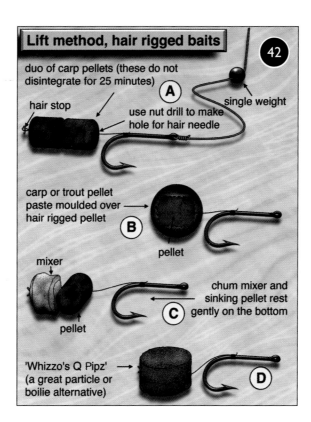

using a short length of 5–7lb test black dacron and, after forming an overhand loop of ¼ inch in length, securing it to the hook's shank with a spade end knot. Follow steps 1–4 and you can't go wrong.

The spade end barrel knot can easily be moved up or down the shank and the hair wound around the shank to accommodate baits of varying sizes, provided it is ¾ inch long to start with. And this is the beauty of using this particular spade end knot because only the end of the dacron is pulled through to secure. The hair loop stays at the position at which it is held against the hook shank.

Now you are geared for experimenting with all kinds of bait which work not only for carp but tench too. When loose feeding with trout or carp pellets as an attractor and fish seem only interested in them and not a different hook bait, put two up on the hair but use a nut drill to make the holes to prevent them splitting. Certain brands of carp pellets are really

A centre-pin reel, the lift method and plump crucian carp not only make summer sense, they bring a smile to everyone's face.

excellent for this technique. Being hard they will not disintegrate for up to 25 minutes (as Diag. 42, Fig. A). Another option is to hair up just a single pellet and cover with a paste (as in Fig. B) made from ground pellets (use a coffee grinder to reduce them to dust) and raw eggs. Paste has the benefit of releasing the bait's aroma much quicker and often results in immediate action.

To pop the bait up just above the bottom (handy for those extra-weedy or snaggy swims) go one step further (as in Fig. C) and hair up a buoyant chum mixer biscuit together with a sinking carp pellet. Or what about hair rigging a boilie or two small boilies (10–12mm) or a boilie alternative such as Whizzo's Qpipz large fishy or fruity pellet baits (as Fig. D)?

WAGGLER FISHING

Basically the term 'waggler fishing' refers to the float being fixed at the bottom end only with locking shots so that upon striking it folds and creates minimal resistance during the retrieve or throughout the fight. However, sometimes a waggler is purposely attached with a band of silicone tubing instead of shots because the entire shotting load is fixed on close to the hook as with the lift method (see Method 12) or on a separate link as when float ledgering (see Method 6).

Wagglers are the most widely used and indeed the most versatile of all freshwater floats for both river and still-water fishing. Most are made from peacock quill (occasionally from clear plastic and common and sarkansas reed) due to is durability and inherent buoyancy.

Insert or tipped wagglers have a narrow-diameter tip inserted into a plain straight stem. Straight wagglers (the most common of all) are simply that, and bodied wagglers (which can be tipped or straight stemmed) are fitted with a polystyrene or cork oval-shaped body at the base which not only increases the float's stability during choppy conditions but also the amount of shot it will take.

As can be seen from Diag. 43 most of the float's shotting load is usually pinched on either side of the bottom ring to lock it at the desired length. However in fast, deep river swims where you need to get the bait down quickly the bulk shot is positioned 2–4 feet above the hook with smaller shots in between. So just a single shot is then used each side of the float to lock it (see page 103, Diag. 47, Fig. D).

Always remember to leave a ¾-inch gap between these shots enabling the float to fold on the strike. As loaded wagglers already contain most of the weight required to cock them (in the form of a brass tube at the base) they too require just a single shot either side of the bottom ring for locking into position, plus one or two small shots down the line. Incidentally when using wagglers it is a good idea not to pass your reel line through the float's bottom eye, because the entire shotting load has to be taken off in order simply to change floats. A plain silicone rubber, or a silicone rubber swivel float adapter, is the answer here, facilitating a change of floats within seconds.

Though all waggler floats work on the same principle, there is a distinct different in the two techniques used to present them in still and in flowing water. In still water, for instance, it is imperative that the line be sunk between float and rod tip to facilitate a smooth sideways (shallow water) or upwards (deep water) strike in order for the hook to penetrate. This also alleviates surface drift. In flowing water, on the other hand, the line should sit upon the surface film and take up a

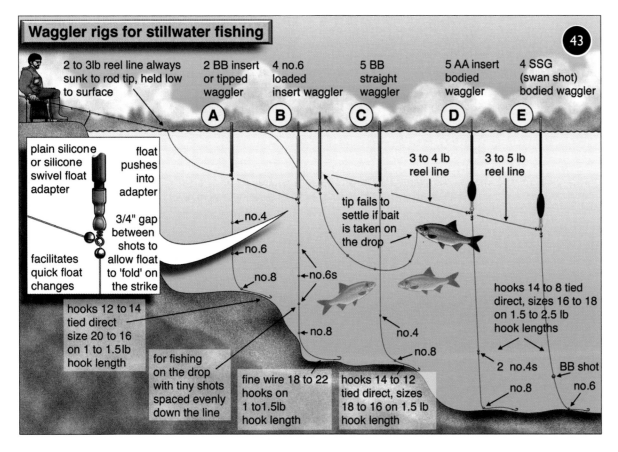

Waggler rigs for stillwater fishing 43

2 to 3lb reel line always sunk to rod tip, held low to surface

2 BB insert or tipped waggler — A

4 no.6 loaded insert waggler — B

5 BB straight waggler — C

5 AA insert bodied waggler — D

4 SSG (swan shot) bodied waggler — E

plain silicone or silicone swivel float adapter

float pushes into adapter

3/4" gap between shots to allow float to 'fold' on the strike

facilitates quick float changes

hooks 12 to 14 tied direct size 20 to 16 on 1 to 1.5lb hook length

for fishing on the drop with tiny shots spaced evenly down the line

no.4
no.6
no.8

no.6s
no.8

fine wire 18 to 22 hooks on 1 to1.5lb hook length

tip fails to settle if bait is taken on the drop

no.4
no.8

hooks 14 to 12 tied direct, sizes 18 to 16 on 1.5 lb hook length

3 to 4 lb reel line

3 to 5 lb reel line

hooks 14 to 8 tied direct, sizes 16 to 18 on 1.5 to 2.5 lb hook lengths

2 no.4s
no.8

BB shot
no.6

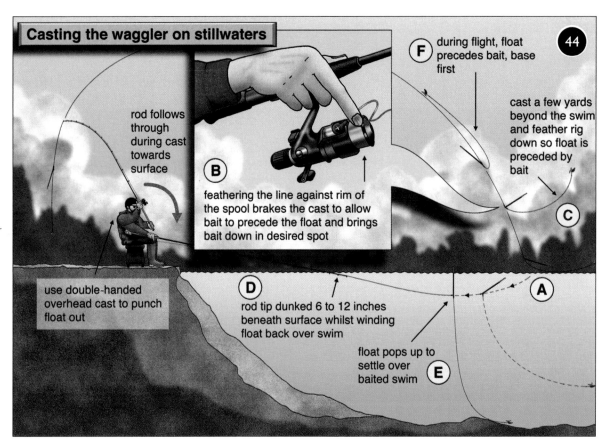

Casting the waggler on stillwaters

F during flight, float precedes bait, base first

cast a few yards beyond the swim and feather rig down so float is preceded by bait

rod follows through during cast towards surface

B feathering the line against rim of the spool brakes the cast to allow bait to precede the float and brings bait down in desired spot

C

use double-handed overhead cast to punch float out

D rod tip dunked 6 to 12 inches beneath surface whilst winding float back over swim

A

float pops up to settle over baited swim E

44

Enthusiastic waggler float fishermen slowly work the deep pool below the weir at Meelick on Ireland's River Shannon for big hybrids and bream.

definite bow between float and rod tip to ensure it stays on course as it trots downstream (see page 102, Diag. 46, Fig. B). If held too tightly (without a bow) the bait will veer away from the feed line and consequently not attract many fish. Only during excessive winds when waggler fishing in really slow-moving rivers should you actually consider fishing with the line sunk between float and rod tip.

But before we delve into each discipline let's consider the kind of outfit required for successful waggler fishing.

RODS AND REELS

Just as stick float fishing warrants a quick-striking, spliced-tip, trotting rod for hitting gentle bites on superfine tackle, waggler fishing also demands a certain action. Fortunately most 13–14 knot match-cum-float fishing rods (sometimes referred to as bottom rods) now produced have a snappy, yet forgiving (in the top third) action complimentary to the long, sweeping strikes so necessary when waggler fishing. You can comfortably use this universal action of a standard waggler rod (a 13-foot model is the best choice) for just about every situation, even stick float fishing. But trying to pull the hook home when waggler fishing at 30 yards in still water using a stick float rod could prove a problem.

Narrow profile, super-lightweight carbon waggler

rods, though at the top end of the price range, are excellent for casting into and cutting the line through wind on the strike. I have a pet hate for rods with overlong handles (why do manufacturers still do it?) because as the reel is always positioned at the top, up to a foot of valuable length is lost behind your elbow. Certainly the handle should be long enough for punching a waggler out double handed, and to this end a 22-inch, at most a 23-inch, handle is quite sufficient. Anything longer is expensive carbon tube wasted. Years ago when glass rods were considerably heavier, manufacturers craftily made handles long because they knew full well that with the reel positioned at the top the long butt protruding over a foot beyond the elbow acted as a counterbalancing weight, thus making the rod feel lighter.

I also have a preference for a slim handle either all

cork or half cork and half duplon of no more than ⅞ inch in diameter with either tough nylon sliding reel fittings or slim screw reel fittings which some manufacturers now put on their waggler rods. Thicker handles only restrict use of the forefinger when applying pressure to the side of the spool on fixed-spool reels or use of the thumb against the rim of a centre pin. This brings me to actual reel choice.

Personally I prefer a centre pin for river work and for close-range still-water fishing and a fixed-spool reel in the 2000 format for greater distances in still water. The third option is a closed-face reel. If I had to choose just one, however, covering all aspects of waggler fishing then it would have to be the fixed spool with a selection of spare spools holding 2, 2½, 3 and 4lb lines. And it's worth shopping around for a low-diameter reasonably stretchy line for close-range situations and one of low stretch for distance work. Take also into account that certain brands sink much quicker than others making them perfect for still-water application. Reels with coned spools for improved casting performance are particularly suited to waggler fishing as forefinger control against the rim is used to feather the float down over the desired spot.

The Drennan range of tipped or insert crystal wagglers was simply made for catching the spooky specimen-sized rudd inhabiting clear-water meres and pits.

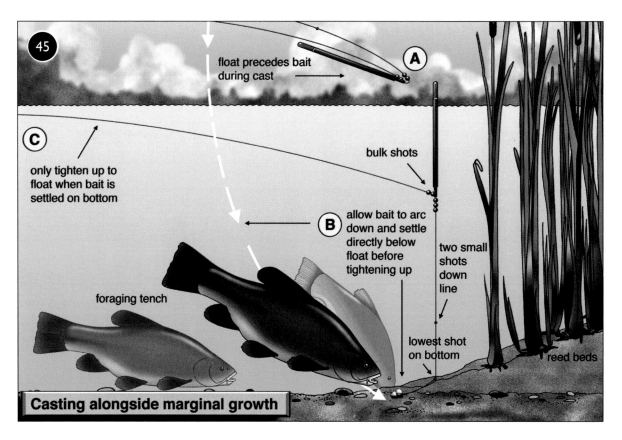

Casting alongside marginal growth

WAGGLER FISHING IN STILL WATERS

Whether using a slim or tipped waggler along the marginal shallows of a small man-made lake or farm pond, or punching out a long-bodied waggler taking three or four swan shots far out into a vast mere or estate lake, the technique does not differ. Most of the shotting capacity is bulked around the float's base, leaving just two or three small shots to be fixed at various points down the line, so it sails through the air base first. Consider Diag. 43 for instance, showing various still-water set-ups. The 2–3lb reel line is always sunk from rod tip to float and starting with close-range tactics a 2 BB insert waggler is ideal, as in Fig. A. See how most of the bulk shot locks the float with three small shots down the line. With this rig you can see bites on the drop and even lift bites, provided the lowest shot actually touches bottom. Careful plummeting is essential therefore.

Loaded insert wagglers (Fig. B) can be rigged for general use with a couple of small shots down the line or several tiny shots spread evenly between float and hook (the lowest a dust shot) for fishing on the drop. This shotting pattern ensures that light baits such as punched bread, maggots and especially dark-coloured casters (being more buoyant) sink to the bottom really slowly. Remember to count how many seconds it takes for the string of evenly spread shots to sink the insert tip down to its final setting, and instantly strike at the merest hold-up which means that a roach, rudd or bream has sucked the bait in on the drop. To achieve the slowest possible descent, use fine-wire hooks in sizes 18–22 on a 1–1½lb hook length.

Sinking the line between float and rod tip is imperative when waggler fishing in still water to avoid subsurface tow and wind drift.

Fig. C shows one of the most popular and versatile floats of all: a 5 BB straight waggler, again with most of the bulk shot locking the float (at least 4 BBs) and a couple of small shot down the line. Hooks in sizes 14–12 can be tied direct to, say, a 2½lb reel line, or a lighter 1½lb hook length when stepping down to a size 16 or smaller. It's all about presentation.

To reach greater distances (use a 3–4lb reel line) and for sensitive presentation in calm conditions, an insert bodied waggler fits the bill. It can be rigged with several small shots spread evenly down the line for fishing on the drop (as in Fig. B), or with the lowest shot resting on the lake bed when in search of bottom feeders like bream, tench and carp (as in Fig. D).

For presenting a bait static on the bottom in choppy conditions at distance, increase reel line to 3–5lb and use a bodied waggler with a shotting load of up to four or five swan shot, most of it locked around the float, and set two shots down low close to the hook, the bottom one resting on the lake bed (as in Fig. E). Incidentally wherever really large fish are expected, increase reel line to suit and tie hooks direct. This of course applies to each and every rig

shown in Diag. 43. What also applies to each rig, particularly when quality bream for instance are feeding aggressively on the bottom but the bait is repeatedly snapped up by nuisance species like young rudd or roach on the drop, is simply to move some of the bulk shot together with shots down the line all to within just 10 inches of the hook. It may not seem a particularly sensitive set-up but then if bream are hard on the feed it won't matter. The waggler will either lift positively or go sailing away.

Sinking the Line

In order to ensure the line is sunk between float and rod tip to alleviate the waggler's two greatest enemies, surface tow and wind drift, you must cast at least 2 or 3 yards beyond your swim, as in Diag. 44, Fig. A. (Note from Fig. F how in flight, the float precedes the bait, base and locking shots first.) Feather the rig down to the surface by using gentle forefinger pressure on the line against the spools; rim (Fig. B) in order that the baited hook and lower shots actually overtake the float (Fig. C).

As the float touches down, simultaneously dunk your rod up 6–12 inches below the surface (as in Fig. D) and crank the reel handle quickly a few turns. The float tip (having disappeared) will then instantly pop up to settle over the desired spot (Fig. E). Then, and only then, you should raise the rod tip to a position a few inches above the surface. In really choppy conditions keep it submerged an inch or so, and set the rod on two rests. To help sink a stubborn line keep a small bottle of detergent handy (washing-up liquid is ideal) and every so often splodge a fingerful around the spool. Alternatively, fly fishing preparations such as liquid leader sink are custom made for the job.

Only trial, error and constant practice will allow you to accomplish this with pinpoint accuracy, but in truth it is not difficult and becomes second nature after a while. The only situation when it becomes impossible

to check the waggler's flight, so the bait goes ahead just before touching down, is when casting tight up against overhanging trees or reed beds situated directly opposite (as in Diag. 45) whereby if unchecked the float continues to precede the bait (as in Fig. A). Cast the float directly to the swim tight up against the feature (overhanging branches or tall reed stems) and dunk the rod immediately it lands – a split second before if possible – but do not wind yet. If the reel line is treated with detergent on a regular basis it should sink straight away. So only when the bait arcs down towards the reeds and settles (as in Fig. B) should you attempt gently to tighten up to the float (as in Fig. C).

This is a fabulous technique for coming to grips with species like bream, rudd, tench and wild carp which work the reed lines whilst foraging natural food items such as snails, and their eggs, plus the nymphs of aquatic insects. Watch out for reed stems knocking and twitching when there is no wind. Don't leave the binoculars at home!

When pursuing specimen rudd along reed lines in crystal-clear water I prefer to use the clear plastic Drennan insert wagglers, which have a similar buoyancy rating to peacock quill, and swap the lower shots for three small ones spread evenly between float and hook in order to present baits like a cube of bread crust or casters – slowly sinking on the drop.

WAGGLER FISHING IN RIVERS

Much of what I have already said about waggler fishing in still waters also applies to river fishing but, as I mentioned earlier, the main difference is not sinking the line between float and rod tip. If you did, current deviations would soon pull the float off course and away from the feed line. In addition the strike would be severely dampened with a sunk line. So endeavour to maintain a floating line at all times (use

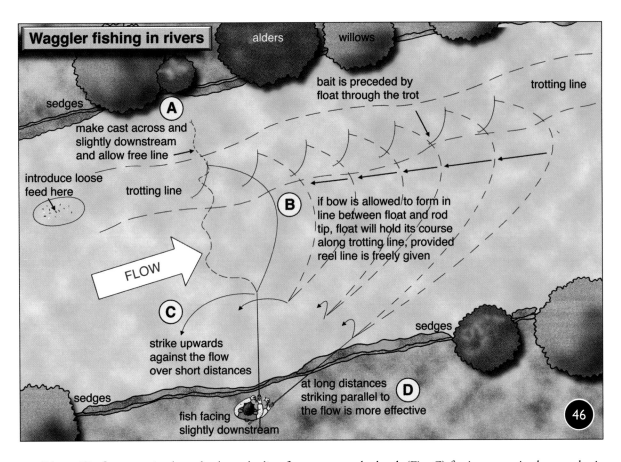

Waggler fishing in rivers

alders

willows

sedges

bait is preceded by float through the trot

trotting line

(A) make cast across and slightly downstream and allow free line

introduce loose feed here

trotting line

(B) if bow is allowed to form in line between float and rod tip, float will hold its course along trotting line, provided reel line is freely given

FLOW

(C) strike upwards against the flow over short distances

sedges

sedges

fish facing slightly downstream

at long distances striking parallel to the flow is more effective (D)

46

In addition to bream, tench and wild carp, casting a waggler tight up against reed lines also produces the colourful rudd. Slowly sinking casters were this specimen's downfall.

a solid mucilin floatant wiped gently along the line for a few yards above the float) always with a distinct bow between waggler and rod tip. Obviously, and taking current speed into account, your loose feed, casters, maggots, or liquidized bread should be fed in either by hand or catapulted well upstream of the swim. Do not start the trot directly in front but cast across and slightly downstream into the head of the swim (as in Diag. 46, Fig. A) remembering to feather the rig down so the bait goes ahead of the float just before it lands on the surface and immediately give line. This allows the float to settle in and precede the bait by at least a couple of feet, as it trips gently over the river bed (Fig. B). Moreover, the float will now hold its intended course as it trots downstream (Fig. B) provided line is freely given to maintain that surface bow. Over short distances strike upwards and against the flow in order

to set the hook (Fig. C) for instance. As the waggler is carried further downstream by the current, however, you may sometimes find that striking parallel to the flow (Fig. D) puts you in contact with the fish far quicker and certainly more positively. Much depends on what angle you sit or stand to the river and how far across the waggler is presented. In a downstream wind, for instance, striking parallel to the water and across the wind is preferable to striking upstream and against it. In really windy conditions when a floating line is forever jerking and pulling the float, thus inhibiting natural presentation of the bait, you have no option but to sink the line between float and rod tip and to strike sideways as though still water fishing. But remember to be generous in paying line out as the float is pulled downstream by the current or it will veer away from your feed line.

As with still-water waggler fishing, remember that sweeping strikes which follow through are more effective by far. Do not attempt at any time (unless guiding the float around trailing branches on the opposite bank) to hold back or straighten the line, or the bait will immediately be pulled away from the swim and more importantly away from the fish. For slow-moving swims, bulk the shots around a straight peacock waggler and distribute several small shots down the line 18–20 inches apart with a tiny dust shot 12–20 inches above the hook (as in Diag. 47,

This lovely net of pound-plus River Wensum winter roach was taken by John waggler fishing maggots in a 4-foot-deep glide at Lenwade, near Norwich.

Fig. A). Straight wagglers are used in running water because unlike the insert or tipped waggler whose tip is drawn under too easily, their inherent buoyancy permits small baits to be trundled smoothly over the river bed without the tip dragging under and registering false bites. Where the bottom is of even depth and completely weed and snag free, fish well over depth so the dust shot itself actually trundles over the clean sand or gravel without catching. This can prove most effective during very low water temperatures when species like dace, grayling, roach, bream and chub really hug the bottom, and at all times for barbel which demand that the bait scrapes bottom (Fig. B). Where the bottom is uneven, however, leave a good 1–1½ inches of the float tip

above the surface encouraging the buoyancy of the peacock waggler to drag the bait over the river bed without the tip being submerged.

As can be seen from Fig. C for trotting in swims where the flow is steady, reel line is increased to 2½–3lb and a 3–4 AA straight waggler is recommended with most of the shotting load bulked around the float, and just two No. 1 shot down the line, plus a No. 4 or 6 16–20 inches from the hook. These distances and shot sizes are not obligatory but are intended simply as a guideline. Be prepared to juggle them about in swims of varying depth and current speed until your waggler drags the bait through smoothly.

Fig. D shows a heavy 4–8 AA straight or bodied peacock waggler shotted specifically for trotting the bait through fast water low down across the river bed

in search of chub and barbel. So only two BBs are used for locking the float in position, and most of the shotting load grouped in a string around two-thirds swim depth, so the bait is taken quickly down. This leaves enough room for a BB or No. 1 plus a No. 3 or 4 between the line of bulk shot and hook. Reel line has been increased to 3–4lb if big chub and especially barbel are the target species and loose feed in the way of maggots, casters or stewed hempseed should be catapulted well upstream to allow for current speed in order that it finally ends up drifting along the river bed at the head of the swim and not three swims downriver. For relatively short-range waggler fishing in fast water, particularly in the swirling currents of a deep weir or mill pool, use a bait dropper to ensure loose feed is deposited exactly where you want it. (See also 'Waggler Fishing' in Method 7, 'Long Trotting'.)

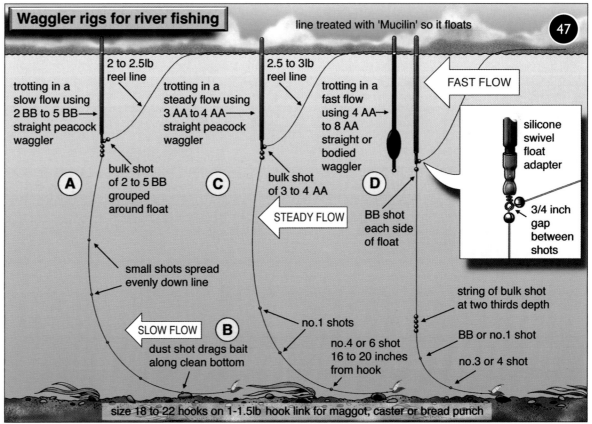

FLY RODDING

FLY FISHING FOR DACE, ROACH, RUDD, CHUB AND GRAYLING

D o you know, after forty years of freshwater fishing I still don't know whether to call the grayling a game or a coarse fish. Daft isn't it? But the truth is most game fishermen, well certainly the Sloanes amongst them, refuse to recognize Her Ladyship as being a game species like char, trout, sea trout and salmon, despite a perfectly adequate adipose fin. Wilson therefore has taken it upon himself in this book to treat the grayling as a coarse species, most worthy of catching by long trotting (see Method 7) and on the fly rod along with dace, roach, rudd and chub.

TACKLE AND SUNDRIES

I shall start at the beginning with the tackle and sundries required. All of these species can be enjoyably taken with a sporting-brook-cum-river outfit comprising a 7½–8-foot carbon rod, small single-action fly reel holding 30 yards of backing and a size 4–5 line, preferably floating.

In cold weather a sink-tip line may prove advantageous in that a leaded nymph can more effectively be presented down close to the bottom, exactly where the fish will be situated. In the case of grayling, which offer superb winter sport, this is indeed critical.

For the present, however, let's concentrate on ensuring that your line matches the rod, otherwise casting will prove troublesome. If for instance the rod's line rating (written just above the handle) says 4–5, that rod will perform best with either a size 4 double-taper line, or a size 5 weight forward. Double-taper lines are best for presenting the dry fly because all the casting weight is in the middle so the last thing to alight on the surface is the fly itself. Weight-forward lines, on the other hand, have most of their weight concentrated into the front third (hence the terminology) making for easier casting especially into the wind when presenting leaded nymphs and wet flies or really buoyant surface attractor patterns for chub. Overall I rate a weight-

Using a floating line and tiny dry fly (a black gnat), Bruce Vaughan casts upstream to a shoal of dace in Wiltshire's lovely River Nadder.

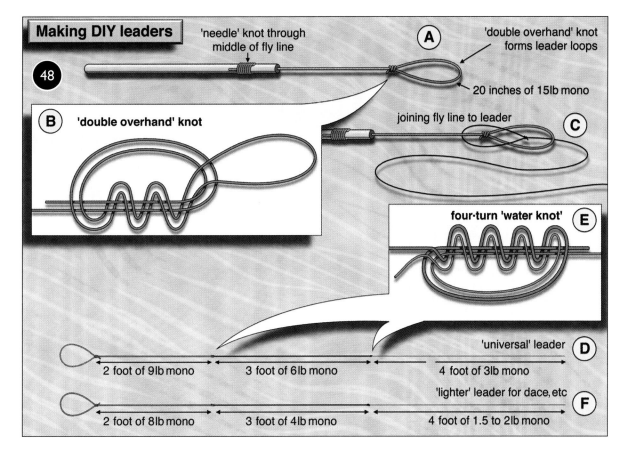

Making DIY leaders

48

'needle' knot through middle of fly line

A 'double overhand' knot forms leader loops

20 inches of 15lb mono

B 'double overhand' knot

joining fly line to leader C

four-turn 'water knot' E

'universal' leader D

2 foot of 9lb mono | 3 foot of 6lb mono | 4 foot of 3lb mono

'lighter' leader for dace, etc F

2 foot of 8lb mono | 3 foot of 4lb mono | 4 foot of 1.5 to 2lb mono

forward line more versatile but for presenting dry flies delicately it is handy to have a double taper; so if you can afford both, enjoy the option.

Joining a tapered cast or leader to the fly line is achieved by first making a leader loop using 20 inches of 15lb monofilament and a needle knot (Diag. 48, Fig. A) through the centre core of the line. This is also shown on page 121, Diag. 54, Fig. A. Once the knot has been bedded down nicely, tie an overhand knot (Diag. 48, Fig. B) on the end to form a loop to which a tapered leader is then attached loop-to-loop fashion (Fig. C). Alternatively sleeve on a short braided connector (with premade loop) over the end of your line, as on page 121, Diag. 54, Fig. B and sleeve over the plastic joint provided. Each new leader is then quickly attached loop to loop.

Wherever possible try to use as long a leader as is

manageable to aid presentation of nymphs, particularly leaded nymphs which you can use to catch dace, chub and grayling from quite fast and deep river runs. When presenting the dry fly however, it is a mistake to use a leader longer than the rod because, weighing next to nothing and greatly affected by wind, a dry fly will not turn over and land where you want it to at the end of the cast.

You can in fact construct your own universal tapered leaders by joining, say, 2 feet of 9lb test to 3 feet of 6lb test to 4 feet of 3lb test (as in Diag. 48, Fig. D) using the four-turn water knot shown in Fig. E. Finish by making an overhang loop at the thickest (9lb) end and you have a 9-foot tapered leader which is extremely economical compared to buying ready-made knotless leaders and suitable for general nymph fishing. Simply shorten and reduce in

strength to suit when making up a leader for dry-fly fishing. I keep several small spools of monofilament in the pockets of my waistcoat for this very purpose so I can construct a leader geared specifically to the situation at hand in minutes. For tippet material (the lightest and last segment of the leader) to which the artificial is tied, I often use a low-diameter, low-stretch brand of monofilament such as Ashima, Drennan Double Strength or Orvis Mirage. Each is considerably thinner than standard mono of identical test and will help induce takes in crystal-clear water from extra-shy or spooky fish. A small tub of leadersink paste (made from fuller's earth mixed with washing-up liquid) or a bottle of liquid detergent is essential for degreasing the leader and encouraging a nymph to sink quickly. You can, as I have on occasion, resort to rubbing river-bank mud along the leader when preparations have been forgotten or simply run out. But it's well worth ensuring these helpful sundries are in your waistcoat by quickly ticking off a mental check list before setting off. Other useful additions are a bottle of floatant for dry flies such as Permafloat, or an aerosol spray, a tin of mucilin leader floatant and a pair each of scissors and forceps.

DACE AND GRAYLING

The quick-rising dace on the dry fly is very much harder to hook than trout. Being shoal fish, however, and extremely free rovers you invariably have several opportunities of missing before they spook entirely. During a prolific hatch their splashy rises at the tail end of shallow runs and pools, with several fish all hitting the surface together, are easily observed.

Leader tippet can be reduced to 1½lb test for dace (with a reduction also in the segments above – see Diag. 48, Fig. F) enabling tiny dry-fly patterns such as black gnat, green wells glory or cock-y-bondu on

Having succumbed to John's leaded nymph presented upstream in the clear shallow water of a southern chalkstream, a big grayling battles for freedom.

John took this superbly coloured grayling from the tiny River Frome in Dorset on a small gold head Fritz nymph tied to a 2lb tippet.

size 16 and 18 hooks to be used. This provides a truly wonderful challenge to the wandering fly rodder, who has the choice of endeavouring to match the hatch of natural insects coming off upon which the shoal is feeding, or simply put up any small fly. Competition amongst a large dace shoal is often so fierce that as long as the dry fly is put down just upstream of the shoal on a snaky line so it does not immediately drag it is liable to be snapped up posthaste.

A quick strike is necessary to set the hook. Waiting a second or two, as with trout, for the fish to get its

head down will not put many dace in the net. Dace have the ability to inhale and spit out your imitation literally like greased lightning. So you must pull into them and lift the rod tip with equal speed. With grayling do not be in so much of a hurry or you will whip the hook form their mouths prematurely. When a grayling rises, sucks in a fly from the surface and dives, it usually leaves a bold telltale circle on the water which is most distinct. You can therefore differentiate as to which species is rising if in any doubt. The rises of dace are anyway quite splashy affairs by comparison.

Remember to make use of any available bankside cover even by wading into position if your outline can be hidden by the foliage behind, so a cast can be made from directly downstream of the rising shoal. Due to the extreme shallowness of mini rivers, streams and brooks which tend to breed dace and grayling reaching to specimen proportions, environments where a bait on float tackle is almost impossible to present during the summer months when weed beds reach to the surface, the dry fly really comes into its own.

Indeed, it is fair to say that just like the trout, coarse species such as dace and grayling can be tempted and subsequently extracted from spots along the river where no other method could be effectively employed.

When both species are not rising, however, and show not the slightest interest in patterns of dry flies, try them with a slowly sinking nymph. The leader is greased to within just a few feet of the artificial which, just like the dry fly, is cast upstream into the flow on a snaky line so the current deviations do not immediately drag it downstream in an unnatural way (as in Diag. 49) Start with a really short throw and progressively lengthen each successive cast to cover the entire run.

The reason for casting directly upstream is so the nymph is not swung unnaturally across, which of course it would be if you placed it directly across the flow. This also applies when presenting the dry fly. As the current carries the artificial, such as a leaded shrimp, mayfly nymph or gold head montana downstream towards you, slowly retrieve the loose line with your left hand in a figure of eight, whilst simultaneously keeping a watchful eye on the leader and the end of the fly line on the surface. Respond immediately with a firm strike and pull (on your left hand) to any sudden jerk or twitch. Strike also to anything which looks odd or remotely like an acceptance. Not all fish bite with aggression and so as the nymph drifts back downstream towards you, watch the leader like a hawk at the point where it hangs down from the surface. Striking intuitively has resulted in many a fine fish being landed, believe me. Incidentally, wherever the occasional specimen grayling is likely to turn up, increase tippet strength to 2lb test.

Dace, and grayling especially, can also be taken by fishing downstream and across using the accepted and traditional wet-fly technique. But you do not necessarily need a team of two or three standard wet-fly patterns to catch fish from a lie which, due to overhanging trees or other obstacles, can only be fished by casting downstream and across. Your single leaded nymph on a degreased leader will score with equal effectiveness, believe me, even on a floating line. Remember to allow the artificial to come around in the flow and to dangle before retrieving it slowly upstream in short erratic pulls. A heavily leaded shrimp can prove deadly for summer grayling and chub when presented in this way.

You can also catch grayling from short and turbulent runs over gravel tight into the bank by a totally unorthodox method. Simply stand or kneel well back from the water's edge and, with just a few feet of line out plus the leader, dunk a heavy goldhead nymph or shrimp with an overhead flip into the head of the run. Then, whilst endeavouring to keep a slight bow in the leader (your bite indicator), follow through with the rod tip kept high as the imitation is drawn downstream over the gravel bed. If there is no joy, repeat for several casts until a grayling makes a mistake and grabs hold. It's really exciting sport this close-range dunking, and it's well worth purchasing or tying up some extra-fast sinking shrimp patterns in order to increase your chances. In recent years I have enjoyed some wonderful sport with grayling using the highly attractive and colourful Fritz range of goldhead nymphs, goldhead buzzers and shellback shrimps. The extra glitter of these artificials really seems to turn Her Ladyship on.

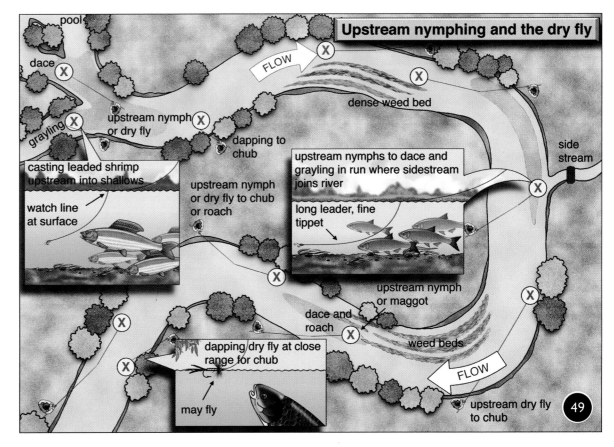

CHUB

With chub in mind most of what I have already said still applies, because this aggressive predatory species will chomp anything you offer it that resembles an item of food. Chub will bang the rod round upon taking large gaudy standard wet-fly patterns fished downstream and across. They will readily suck in leaded shrimps and mayfly nymphs, and go ballistic should a dog nobbler or similar jig-style pattern of lead-headed artificial dare to invade their territory. With this in mind increase tippet strength to 4–5lb test.

When presented on a greased leader chub are real suckers for large bushy dry-fly patterns such as sedges, soldier palmer, daddy longlegs, hoppers and mayflies. They also love chasing skating flies like a deerhair sedge or muddler minnow fished across the surface as dusk starts to fall.

To set the larger hooks of chub-sizes flies – 10s, 8s or even 6s – you need to step up to a 5–6 line and 9-foot rod with a leader tippet of no less than 5lb test. Then you can effectively work life into all the very latest deerhair surface poppers. They are still classed as flies, I suppose, but definitely borderline. I have mentioned many of these creations including the fluffy mouse complete with leather tail in Method 3, 'Working Top-water Lures', because in addition to a powerful fly-fishing outfit they can also be worked on an Avon rod/fixed-spool reel combination and 6lb test line.

Personally I prefer the smaller patterns such as sculpin and bumble bee for fly rodding. They have great buoyancy, being tied purely from deerhair, and when popped, gurgled or simply stripped in fast or dragged across the flow, seem to pull chub out from the thickest cover. Pike grab them too, so no doubt you'll experience the occasional bite-off. But what the hell – it's all unbelievable fun!

ROACH AND RUDD

We must now come down from cloud nine and the explosive fights of chub in shallow, turbulent water to the gentle delight of persuading roach and rudd to suck in an artificial. So it's back to the light 7½–8-foot rod taking a size 4–5 line suggested for both dace and grayling, which is tailor-made for obtaining the utmost enjoyment from catching roach and rudd. Of the two, rudd are far more receptive, particularly when it comes to accepting dry flies from the surface. Only during the hottest summer weather will you intentionally tempt roach off the top. But rudd are custom built to occupy the upper water layers and sip in food from above, be it a slowly sinking nymph or dry fly sitting in the surface film. Just look at their undershot mouth with its protruding lower jaw.

Spending time observing rudd shoals during the heat of a summer's day through binoculars can quickly put you on to their whereabouts. Their splashy rises are really noticeable even with a chop ruffling the surface. You can of course create your own rises by catapulting out floating casters and when the rudd start feeding upon them fish a single maggot on a fine-wire size 16 hook tied direct to a 1½lb tippet. With close-range casting you may actually be able to get a caster to stay on. Overall, however, a maggot withstands the rigours of casting much better. You then simply watch the leader on the surface as the maggot slowly sinks and strike when it suddenly tightens. In really clear-water estate lakes and meres, even gravel and clay pits, you can actually see the slowly falling maggot being sucked in. I have taken some wonderful hauls of daytime

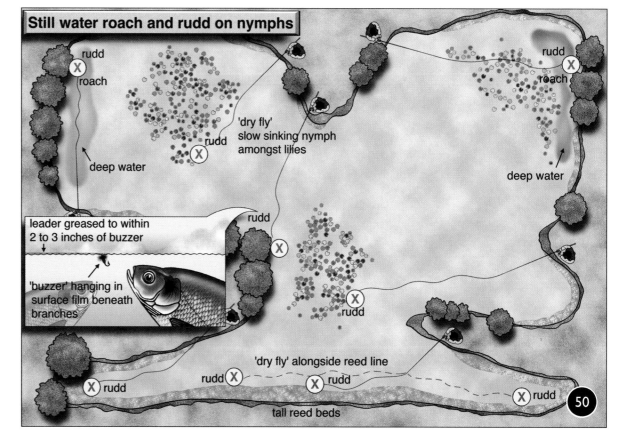

Still water roach and rudd on nymphs

rudd
roach

'dry fly'
slow sinking nymph
amongst lilies

deep water

rudd

leader greased to within
2 to 3 inches of buzzer

'buzzer' hanging in
surface film beneath
branches

rudd

rudd

rudd

deep water

rudd

'dry fly' alongside reed line

rudd

rudd

rudd

tall reed beds

50

Proof of the pudding are these leaded nymphs, shrimps and bugs from the highly reflective Fritz range of imitative patterns to which grayling are particularly attracted.

rudd in this way from fisheries where no other method could be employed.

Alternatively you can match the hatch when rudd are nymphing just below the surface or actually from the top sucking down emerging midges, by presenting a buzzer. Treat the leader well with mucilin to within an inch or two of the artificial so it literally hangs, as indeed it should, in the surface film (as in Diag. 50). When fishing a slowly sinking nymph beside reed beds, overhanging trees or lily beds – the favourite haunts of summer rudd – I suggest patterns like a sedge pupae or a pheasant tail. Watch the leader carefully as the nymph slowly descends for those takes on the drop, then retrieve in a slow figure of eight.

Rudd obtain much of their natural food during the summer months from the warmer upper water layers,

in the way of hatching aquatic life, and they love to bask beside and amongst the trailing branches of willows in particular, where falling caterpillars and other terrestrial bugs help supplement their diet. So even when absolutely nothing is actually rising, always try a few exploratory casts close to feature lies. You will no doubt also catch the occasional still water roach in the same way.

By far the most fascinating approach, however, is to take rudd off the top with a dry fly when they are up and gorging upon hatching insects. If you can identify and then match the hatch, fine; if not, then use small, very buoyant winged dry flies that will float for several minutes (once treated) without waterlogging. Either an alder or winged black gnat tied on a size 16 hook is ideal here. Coachman, blue dun, olive dun, a ginger quill, even a tiny winged Lee Wulf sedge are all patterns

worth trying. If rudd are on midges and won't accept relatively large imitations, be prepared to step down in hook size to an 18 or 20 black gnat. It's fair to say though that being a shoal fish, rudd are more competitive than and rarely show the preoccupational indifference of the brown trout.

RIVER ROACH

Roach are arguably the hardest, certainly the less cooperative, of the five species within this method to catch by design using fly tackle; so whenever the opportunity presents itself, take it. I have in fact caught some superb pound-plus roach from slow-moving summer rivers where density of weed beds virtually ruled out any other technique. But in truth most have been lured by the method mentioned earlier of dispensing with an artificial in preference for a single maggot presented on a size 16 fine hook (so it sinks ever so slowly) into clear runs. Then watch the maggot through Polaroid glasses or the cast for a take. I guess it's not that far from freelining really – but who cares!

Purely with chub in mind, consider these extremely buoyant deerhair surface-popping bumble bees, sculpins and mini frogs, etc. They produce slamming takes.

FLY RODDING FOR PERCH AND PIKE

In my experience neither perch nor pike drift up to the surface and suck in a dry fly. If they do it must surely rate as an extremely rare occasion! Both can provide fabulous sport on a fly-fishing outfit if you are not too worried about the type or size of artificial used, which is why I refer to fly rodding for carp or pike, for instance, as opposed to calling it fly fishing.

Frankly I am not out to kid anyone but simply to help you enjoy the fabulous fight involved in catching predators like pike and, to a much lesser extent, perch and even zander using just a few ounces of carbon fibre. It makes even the most mediocre fish seem big. Without exception I'll literally present anything that works, provided it can be cast or even plopped out including huge flies, deerhair poppers, baby plugs, spinners, leadheaded jigs, fly spoons, plastic worms, deerhair mice, and so on; they are all really great fun.

RODS AND LINES

Let's start with tackle because any old fly outfit simply won't do. For starters you need a 9½–10-foot two piece (as opposed to an easy actioned three-piece loch-style fly rod) powerful carbon reservoir casting rod capable of throwing a size 10 or even an 11 weight-forward line. Or, better still, go for a saltwater taper or bass bug taper line.

As this technique is well established in the US, specialized weight-forward lines with really steep, condensed tapers at the front end are readily available over there. They are now slowly becoming more available in the UK and the Mastery pike series from Scientific Anglers, which is custom built for casting extra-heavy flies and lures, has an extra-powerful front taper for minimal false casting and accurate delivery of the largest artificials tied specifically for predator fishing. What's more, this high-visibility sunset-orange floating line, available in sizes 7–10, sits especially high in the water for easy pick-up.

Distributed throughout the UK by Normark, the Cortland Fly Line Company also produces lines of a similar nature. However, you may need to talk your local tackle dealer into ordering one in especially for you. While Normark's bass bug taper and saltwater taper lines are the ideal types for our European pike-fishing requirements, their Pike/Musky line which comes in a distinctive red colour has an even shorter front taper making it perfect for larger flies and lures (see Diags 51 and 52).

You see, to be able to cast heavy artificials it is imperative that the weight of the lure and the casting weight (condensed into a rapid taper) zoom through

TAPER DESIGN

TIP: Connect the leader to the tip, which is thin and short (six to twelve inches). If you cut a portion of the tip off each time you change leader connections, you can still make many changes before you reach the front taper.

FRONT TAPER: The front taper decreases in diameter from the body to the tip. This gradual change in the line's mass (weight) effects how your casting energy is transferred to the fly and how delicately or powerfully the fly is delivered.

BODY: Most of the weight is concentrated in this section. It's the longest section of the head and has the largest diameter. Its weight is what carries your cast.

REAR TAPER: This section decreases in diameter from the thicker body to the thin running line. This gradual change provides casting smoothness on casts beyond 30 feet.

HEAD: The head is the combination of the front taper, body and the rear taper. The weight of the front thirty feet dictates the line-weight designation.

RUNNING LINE: When you make a long cast, the weight and energy in the head pulls the running line out through the guides. Because the running line is lightweight and has a small diameter, it passes through the guides easily on long casts, which enables you to shoot line for even longer casts.

Reproduced by permission of Cortland Lines

the air together. If they are any more than a few feet apart, not only is the action of the cast delayed (because the lure has to catch up on each forward and backward movement during this false casting) but you are quite liable to end up with a hook in the back of your neck.

With a double taper line, for example, its casting weight and that of the artificial would be more than 10 yards apart and fighting each other all the way. Unfortunately American-style bass bug and saltwater taper lines are not cheap, but there is nothing to stop you from purchasing an inexpensive weight-forward floating line (a size larger than your rod suggests) and cutting it back for several feet at the front end. This enables the heavy forward taper casting part of the line to come immediately into play.

REELS

For this very specialized form of fly rodding I suggest you use a single-action fly reel and one with a larger diameter than is actually required, loaded well with 20–30lb test braided nylon backing. Because the fly line comes off the reel in large, limp loose coils, casting performance will be automatically enhanced. I much prefer single-actioned reels whereby a fish is played by rim control alone through exerting pressure with the flat of the hand. Pike are not bonefish and so an expensive, complicated drag system is not required. Far better that you invest your money in a line tray which belts around the waist and contains the line nicely for retrieving and casting without it becoming caught around marginal plants or being trod upon. A line tray is also a great boon when fly rodding from a boat where the line seems to find all kinds of obstacles to become caught around, usually when midway through shooting a long cast.

52

FLY LINE TAPER PROFILES

FLY LINE PROFILES

Listed below are the types of fly lines that Cortland Line Company has to offer.

DOUBLE TAPER

TIP   FRONT TAPER   BODY   BACK TAPER

The double taper is a reversible fly line with an identical taper at both ends. A double taper line does not cast as long as a weight forward but is easier to mend.

ROCKET TAPER

TIP   FRONT TAPER   BODY   BACK TAPER   RUNNING LINE

Specially designed weight forward line with long slender front taper for delicate presentation of small flies. Weight distribution of body section allows extra distance when required.

BASS TAPER

TIP   FRONT TAPER   BODY   BACK TAPER   RUNNING LINE

Weight forward line with short front taper to "turn over" heavier, wind resistant cork and hair body bugs. The most practical choice for bass popping bugs.

PIKE/MUSKY LINE

TIP   FRONT TAPER   BODY   BACK TAPER   RUNNING LINE

Similar to bass taper with an even shorter front taper. Perfect for larger flies.

SALT WATER TAPER

TIP   FRONT TAPER   BODY   BACK TAPER   RUNNING LINE

Weight forward line for casting larger flies during windy conditions. Small diameter running line feeds through rod guides with less frictional resistance.

CLEAR CREEK TAPER

TIP   FRONT TAPER   BODY   BACK TAPER   RUNNING LINE

Extended tips for pinpoint accuracy and most delicate presentation.

SHOOTING TAPER

TIP   FRONT TAPER   BODY   LOOP

Specialized for long distance casting. It has a 30' head with a factory spliced loop for attaching monofilament or running line.

LEVEL

BODY

For live bait fishing and when delicate fly presentation or long casts are not essential. An economy line.

LEADERS AND TRACES

To reduce the distance between the end of your forward taper line and artificial further, only a very short leader should be used. I suggest starting at somewhere between 4 and 6 feet. Don't use tapered leader, simply 4–6 feet of 10–12lb test monofilament joined to the fly line using a needle knot through the centre core of the line (as in Diag. 53, page 117). Then add a 6-inch braided alasticum wire trace of 10lb test with a size 12–14 swivel for joining to the leader and an equally small American snap swivel at the other end to facilitate rapid lure changing. The wide clip of American snap swivels allows for maximum side-to-side movement of the artificial, something which is most important.

Incidentally, whilst talking traces, as an alternative material to braided alasticum, you might like to try one of the new supersoft low-diameter wires such as Wonder Wire marketed through Caliber Tackle which is braided from no fewer than forty-nine fine strands. This incredibly supple wire results in more takes because the artificial works far more attractively and it is extremely kink resistant. In 15lb test, for instance, Wonder Wire is little more than the diameter of 6lb monofilament and is perfect for fly rodding. One word of warning however; it cannot be twisted like alasticum and seven-strand type wires. Either use mini crimps or simply tie a two-turn half blood knot, pulling on the short end only, otherwise you will create kinks in front of the artificial. Also called the figure-of-eight knot, the two-turn half blood would seem

Even a mild winter's day presents opportunities for enjoying fly rodding in shallow water. John used a marabou creation to tempt this nicely marked pike.

ridiculous if tied using monofilament because it would instantly slip, but with Wonder Wire it really works. So try it and see, but don't trim the ends too close.

CASTING AND RETRIEVING

It is perhaps worth mentioning at this point that instead of holding the rod upright when casting, angle it over slightly at around 45 degrees, which almost borders on side casting. At least you can then keep an eye on the back cast and ensure you don't experience the pain of a treble or large single entering warm flesh at the back of your neck at 50 miles an hour! Not nice – believe me! This is good reason indeed, be the conditions bright or dark, sunny or wet, for always wearing a peaked hat and Polaroid glasses for facial protection. Polaroid glasses will, of course, also allow you to observe the reactions through clear water of pike which follow the artificial but decline from taking, and to spot individual fish than can be targeted.

Very often it is the fly line itself landing upon the surface that inhibits a predator from grabbing hold, so don't cast across a particular fish. Place the artificial a few feet to the side so it comes within the pike's striking distance during the retrieve. Hook penetration is of course greatly helped when pike zoom in at speed to grab the artificial, adding their own weight to your own lifting – strike on the rod and yank hard with your retrieving hand to keep the line tight.

To achieve fair distances when fly rodding with relatively weighty artificials and using minimum false casting, you will find the ability of being able to double-haul cast a great benefit because it dramatically increases line speed. Start by making just one false cast after the retrieve, say with around 10–12 yards of line in the air directly in front and, as

To prevent the line catching up when you shoot, a line tray belted around the waist aids casting enormously whether fly rodding from bank or boat.

you bring the line back into the power stroke with the rod almost vertical, pull down on the fly line with your left hand (assuming you are right-handed) which accelerates its backward passage. Your left hand should be close to the top of your head when pulling this first haul for maximum leverage.

As the line starts to unroll on the back cast, bring your left hand up again at head height and pause momentarily before pulling the line down forcibly (thus accelerating it again) on the forward power stroke which is your second haul. Hence the terminology 'double haul'. It is actually very much

Reservoir perch often take attractor flies intended for trout. So why not set out specifically to catch them using larger flies, jigs and even tiny spinners?

nothing out of the ordinary with pike which, if not frightened by your shadow, cannot possibly stand seeing the chance of a meal getting away.

Perch (and to a much lesser extent zander) require a different approach from pike in that lifelike presentation is far more important than the speed at which the artificial is retrieved. Tiny size 00 Mepps-type bar spinners for instance, or dog nobbler lead-headed-type flies with marabou tails that pulsate attractively, can be retrieved relatively slowly in short sharp pulls of 4–6 inches. Tiny wormtail spinning jigs work well too, though you do need perseverance when trying to cast these heavier, less aerodynamic artificials. If in difficulty your leader is probably too long, so reduce it in length until casting becomes less hazardous. In deep waters and with perch and zander still in the frame, particularly during the cold winter months, it is well worth investing in a sink-tip or even a fast-sinking fly line in order that your artificial, be it fly or spinner, can be presented low down at the level where the shoal is situated. In so far as very cold conditions are concerned, this also applies to pike, however as fly rodding is a technique for enjoying all season through and not, like most other methods, limited to winter months only, make the most use of those summery feature lies where pike and perch are guaranteed to be lying in wait. You know the kind of spots – dark areas of dappled water beneath overhanging willows or alders, beneath bridge arches, beside fallen and part-sunken trees, reed lines, rush beds, piled banking, old boathouses and lily beds. In both rivers and lakes all provide, in one way or another, the cover and ambush points from where predators can survey the surrounding terrain and instantly pounce out upon an unsuspecting fish or frog, or in the case of pike perhaps a mouse, vole or even a duckling which ventures too close.

This brings me to the subject of artificial fly-rodding-lures which could almost take up a book in

easier to achieve than to explain and once you have mastered the double haul you will be able to get your artificial out quickly with just one or two false casts.

Generally speaking there is no set pattern of retrieve. Fly rodding for pike using artificials is in fact not so very different from catching rainbow trout on brightly coloured flies when the retrieve usually needs to be quite fast in order to instigate a follow. Much, of course, depends upon water clarity. In coloured fisheries the retrieve must be slowed right down. In

crystal-clear water it is sometimes impossible to strip in fast enough, once a bow wave appears immediately behind the artificial, and the pursuing pike finally swims away in disgust, right at your feet. This happens if you stand close to the water's edge, which I admit is tempting in order to put a few more feet on the cast, but be wise and try to keep well back so the artificial can be worked right up to and even through mere inches of water and sparse marginal growth such as reeds and rushes. An explosive last-second take is

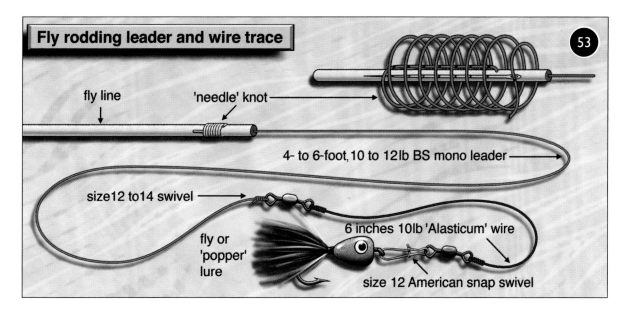

A peep into John's fly-rodding predator box reveals all sorts of weird and wonderful creations from the tiniest plugs to deerhair mice complete with eyes and tail.

itself, such is the variety of choice. But let's try to make matters relatively simple by having just two categories: floating and sinking.

FLOATING ARTIFICIALS

I won't call floating artificials flies, because the majority of my fly-rodding patterns are nothing like aquatic insects. Rodents, amphibians and fish, yes, but not insects – except perhaps for deerhair bumble bees. Actually I just love collecting these wonderful American-style popping bugs which have bulbous bodies tied on large single hooks and come in all shapes and sizes from muddler minnows to mice. Most are made of deerhair to which rubber frog's legs and wagtails have been added. These lures are super-buoyant and will float without any form of dressing. I particularly love to catch pike on the mouse imitation complete with eyes, ears, whiskers and a leather tail. It looks so lifelike when being plopped and gurgled upstream beneath overhanging trees or beside beds of bullrushes. And I wish I had a fiver for every chub that has also succumbed to its lifelike form, wire trace and all. Some deerhair patterns are

tied on long shank hooks up to size 3/0 but have small buoyant heads with bodies and wings made from light-reflecting coloured materials plus marabou for its unique pulsating lifelife qualities. Being light in overall weight these are by far the easiest big artificials (in size) to cast accurately with the rod.

SINKING (WET PATTERNS) ARTIFICIALS

This group can more or less cover everything from the long-shank predator flies just described (minus the buoyant head so they sink quickly) to the tiniest spinner or fly spoon. Overall, large streamer-type flies with hair or long feather wings are amongst the most effective patterns for pike because they can be stripped in fast and really do look like a good mouthful. Imitative crayfish and prawn artificials of up to 3 inches along also work along similar lines.

Smaller lead-headed artificials such as the dog nobbler or any similar jig with a marabou tail are favoured more by perch and zander but pike certainly won't refuse them. It is that irresistible

twitching, falling, jerking action which turns most predators on. Large salmon flies tied on single hooks will also catch pike, particularly patterns such as silver doctor, green highlander and thunder and lightning, all of which have a jungle cock feather tied in at the head to represent the eye of a small fish.

Other standard patterns of wet flies, especially those tied with mylar bodies to imitate fry such as the silver zonkers and Micky Finn, are also good catchers of both perch and pike.

As I mentioned earlier, even small spinners may be effectively used (for perch especially) with the fly rod. Tiny bar spinners as Landa Flipz-x which have fluorescent blades, or any of the Mepps range in size 00 or 0 weighing up to just 2g are highly recommended. It is well worth shopping around and delving through the catalogues of specialist tackle and lure companies to locate a comprehensive source of these tiny spinners, because the average tackle shop may not stock them. I do occasionally even use tiny sinking plugs marketed by Normark. Being little more than 1¼ inches in length, they can be cast with ease just like all those artificials already mentioned. No doubt, like me, you'll find that there is no end to it.

FLY RODDING
FOR CARP

American sports fishermen working the shallow flats between mangrove islands in the Florida Keys regularly beat 100lb tarpon using fly rods. A world-wide multi-million-pound industry has in fact evolved around even gladiators such as marlin and sail fish being pursued by fly-rodding techniques. So let me point out right from the start that catching carp on fly tackle is within the capability of everyone. It's great fun too.

If you own a 9–10-foot fly rod, say a standard still-water rod that maybe throws a size 7–8 floating line or thereabouts and you are really keen on catching carp with floaters, then how about experimenting a bit and enjoying just about the most exhilarating summer technique available to coarse fishermen in the UK short of catching a plane to Miami and bonefishing the Keys.

Fly rodding is off-beat maybe but it's something which for me came about several years ago whilst trying to extract double-figure carp from a local lake simply covered in lilies. You know the type, Nuphar lutea, our native yellow lily (often called brandy bottle), with huge green surface pads, hiding a mountain of subsurface lettuce-like leaves (called cabbages by most) which is also recognizable by its tight bright yellow flowers on thick, erect stalks. To minimize break-offs amongst this veritable cabbage jungle, only one kind of rod surpassed the old, sloppy, glass carp rods for this particular close-range, make-or-break situation. It was a 10-foot carbon reservoir fly rod which under full pressure just carried on bending and bending and bending like a huge elastic band.

This of course is the fly rod's secret when it comes to being able to subdue huge fish on seemingly impossible, inadequate tackle. You just have to get over that silly mental blockage which suggests that only 2½–3lb test curve meat sticks and jumbo-sized fixed-spool reels with shock rigs and 3–4oz leads (anyone seen my lips?) are necessary for putting carp on the bank. It simply isn't true. At extreme range, OK, but from the marginal shallows to however far out you can sensibly cast a floating fly line (around 20 yards) then I do urge you at least to give fly rodding for carp a try. You won't regret it though no doubt other anglers will think you have flipped your lid. But who cares? Naturally I am not talking here of huge, spooky, extremely difficult to catch (on anything) carp which live in small numbers in huge still-water fisheries, but in the average well-stocked modern carp lake where everything needs to nosh regularly to survive, fly rodding can be wonderful fun. So treat it as such.

Now you can, of course, fool surface and even sub-surface carp into sucking in artificial flies. As dusk falls, big bushy dry flies like mayflies, sedges and daddy long legs are quite liable to be sucked in from the surface film, especially when carp are in a slurping mood and working beneath a scum line.

You don't even need to cast; simply crawl into a close-range position and dunk your artificial amongst open mouths directly beneath the rod tip. If actually catching carp on an artificial is what grabs you in preference to bait, there is nothing in the rule book from stopping you attracting them up with small floaters – but fishing a dry fly amongst them. On a personal level I just like bending into hard battling carp on a fly rod for the ensuing fight. Trying to match the hatch, so to speak, simply doesn't come into it.

Slowly sinking nymphs work well too, especially when carp are noshing on natural food items. In clear water you can sometimes actually observe the artificial being sucked in, and of course in coloured water you must watch the cast for a take as the nymph slowly descends. But, and immensely satisfying as this purist approach might be, what I am suggesting you use when fly rodding for carp is more or less the same hook rig and floater you would present on a standard carp rod and fixed-spool reel combo. The only difference is that instead of getting your floater out with the aid of a surface controller float you cast it out with the fly rod outfit.

LEADERS, LINES AND REELS

Instead of the traditional dry-fly fisherman's tapered cast or leader I simply use 9–10 feet of 8–12lb mono (depending upon the size of fish expected) tied with a needle knot to the front end of a weight-forward floating fly line (Diag. 54, Fig. A). This is not imperative as you can quite happily use a braided leader connector which comes with a preformed

Due to the elastic-band action of the fly rod, even quite sizeable carp can be extracted from lily-clad marginal swims.

Keeping well back and kneeling amongst marginal grasses, John waits for a mouth to engulf his single mixer slowly drifting downwind amongst a handful of loose biscuits.

surface plants it doesn't really matter. If in doubt purchase a mid-green line and be sure it matches the suggested sizes written just above the cork handle of your rod. The numbers 6–8 or 7–9 simply relate to the size (or weight) of lines that will marry nicely with your particular rod. If there is any doubt, use the highest number. Being slightly heavier it will allow you to cast more easily and further over the generally short distances required to catch carp.

A single-action fly reel (as opposed to a geared reel) which can hold say 100 yards of 15–20lb braided backing beneath the line is advisable. On two occasions I have been taken halfway down the backing line by 25lb-plus carp in large waters where they decided to really run off, so don't economize on the backing. Besides you need plenty to ensure the reel is full so the fly line itself comes off in loose coils. Choose one without any kind of braking system so that only pressure upon the rim with the palm of your hand is used to slow down big fish.

USING FLOATERS

The leader or cast itself is smeared lightly with mucilin to within a few inches of the hook, otherwise as the 8–12lb monofilament sinks it will actually draw a small floating bait unnaturally across the surface. Hooks should match bait size and be strongly forged. I have used Drennan's Super specialist for many years and have yet to experience one opening under even severe strain. Try however to use a size smaller rather than larger to aid presentation. It's all about exactly that. There are numerous ways of attaching small floaters to your bare hook. You can dampen biscuit-type cat and dog floaters and put into a polybag (seal the end) for 20 minutes so they become rubbery and then almost the entire hook can gently be hidden inside. Alternatively you can tie a short dacron hair (see

loop. This is sleeved over the end of the fly line and secured by the plastic joint provided (Fig. B). Then tie an overhand loop on the end of your monofilament and join loop to loop as you would a hook to nylon with your reel line (Fig. C). The choice is yours.

A few words about various fly lines are, I think, warranted here because it is important that you use a weight-forward floating line instead of a double taper. As most of its casting weight is in the front third of the line, a weight-forward line is perfect for casting baits. Double taper lines have their weight in

the middle which, though they are perfect for delicately landing a tiny dry fly on the surface parachute style, makes them hopeless for achieving any degree of accuracy with baits. Actual casting distance will also be reduced if you use a double taper line.

Weight-forward floating lines are available in various colours from white to dark mahogany. In bright sunshine coupled to crystal-clear water and spooky carp, a white line is perhaps not a good idea, but then if only the leader actually lands upon the surface while the line drapes over lily pads or thick

Diag. 55 on page 122) on to your hook shank and sleeve on one or two floaters such as chum mixers, munchies, carp or trout pellets, or even mini boilies.

Generally when floater fishing I like to dampen the biscuits slightly so they do not break as the baiting needle is pushed through. However, with the fly rod this only limits the number of casts I can make before having to rebait, so I suggest only dry floaters are used. Simply use a nut drill to make the hole first, so the biscuit or pellet does not break, then hair rig in the normal fashion (as in Diag. 55, Fig. A).

With floating baits presented on a hair you need to ensure that the hook itself floats horizontally in the surface film and does not hang down, or numerous refusals could result. The best way of doing this is by gluing a slither of floating foam (black duplon – rod handle material) along the shank of the hook (Fig. B). But far and away the best kind of presentation is to ensure the floater actually sits on top of the hook and there are two ways of achieving this. You can either use a John Roberts' silicone bait band (as Fig. C – there are two sizes to fit chum mixers/boilies and carp and trout pellets) or carefully cut a shallow groove into the floater – any floater even floating sweetcorn – and literally superglue it on to the shank of your hook (Fig. D).

Personally I much prefer the latter method which in practice is far easier and quicker than it might sound. I keep half a junior hacksaw blade (bend and break into two) and a tube of superglue permanently in my waistcoat pocket. Until you have actually presented small floaters using the 'groove and glue' technique as I call it, you probably think it's a lot of hassle, but I do urge you to give it a try. The adhesive powers of superglue are unbelievable and such that virtually any small food which has inherent buoyancy can be used as bait simply by gluing to the shank of the hook. Most important of all, though, which is why I prefer this method, they will not fly

off or become dislodged and ruin presentation when being cast with your fly rod. Even gluing floating sweetcorn or a ¼-inch diameter floating trout or carp pellet to the shank of a size 12 hook is no problem. A little ruse that works on occasion, when a good mouthful is required, is to glue one floater on to the hook shank and present a second on a really short hair (as in Fig. E).

Generally speaking the baited hook needs to be as light as possible for casting accuracy and presentation. However, when really close-range fishing beneath trees for instance where casting is impossible, the heavier hook bait is advantageous. You simply use a catapult cast to get the bait out by holding the hook bend tightly and then pulling back with your left hand, while flexing the rod like a bow with your right, assuming you are right-handed.

When you let go the bait will fly out to the full length of leader beyond the rod top. It will only go a few yards, perhaps, but when marginal stalking this is usual sufficient (as in Diag. 56).

CASTING AND RETRIEVING

Providing you can cast out a leaded nymph or a lure to put and take rainbow trout, then taking carp off the top with more or less the same outfit should give you little trouble. It will, I'll guarantee, provide you with enormous enjoyment. I will even suggest that following a hectic fight, you might actually find your carp safely in the net very much quicker than had it been caught on standard, more powerful carp tackle, which as I said at the start, is totally due to the unique elastic-bend action of the fly rod

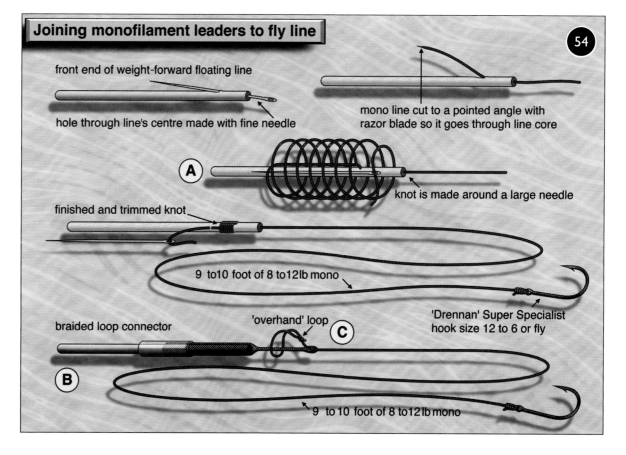

Joining monofilament leaders to fly line 54

front end of weight-forward floating line

hole through line's centre made with fine needle

mono line cut to a pointed angle with razor blade so it goes through line core

A

knot is made around a large needle

finished and trimmed knot

9 to 10 foot of 8 to 12lb mono

'Drennan' Super Specialist hook size 12 to 6 or fly

braided loop connector

'overhand' loop C

B

9 to 10 foot of 8 to 12lb mono

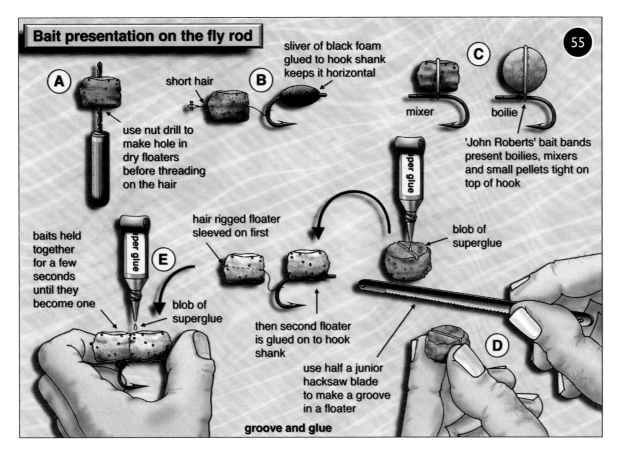

Bait presentation on the fly rod 55

A use nut drill to make hole in dry floaters before threading on the hair

short hair

B sliver of black foam glued to hook shank keeps it horizontal

C mixer boilie

'John Roberts' bait bands present boilies, mixers and small pellets tight on top of hook

baits held together for a few seconds until they become one

E blob of superglue

hair rigged floater sleeved on first

then second floater is glued on to hook shank

use half a junior hacksaw blade to make a groove in a floater

blob of superglue

D

groove and glue

By wearing shorts and old shoes or trainers during the summer months you can even get in to land the whoppers.

itself. It just carries on bending and bending and each time the carp thrusts its tail, the power is absorbed. Super-lightweight, thin-wall, soft-actioned loch-style fly rods are not recommended for the heavy handed approach association with catching carp. I recommend a 10-foot, powerful reservoir (bank) rod capable of punching out a size 9 line into a wind. Then you can go as hard on carp as you like.

Just a few words about casting are, I think, in order at this point because punching out a floating bait is slightly different from gently laying down a dry fly. On the forward cast for instance you really do need an extra-firm wrist action (as though knocking a 6-inch nail into an oak post) to straighten the leader fully and propel the floater ahead of the fly line. Ease up or be caught by a strong facing wind

and you'll find that both leader and bait will fall in a heap. Most other aspects are of course the same, and being stealthy, wearing Polaroid sunglasses and keeping low down below the skyline are equally as important as wearing drab clothing. A most useful item for observing the comings and goings of carp are Polaroid binoculars which haven't been around too long. Mine are 8 x 25 magnification, incredibly light and made by Bushell. I rate these binoculars as the most useful single item of tackle for viewing fish and general waterside wildlife since I purchased my first pair of Polaroid sunglasses way back in the late 1950s. It is always so difficult to observe beyond distances of 10 yards when wearing Polaroid sunglasses, but at this point Polaroid binoculars now take over and open up a whole new field of subsurface vision.

Actually, I probably spend more time in observation when fly rodding for carp than I do fishing. This is because continually false casting the floater is bound to spook the fish. So I wait until most of the fish before me are up on the top gorging down everything with gay abandon before casting in my floater. I really do enjoy getting them up to the top through catapulting out regular helpings of free floaters. Quite apart from gaining their confidence, it perhaps allows me to select a particular fish — or at least know which fish are more receptive than others. If due to a chop of the surface, or too many mouths, or too many floaters, or both dimpling the surface, you cannot actually see when the hook bait is slurped down watch the fly line itself. Instigating bold, positive takes is imperative when fly rodding. Due to the fly rod's

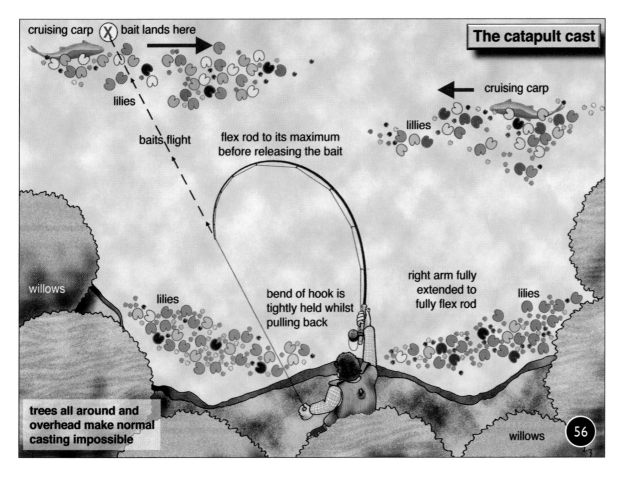

Though splattered by mud and weed, by the look on John's face he was more than pleased to land this superb 20lb-plus leather carp.

sloppy action, trying to set the hook quickly on a half chance before the fish ejects it is simply not on. You need to see those lips come up, suck in and go down, and wait for the leader to tighten before pulling on the line with your left hand and heaving on the rod with your right. Simply striking by using only your arm is not enough. As when using standard tackle for presenting floaters to carp, a proportion of fish will inevitably panic off, virtually hooking themselves immediately upon sucking in the bait. Most of them need to be struck and so everything needs to be tight for the hook to be driven home.

Remember to jump quickly to your feet (of course you have been keeping low down) and hold the rod up really high when a good fish goes charging off through dense lilies, so the line doesn't catch around stalks and pads, just as you would on a regular outfit. Small- to moderate-sized fish can quite easily be played like rainbow trout, by holding the line and paying out or retrieving by hand.

When a big fish grabs hold, however, and if you are not quickly taken down to the backing (lovely stuff), endeavour before you tread on it, to get any loose line cluttering marginal growth straight back on to the reel and continue playing the fish entirely from the reel, breaking the rim with the palm of your winding hand in order to slow it down. This is where a reserve of up to 100 yards of backing beneath the fly line may well prove its worth. Above all try not to panic. You'll get it all back on the reel eventually. With most of the fly line out being towed around by the carp, you will come to realize how it is that massive fish can eventually be landed on just a few ounces of carbon. Put in simple terms, it is like the action of a giant elastic band under constant pressure.

If carp are really loath to suck in your floater but take all the others, try a slowly sinking bait and watch the cast like a hawk. Glue half a small floater on to the shank of the hook, like those with which you have been loose feeding, and then put enough maggots on to the bend of the hook to make it just sink. Actually a bunch of maggots slowly descending through the swim has taken no small number of carp for me over the years. Unlike most baits, maggots withstand the rigours of casting exceptionally well. Give them a try, but hang on!

LEDGERING

Ledgering is arguably the most effective method of catching specimen tench from shallow reservoirs and estate lakes.

BOBBIN LEDGERING

While it is fair to say that a large proportion of anglers who ledger in slow-moving rivers and still waters now opt to use a built-in quivertip in preference to all other indicators (particularly match fishermen), there are nevertheless numerous situations especially if ledgering with two rods or at distances in excess of say 50 yards when using clip-on bobbin bite indicators is preferable.

Whether presenting a ledgered lobworm for tench or bream, with or without the addition of a swimfeeder, or a small livebait for perch or zander, bobbin ledgering offers an extremely versatile method of bite indication. For instance bobbin indicators can be most effectively used in conjunction with electronic bite alarms, permitting maximum enjoyment of the surrounding environment. With or without binoculars you can be looking around at various aspects of natural history and watching for signs of feeding fish, yet be able instantly to switch your eyes back to witness a bobbin move up or down whenever the bleep tone of the electronic alarm sounds. This of course is in complete contrast to and simply not possible when quivertipping where eye contact is imperative at all times.

Another definite plus factor for bobbin ledgering as opposed to using the quivertip (where the rod must be set at an angle parallel to the bank in order for bites to be seen) occurs whenever marginal shrubbery is dense. A pair of rods may be set up in the tiniest of gaps between trees pointing straight out directly at the ledgered baits for maximum line pick-up on the strike and the bobbins clipped on – an impossibility when quivertipping. And as far as lengthy sessions are concerned, stints of several hours or longer, which are dictated by really large sheets of water where fish density of specimen bream or tench for example is extremely low, quivertipping is just not practical. So once again bite indication provided by ledger bobbins is the answer, permitting a relaxed yet expectant mode of approach.

Yet another reason for employing bobbins occurs whilst bream fishing in still waters when fish are

This superb 12lb bream caught bobbin ledgering in a Norfolk gravel pit on lobworm, proves the effectiveness of this method. Note how the rods point straight out.

packed so tightly together that tiny pulls and plinks constantly register on the supersensitive quivertip, most of which are actually false indications, better known as line bites. During these frustrating periods a switch over to a bobbin instantly provides a more reliable indication. Line bites merely jingle the bobbin up and down or occasionally zoom it up to the butt ring at lightning speed and return it just as quickly; genuine bites, on the other hand, invariably take the bobbin slowly up and keep it there. Indeed a point well worth remembering is that there are occasions when it is just as necessary to be deliberately slow in striking, as it is to be quick.

When ledgering in really slow-moving rivers and the target species are quality-sized roach and bream attracted by large hook baits – baits such as breadflake, lobworm or sweetcorn – where I expect a confident bite to materialize, once again I much prefer to use a bobbin indicator. Premature striking by using a supersensitive quivertip can all too easily spook a specimen fish before it moves away with the larger bait well inside its mouth.

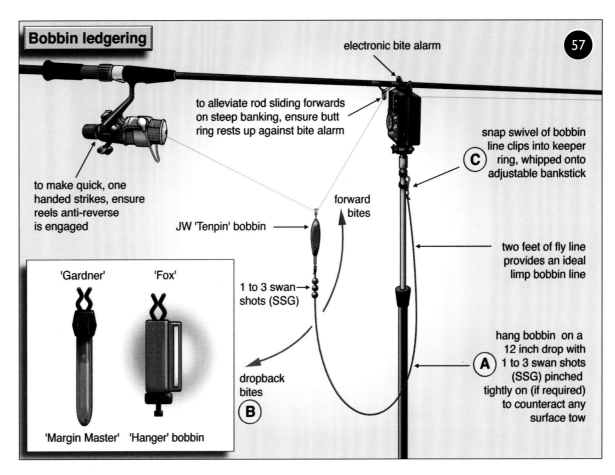

Bobbin ledgering — 57

electronic bite alarm

to alleviate rod sliding forwards on steep banking, ensure butt ring rests up against bite alarm

to make quick, one handed strikes, ensure reels anti-reverse is engaged

JW 'Tenpin' bobbin

forward bites

snap swivel of bobbin line clips into keeper ring, whipped onto adjustable bankstick — C

two feet of fly line provides an ideal limp bobbin line

1 to 3 swan shots (SSG)

'Gardner'   'Fox'

'Margin Master'   'Hanger' bobbin

dropback bites — B

hang bobbin on a 12 inch drop with 1 to 3 swan shots (SSG) pinched tightly on (if required) to counteract any surface tow — A

TACKLE COMBOS

There is no hard-and-fast rule for the tackle set-ups I might use when bobbin ledgering. When seeking quality roach, rudd and medium-sized bream, for instance, an 11–12-foot Avon-style rod with a test curve of around 1¼lb, coupled to say a 3lb reel line is ideal. But I step up to a reel line of 4lb for close-range tench and bream fishing in snag-free swims and for quality perch.

For extracting the same from snaggy, overgrown or weedy, marginal swims however, and especially for the rigours demanded by distance fishing which often includes the constant casting of heavy feeders or bomb plus a large bait, a 6lb reel line is imperative. I also use a 6lb reel line when bobbin ledgering

worms, livebaits or deadbaits for specimen perch and zander, again relying on the versatility of a 1¼lb test curve Avon rod which permits enjoyable yet firm playing of these two predators with little fear of the hooks pulling out, a near impossibility if rod strength is greatly increased to cover the eventuality of a pike turning up.

It's worth noting here that while many anglers choose to fish far heavier for zander I feel they must sometimes pay the price and the consequences of inhibiting these extremely sensitive biters from providing a hittable run by the use of over-the-top tackle, lines and terminal rigs especially. An 8lb test line for instance would be my absolute upper limit for zander which, let's face it, are far more commonly caught well short of double figures rather than over.

The only exception I would make to this personal yardstick is when fishing certain Fenland drains, namely the Great Ouse Relief Channel or the Middle Level Drain, which are renowned for breeding huge colonies of the dreaded zebra mussel which have razor-sharp edges to their shells and literally pave the bottom in places. They are famous for ripping all too easily through a ledgered line, so a step up in diameter would then seem to be a sensible precaution.

FISHING THE BOBBIN

First, always endeavour to point the rod tip directly at the ledgered bait. This minimizes on the amount of subsurface tow or drag on the line which has to be taken up on the strike, thus ensuring maximum pick-up for firm hook setting.

After casting and taking up most of the slack, clip the bobbin on to the line just behind the butt ring (on the reel side) and, to ensure the line remains taut, press down your forefinger on the line in front of the bobbin until it comes to rest hanging almost straight down from the butt ring on a drop of 12–24 inches depending upon whether you are expecting mere twitches or long positive runs.

From studying Diag. 57, (Fig. A) you can see that on a 12-inch drop, for instance, the fish can move the bait away from the rod for a distance of at least 12 inches before the bobbin hits the butt ring or dislodges the bomb or feeder and swims directly

towards the rod thus indicating a drop-back bite by the bobbin falling towards the ground (Fig. B).

If the bobbin does not hang down on a long enough drop, switch the reel's antireverse off (it should be switched on at all other times) enabling extra line to revolve backwards from the spool. As soon as the bobbin hangs on the desired drop, switch the reel's antireverse on again. If it simply refuses to settle or keeps dropping back this invariably means that a fish has grabbed the bait and swum towards the rod within seconds of the ledger or swimfeeder landing on the bottom. This is a common occurrence when tench or bream are really on the feed and an instant drop-back bite occurs (Fig. B) which should be hit straight away in a sweeping back strike to maximize on line pick-up.

Rather than feeder fish, John catapults out broken worms whilst bobbin ledgering for perch just 20 yards out.

When using two rods it is worth taking the trouble to ensure that both bobbins hang at exactly the same height. This is not for reasons of neatness, but simply because the slightest twitch bite will then be evident in an instant even if the alarm fails to bleep.

WHICH BOBBINS?

Now let's look at the merits of various bobbins. I have purposefully excluded monkey climbers here, although they are simply bobbins on a stick and despite the fact that they are extremely useful when ledgering in gale-force winds, because monkey climbers are not in my opinion anywhere near as versatile as clip-on bobbins.

For much of my ledgering I use my own JW tenpin bobbins which have a stainless steel sprung wire clip into which the reel line is pushed. This clip can easily be tensioned by moving the short length of silicone tubing up or down. To eradicate bobbin

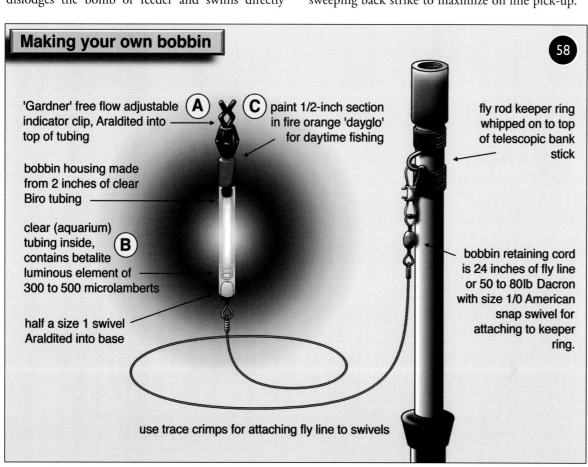

Making your own bobbin

58

'Gardner' free flow adjustable (A) indicator clip, Araldited into top of tubing

(C) paint 1/2-inch section in fire orange 'dayglo' for daytime fishing

bobbin housing made from 2 inches of clear Biro tubing

clear (aquarium) tubing inside, (B) contains betalite luminous element of 300 to 500 microlamberts

half a size 1 swivel Araldited into base

fly rod keeper ring whipped on to top of telescopic bank stick

bobbin retaining cord is 24 inches of fly line or 50 to 80lb Dacron with size 1/0 American snap swivel for attaching to keeper ring.

use trace crimps for attaching fly line to swivels

snap back on the strike which all to easily happens with a stretchy retaining cord like monofilament, I suggest a 2-foot length of fly line (heavy duty dacron is also ideal) attached to the bobbin with a trace crimp. At the other end a large American snap swivel is crimped on, so the retaining cord can be quickly attached to the top of the front bank stick, on to which is whipped a small keeper ring as used just above the handle of fly rods (Diag. 57, Fig. C).

For ledgering after dark various commercial betalight bobbins (which incorporate a 300–500 microlambert luminous element) are available such as the Glo Bobbin. An excellent range of bobbins that come fitted with a clear tube to accept a betalight element are made by Fox International and known as the Hanger bobbins. Though the range was initially designed for bolt-rig carp fishing these lightweight hangers make great all-purpose ledger bobbins. They are fitted with a micrometer adjustment line release clip, a light-reactive, tough acrylic head in green, red or yellow, plus a quick-release dovetail tag which fits on to the bank stick just below the bite alarm or rest head. The Hanger bobbin then simply dovetails on in an instant. Its only drawback is the 11½-inch dacron retaining cord which is too short by far for general use, but this is easily replaced by 2 feet of heavy dacron or fly line.

A similar bobbin complete with recess for a luminous element called the Marginmaster is made by Gardner Tackle. Available in green, red, amber or clear, it has an adjustable free-flow line clip and simply needs to be rigged with a retaining cord. Again 2 feet of fly line is perfect for the job.

The free-flow adjustable line clip is actually available as a single item enabling you to construct your own designer bobbin, as in Diag. 58, Fig. A for instance, with built-in provision for a betalight element (Fig. B). A ½-inch section (Fig. C) is then painted in easy-to-see fire orange for daytime viewing.

STRIKING WITH BOBBINS

Regardless of which bobbin is used, it is imperative that it falls easily from the line on the strike but does

There's nothing to beat bobbin bite indication when summer tench fishing at mid to long range. John's brother, Dave Wilson, returns a 5-pounder.

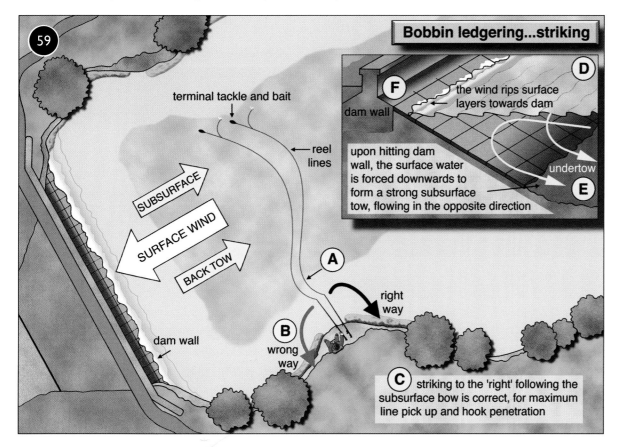

Diagram 59: Bobbin ledgering...striking

terminal tackle and bait

reel lines

SUBSURFACE
SURFACE WIND
BACK TOW

dam wall

A

B wrong way

right way

C striking to the 'right' following the subsurface bow is correct, for maximum line pick up and hook penetration

F dam wall

D the wind rips surface layers towards dam

upon hitting dam wall, the surface water is forced downwards to form a strong subsurface tow, flowing in the opposite direction

undertow

E

Note how John strikes sideways to hook tench in the shallows of a Norfolk estate lake, pulling the line through the water as opposed to up and against surface tension.

acute problem whenever the wind rips across the surface parallel to the shoreline from which you are fishing.

Just look at Diag. 59. The way in which both lines have been angled to the left by the wind (Fig. A) would indicate an upwards strike to the left, yet this is wrong (Fig. B). Far more line will be picked up (and the hook banged home with maximum force) if the strike is executed upwards and to the right, following the curvature of the subsurface bow (Fig. C). It is always best to pull the line through the water on the strike as opposed to pulling or lifting it against water pressure.

Consider Fig. D and you can appreciate what actually happens beneath the surface. As the wind rips the surface layers (Fig. F) down the lake from right to left, upon hitting the dam all the water is pushed downwards (Fig. E) and subsequently flows back down the lake in the opposite direction.

When bolt-rig fishing for carp and tench using a heavy lead incorporated within the terminal rig which causes the fish virtually to set the hook itself, being aware of subsurface tow is perhaps not so important (see Method 18, 'Bolt-Rig Ledgering for Tench and Carp'). But when ledgering (especially at distance) using a standard bomb/feeder, fixed paternoster or running terminal rig, where striking the hook home hard is of paramount importance, think seriously about how your line will be lying along the bottom between bait and rod. It is perhaps also worth pointing out that in deep water it makes sense to strike upwards in order to continue the angle at which the line is lying between bait and rod tip. Whereas in really shallow waters, striking sideways and low to the ground in order to pull the line *through* the water is imperative for maximum line pick-up, striking upwards in shallow water *against* surface tension (and the problem is compounded the further out you cast)

not rise prematurely due to subsurface tow or through wind drift. The answer is to pinch sufficient weight in swan shots tightly on to the retaining cord immediately below the bobbin. The 2 x SSG and 3 x SSG shots are simply perfect for the job.

Actually, being aware of subsurface tow which causes the line to form a huge (unseen) bow beneath the surface between bait and rod tip and then subsequently striking in an arc complimentary to the angle at which the line is bowed, instead of against it, will put many more fish in the net and preclude the missing of seemingly unmissable bites. This phenomenon (which of course you can never actually see) happens in all large sheets of water, becoming an greatly reduces the chances of the hook being driven home.

INDUCING BITES

What I particularly enjoy about bobbin ledgering, especially when sport is slow, is being able to induce bites and thus encourage lethargic fish to grab hold of the bait, simply by yanking the bobbin down with my left hand whilst turning the reel handle and taking up the slack with my right. You may have gathered from this that being right-handed I always sit with both rods positioned slightly to my right for an instant right-handed strike and so I can twitch the bait in whenever positive indications are not happening when they should. You can just imagine a big old perch, for

instance, that is not really in an active mood sitting there looking at a lobworm doing nothing on the bottom. Then all of a sudden the meal it thought it didn't want looks like getting away. And that's the secret of twitching the bobbins to move the bait and instigate action.

TWITCHER HITTING

Actual twitch bites are different altogether. I am referring of course to those tiny, barely perceptible movements of the bobbin which, for argument's sake let's say, do not go up or down more than ¼ inch. The fact is, however, many is the time when a fat tench, big roach or a bream might be sitting munching on the spot having sucked the bait in back to its pharyngeal teeth for chewing but failing

to move off and provide a hittable lift of the bobbin.

Contrary to general thought these twitch bites are in fact signs of fish feeding with extreme confidence and once you have realized the situation the best course of action is to reduce the hook length severely, say from 20 inches down to just 6 inches which automatically produces a more positive registration on the bobbin.

To see any subsequent bites more clearly, hang both bobbins (assuming you are using two rods) on really short drops, say 6–8 inches, and be prepared to hit anything – even the slightest jingle. And I mean anything: strike even if you think one of the bobbins shifted slightly. Or, better still, refocus your eyes on the reel line between rod tip and the surface and hit the merest twitch.

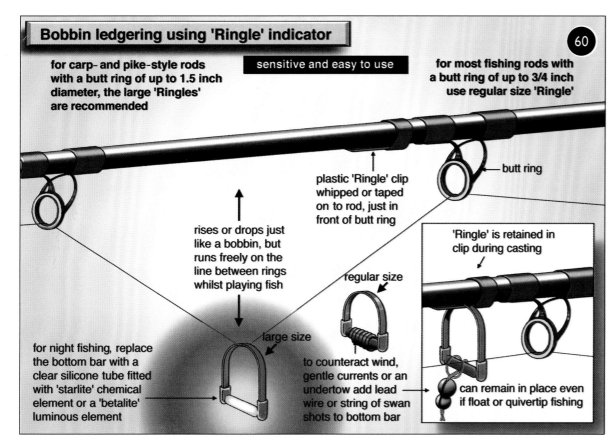

Bobbin ledgering using 'Ringle' indicator

60

for carp- and pike-style rods with a butt ring of up to 1.5 inch diameter, the large 'Ringles' are recommended

sensitive and easy to use

for most fishing rods with a butt ring of up to 3/4 inch use regular size 'Ringle'

plastic 'Ringle' clip whipped or taped on to rod, just in front of butt ring

butt ring

rises or drops just like a bobbin, but runs freely on the line between rings whilst playing fish

regular size

'Ringle' is retained in clip during casting

for night fishing, replace the bottom bar with a clear silicone tube fitted with 'starlite' chemical element or a 'betalite' luminous element

large size

to counteract wind, gentle currents or an undertow add lead wire or string of swan shots to bottom bar

can remain in place even if float or quivertip fishing

Proof of the pudding. Tench weighing 7lb and 8lb respectively caught bobbin ledgering on a lobworm/feeder rig from a Midlands reservoir.

BOLT-RIG LEDGERING FOR TENCH AND CARP

With bolt-rig ledgering we are into a completely different situation from ledgering in general and deliberately using what would seem ridiculously extra-heavy leads in the 2–4oz range. These are used in order to shock tench or carp into panicking or bolting off (hence the term 'bolt rig') and hooking themselves in the process, whilst simultaneously providing a most positive bite indication on the electronic buzzer/indicator set-up

as they run off. Some would perhaps say that this is computerized fishing but the fact remains there are situations when unless bolt-rig ledgering is used few fish will be caught. Take extreme-range ledgering for example, let's say distances in excess of 75 yards, where unless the fish panics off and helps the hook to prick home, the likelihood of a hook being pulled from a ball of paste and driven home beyond the barb is remote.

The simple principle of this method works on the fact that both tench or carp realize the bait must be vacuumed back to their powerful pharyngeal (throat) teeth for mastication prior to swallowing but forget that it's inside their mouth upon feeling that strange resistance caused by a heavy lead and promptly close their lips before doing a runner. At this point the weight of the bomb helps in hook penetration. This naturally calls for specialized terminal rigs as can be seen from Diag. 61. For close-range fishing, where casting tangles do not pose a problem, there is little reason to load up with unnecessary beads and antitangle tubing. Instead use the simple rig in Fig. A which consists of a 2oz pear bomb on a 3-inch length of just 6lb mono (covered in fine-diameter black silicone tubing) with a size 10 swivel at the end. To the opposite end of the swivel is tied both the 4–6-inch mono hook link with a size 8–6 hook (depending on bait size) and hair-rigged or side-hooked particles or boilie and the 10–12lb reel line. In 12-inch divisions immediately above the swivel junction, pinch on size AA shot or mould on a blob on tungsten-type putty. This ensures the reel line closest to the rig is ironed flat to the bottom, or actually disappears into the surface layer of silty lakes and ponds. Excellent for presenting particles, this rig.

Diag. 62, Fig. A shows a basic helicopter rig which means the hook length is free to swivel around the reel line between the two beads during flight and thus not tangle even when long-range casting. To ensure it remains separate, a 12–14-inch length of fine-diameter silicone tubing is sleeved on to the reel line above the end rig set-up (which comprises a 2–2½oz bomb) and kept in place by a rubber float stop or sliding knot tied from 25lb power gum. The

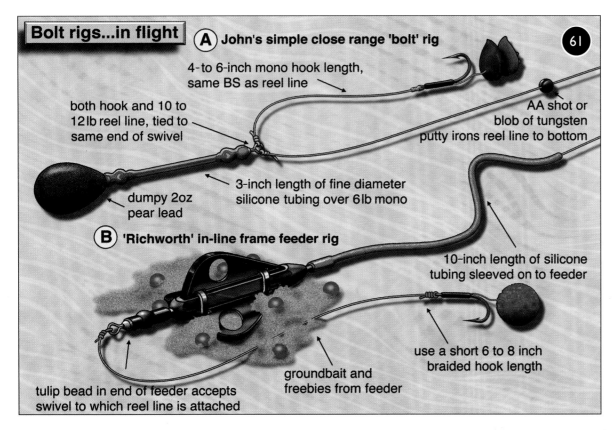

Bolt rigs...in flight   (A) **John's simple close range 'bolt' rig**   61

4- to 6-inch mono hook length, same BS as reel line

both hook and 10 to 12lb reel line, tied to same end of swivel

AA shot or blob of tungsten putty irons reel line to bottom

dumpy 2oz pear lead

3-inch length of fine diameter silicone tubing over 6lb mono

(B) **'Richworth' in-line frame feeder rig**

10-inch length of silicone tubing sleeved on to feeder

use a short 6 to 8 inch braided hook length

tulip bead in end of feeder accepts swivel to which reel line is attached

groundbait and freebies from feeder

Hooked at long range, an angler controls a big tench that accepted a boilie-baited bolt rig.

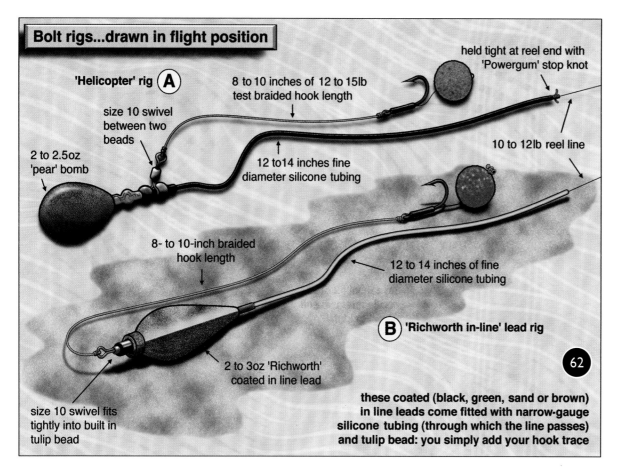

Bolt rigs...drawn in flight position

'Helicopter' rig (A)

size 10 swivel between two beads

2 to 2.5oz 'pear' bomb

8 to 10 inches of 12 to 15lb test braided hook length

12 to14 inches fine diameter silicone tubing

held tight at reel end with 'Powergum' stop knot

10 to 12lb reel line

8- to 10-inch braided hook length

12 to 14 inches of fine diameter silicone tubing

(B) 'Richworth in-line' lead rig

2 to 3oz 'Richworth' coated in line lead

62

size 10 swivel fits tightly into built in tulip bead

these coated (black, green, sand or brown) in line leads come fitted with narrow-gauge silicone tubing (through which the line passes) and tulip bead: you simply add your hook trace

which have a tulip bead (to take the hook length swivel) at the wide end and 12 inches of ready-fitted narrow-diameter, black silicone tubing through which the reel line is passed at the other. These in-line ready-mades also come with side grooves to accept dissolving capsules (into which your chosen bait flavour can be injected) held in place with a small band provided. Coated colours are available in green, sand, black and brown to match the bottom and sizes vary from 1½oz to 4oz. For general bolt-rig fishing use no more than 2½oz.

ROD ANGLES

OK, so you cast out your chosen bolt rig and bait, after tightening up, and what happens at the rod

This simple set-up, for catching carp in waters where the banks are made up, shows a rod pod with buzzer bars, electronic bite alarms and swinger arm indicators.

8–10-inch hook length is made from supple, low-diameter braid of which there are numerous makes from which to choose. As always hook sizes depend upon that of the bait. Consider Diag. 63, Figs A to F, for some of the most effective options. As can be seen from Diag. 64 when fishing over bottom weeds or debris simply to offer a buoyant off-the-bottom bait using pop-ups is the answer.

Diag. 61, Fig. B shows an in-line bolt-rig set-up with a Richworth built-in frame feeder bomb (1–2oz) around which a groundbait made from your bait's basic mix (prior to rolling into balls and boiling) can be moulded. A carp pellet boilie on the hook with a handful of the same base mix around the feeder is one of the most effective combinations.

As fish quickly gather around the frame feeder in

order to peck off the attractor ground-bait, use a short 6–8-inch hook line so the bait comes to settle close by. These very latest in-line feeder bombs manufactured by Richworth Products save any messing about converting frame feeders. Available in 1oz and 2oz models these are feeder and lead combined through which runs a length of tubing so a suitable rig can quickly be made up. If you make up exactly the same rig as Diag. 61, Fig. B, substituting the frame feeder for an in-line lead (Diag. 62, Fig. B), you have an excellent in-line bolt rig for general fishing which many top anglers actually prefer to a helicopter rig (as in Diag. 62, Fig. A) because the lead is in line with the carp as it moves off with the bait. Again Richworth Products also come to the rescue here with their range of coated premade bombs end? Well to start off with it's worth considering at what angle to set the rod. Generally speaking it is ideal to have the rod in two rests or on a rod pod (for gravel pit or reservoir banks) set at an angle more or less pointing directly at the ledgered bait when bolt-rig fishing. This is just as it is when bobbin ledgering using a feeder or bomb rig. However, as can be seen from Diag. 65, Fig. B, there are situations when the line hangs over shallow bars situated between rod tip and the ledgered bait (as is so often the case when fishing irregular-bottomed gravel pits, from which problems can arise). Either coarse gravel or, worse still, a colony of freshwater mussels can damage the line or, due to the line draping over these bars, bite indication is impaired. Therefore winding up tight after casting and angling the rod tip upwards (Fig A) to keep the line away from shallow bars or ridges is

much preferred. The down side however is that some fish will become spooked and not swim anywhere near the bait, but you can't have everything.

LINE LOOPS AND BACK LEADS

In order to stop a strong subsurface tow, wind drift or strong winds from continually lifting the bite indicator and creating irritating bleeps on the buzzer, clip a loop of line up beneath a plastic run clip positioned on the rod just ahead of the buzzer and indicator set-up (Diag. 65, Fig. C). But remember that drop-back bites cannot then register on the buzzer/indicator set-up, only forward runs.

In addition, for certain situations in close-range swims for example, Diag. 66, Fig. A, and when

John caught this wonderfully scaled 24lb estate-lake mirror carp on a hair-rigged Q-pipz fished bolt-rig style during his TV series 'Go Fishing'.

presenting the bait over areas where a hauser tight line causes irritating line bites or simply spooks fish from approaching the bait (Fig. B), you need to consider using a back lead. These handy items which clip on to the reel line ahead of the rod may be secured to the front rod rest (Fig. C) with a length of dacron retaining cord and slid down the line to iron it to the bottom, enabling fish to move freely about without bumping into it or being spooked by its existence. Some back leads, like the Gardner Captive models are fitted with a retaining loop and have adjustable clips for instant line release with a sharp jerk – or, in the case of a positive run, your strike of course. Alternatively, the cordless Fox back leads simply clip over the line by way of a split flexible top ring and slide down the line at the rod tip, ironing it to the bottom contour. These stay on the line above the rig throughout the fight and are simply removed prior to rebaiting.

REEL SETTING

Without question the best reels for bolt-rig fishing are those with a built-in bait runner-type facility which

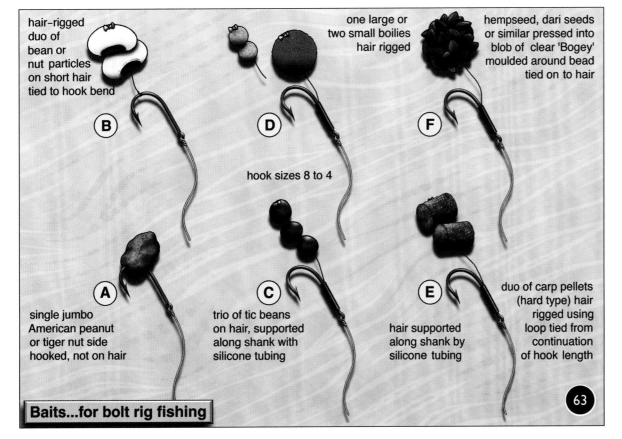

hair-rigged duo of bean or nut particles on short hair tied to hook bend

(B)

one large or two small boilies hair rigged

(D)

hempseed, dari seeds or similar pressed into blob of clear 'Bogey' moulded around bead tied on to hair

(F)

hook sizes 8 to 4

single jumbo American peanut or tiger nut side hooked, not on hair

(A)

trio of tic beans on hair, supported along shank with silicone tubing

(C)

hair supported along shank by silicone tubing

(E)

duo of carp pellets (hard type) hair rigged using loop tied from continuation of hook length

63

Baits...for bolt rig fishing

disengages the rotor and allows a fish to go belting off taking line (under a preset tension) around the closed bale arm from a spool which freely revolves. You simply crank the handle in order to re-engage the spool to its (preset) clutch setting suitable for the strength line being used and lift the rod into the tench or carp. It's so easy your granny could do it.

If your reel is of the stern drag type but does not have a free spool facility you can still fish with the bale arm closed but must of course, after casting and putting the rod down, slacken off the clutch setting by turning the calibrated drag knob fully one whole turn anticlockwise. With most reels this is sufficient to allow a fish that has hooked itself to go belting off without pulling the rod in. But of course you must turn the drag knob back clockwise again immediately before lifting the rod into the fish and

be prepared quickly to make a minor clutch adjustment with the drag knob during the early stages of the fight This is not a difficult skill to master with modern stern drag reels which have extremely sensitive drag systems even on low-price models.

Front drag reels are not recommended for bolt-rig fishing, as trying to readjust the clutch whilst the spool is revolving in a blur and line evaporates around the bale arm roller is far from easy.

Of course some tench and carp anglers don't worry about the slipping clutch anyway and simply play fish by backwinding through the gears with the drag knob done up tight. It is not, in my opinion however, the most effective nor the most enjoyable way of subduing particularly large or really fast-moving carp. So get used to the capabilities of your

reel's slipping clutch system. Once mastered it will not let you down, and playing fish is, of course, what it was designed for.

BUZZERS AND INDICATORS

Now let's consider a subject which to the newcomer must at first appear confusing to say the least. Which electronic bite alarm (buzzer for short) and indicator system should you use? The plain truth of course is that if you sit close beside your rod or rods and simply fix a bobbin or clip the line beneath the body of a monkey climber set midway between a simple front rod rest head and reel, you do not actually need any form of electronic alarm, provided you keep your eyes on the indicators.

However, as bolt-rig ledgering tench and carping sessions can lead into hour upon hour of concentration, to have en electronic bite alarm in place of a front rod rest head through which the line passes does allow immense overall enjoyment of the location being fished, whilst in addition even encouraging the eventual capture of bonus fish which, for instance, you might well have identified as bubbles through binoculars when viewing around and capitalized upon by immediately placing a bait close by. So do not be afraid of winding a bait in and instantly relocating to a potentially productive spot, or you will not land many bonus fish.

Today most top-quality alarms work with the line resting across a frictionless roller set in a deep groove in the centre of the head and thus becoming the front rod rest. They work either through a photoelectronic cell or reed switch principle which gives a single bleep tone for every ½–1 inch of line going backwards or forwards across the supersensitive roller. Simultaneously an LED (light emitting diode) comes on, so from both sight and

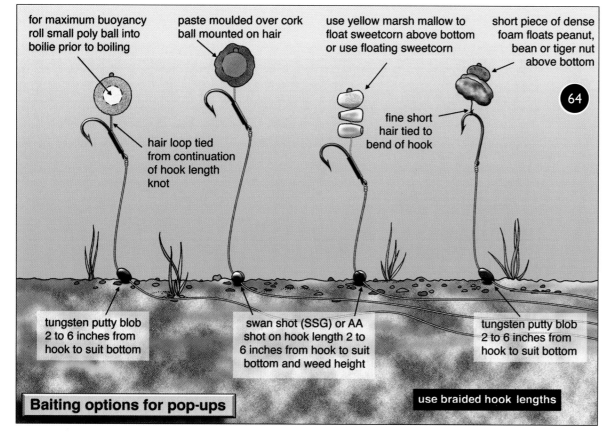

for maximum buoyancy roll small poly ball into boilie prior to boiling

paste moulded over cork ball mounted on hair

use yellow marsh mallow to float sweetcorn above bottom or use floating sweetcorn

short piece of dense foam floats peanut, bean or tiger nut above bottom

64

hair loop tied from continuation of hook length knot

fine short hair tied to bend of hook

tungsten putty blob 2 to 6 inches from hook to suit bottom

swan shot (SSG) or AA shot on hook length 2 to 6 inches from hook to suit bottom and weed height

tungsten putty blob 2 to 6 inches from hook to suit bottom

Baiting options for pop-ups

use braided hook lengths

sound you can immediately relate to whether the bite is a mere twitch (which just could be a line bite of course) or a tearaway run. Also as the indicator rises or falls, you instantly know whether it is a forward or a drop-back bite. However, more of the latter later on.

Whilst a heavy bobbin or monkey climber clipped on to the line for indication would have been sufficient several years ago, indicators designed specifically for the method of bite detection whilst bolt-rig ledgering have now become quite sophisticated, being completely free of frictional drag. Among dozens of varying models on the market, arguably the most versatile is the swinger MK2 made by Fox. This particular indicator has a 9-inch stainless steel arm along which a stainless steel counterbalancing weight can be moved to suit conditions at hand with adjustment from zero to 2oz. It is thus perfect for registering tiny forward twitches in a flat calm and equally small drop-backs when fishing at distance.

At the line end is an acrylic, light-reactive head (available in red, yellow or green) which has provision for a betalight luminous element and a totally unique line-release gate. As this indicator simply moves (swings) up and down from its pivot lug which dovetails on to a clip that fits around the buzzer thread on the front bank stick and does not sway from side to side, it remains steady in the windiest weather. Functional whether you opt for two outfits set on separate bank sticks, or a 2/3 rod pod set-up when fishing over hard gravel or from a wooden staging, these swinger-type indicators are excellent.

BAITS FOR BOLT-RIG LEDGERING

As can be seen from the variety of baits and how they can be presented in Diag. 63, generally

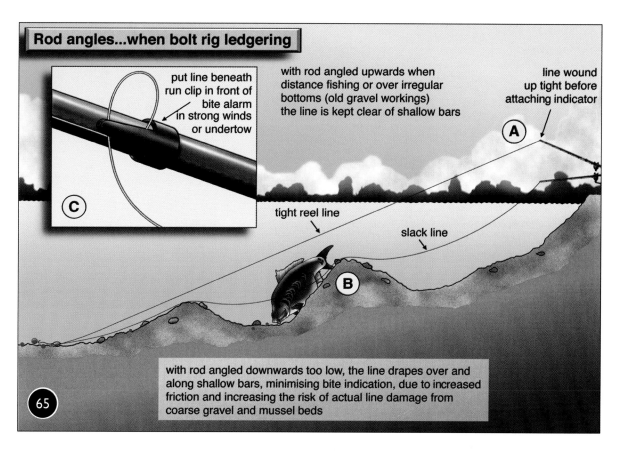

Rod angles...when bolt rig ledgering

put line beneath run clip in front of bite alarm in strong winds or undertow

with rod angled upwards when distance fishing or over irregular bottoms (old gravel workings) the line is kept clear of shallow bars

line wound up tight before attaching indicator

tight reel line

slack line

with rod angled downwards too low, the line drapes over and along shallow bars, minimising bite indication, due to increased friction and increasing the risk of actual line damage from coarse gravel and mussel beds

65

Carp pellets are unbelievably versatile. You can drill and hair rig them or grind to dust, mix with eggs into a paste, then roll into boilies.

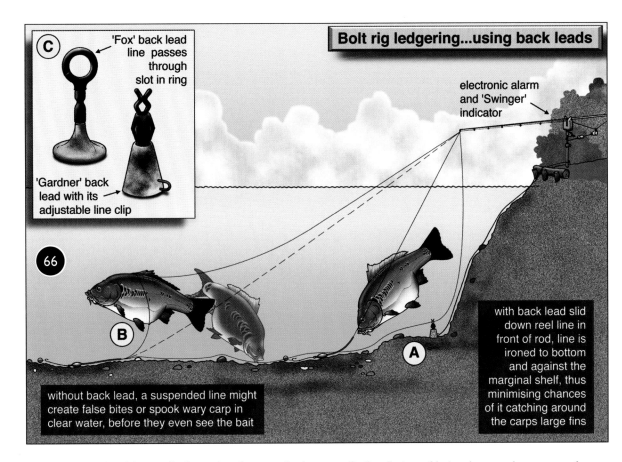

C 'Fox' back lead line passes through slot in ring

'Gardner' back lead with its adjustable line clip

Bolt rig ledgering...using back leads

electronic alarm and 'Swinger' indicator

66

B

A

without back lead, a suspended line might create false bites or spook wary carp in clear water, before they even see the bait

with back lead slid down reel line in front of rod, line is ironed to bottom and against the marginal shelf, thus minimising chances of it catching around the carps large fins

speaking only hard baits which need to be crunched by the fishes pharyngeal teeth are suitable.

Soft baits, such as breadflake or pastes, are quite liable to disintegrate before reaching the tench or carp's throat teeth or be picked to bits by nuisance species, leaving you sitting there waiting for a run with a bare hook. This is why offerings such as large particles and boilies are so effective. Not only are they selective, in that small unwanted species cannot peck them to bits, but they remain intact on the bottom often for hours. This, let's face it, is a wonderful confidence booster when fishing a water extremely low in fish density where only the occasional bite is expected. After all you don't want to be winding in every twenty minutes just to see if the bait is still there, do you?

Nowadays the carp and tench angler is literally

spoilt for choice of baits that can be presented on a hair rig (see Diag. 63) in conjunction with a bolt rig. Brought about by the fact that both carp and tench do eventually learn to be suspicious of anything offered in the shape of a round ball (boilies), bait manufacturers are continually coming up with alternatives. One of the most effective in my opinion is the large hard pressed pellet-type baits called Qpipz made by Whizzo products which can be hair rigged just like boilies. Actually almost any hard pelleted food becomes an effective bait provided it does not disintegrate within a short while. I particularly favour small $5/16$–$1/2$-inch diameter carp pellets which remain on the hair without disintegrating for at least half an hour. In addition to being presented on the hair from one to three up (use a nut drill to make the holes) they can easily be catapulted out as loose feed.

There are now numerous very similar products on the market, the most effective I've used being the pelleted Coarse Fish 80 food produced by BOCM Pauls Ltd which is in fact a complete formulated food purposely made and sold for growing on coarse fish as opposed to trout pellets which have a higher protein content and in fact break down in water far quicker.

It's well worth visiting pet stores, aquatic centres and of course your local specialist tackle shop in search of new baits within this pelleted field. But do test them all, threaded on to a hair rig and left in a jar of water for various lengths of time, before using as bait. There is nothing more disturbing and unsettling than sitting there behind a pair of rods wondering if your baits are still there.

STRIKING

In many cases, particularly when fishing at close range, you need merely to put the reel back into gear or tighten the drag before picking up the rod and going straight into playing the fish. There is no heavy striking involved. At medium range, say 40–60 yards, a firm lift of the rod after engaging the clutch or tightening up will help secure an immediate bend in the rod to keep everything tight. While at extreme range, say 80 yards plus, a sweeping back strike is necessary for keeping that hook point in, due to the inherent stretch in monofilament reel lines which is up to 25 per cent. This of course is assuming that all bites consist of the fish running off in the opposite direction from the rod, which they do not.

Drop-Back Bites

Inevitably a proportion of bites will be drop-backs whereupon feeling the lead and the hook biting home (which is why it is essential to have the entire hook exposed) the fish promptly sets off towards the rod. And when this happens the indicator usually falls back or drops down (depending upon which type is used) so you need to engage the reel quickly from free spool and wind in like the clappers to put a firm bend in the rod, before the fish rids itself of the hook.

Drop-backs can really become an acute problem when ledgering at extreme range, which is why some carp fishermen prefer to use a rigid quiver-type indicator incorporating an adjustable line clip that can be tensioned and in effect drag the lead back towards the rod. Even tiny movements of the lead are then registered by a relaxing of the quiver arm, despite the bait lying on the bottom over 100 yards out. But this should really be classed as advanced bolt-rig fishing. Newcomers to the method are best advised first to perfect the method over close- to medium-range situations and not to overcomplicate their set-ups.

THE BOLT RIG IN RUNNING WATER

Strangely, and I say strangely because at the time bolt or shock rigs were unthought of, I first used the very simplest of bolt rigs when winter chub fishing during the late 1950s. At that time the Taylor brothers were catching numbers of big chub from the Upper Reaches of the Great Ouse by ledgering with a large cube of breadcrust stopped only an inch or two from a heavy bomb by a single split shot (as in Diag. 67), and I was not slow in emulating their methods. Of course along came a chub, sucked up the crust and promptly did a runner because it felt the weight of the bomb moving – and in the process it produced an absolute slamming bite. It was a bolt-rig bite nonetheless, although to the best of my knowledge no one identified it as such in those days. We simply knew that when you ledgered crust (which had to be presented on a bomb stopped close to the hook of course as in Diag. 67) during the winter months, chub bites were invariably slammers.

They do say that nothing is new in fishing and much of the time I can only agree. Take boilies for instance, a fabulous extremely selective bait which, along with the bolt-rig technique, has virtually revolutionized carp fishing since the 1980s. Yet in India boiled baits were used to catch mahseer over 100 years ago. I refer to a bait called ragi, which is made from the local millet flour. This is mixed with water and kneaded into chicken-egg-sized balls and then boiled in water for 20 minutes. This process brings out the natural gluten of the flour and thus makes the bait rubbery and impervious to the attentions of other very much smaller mahseer-like species which abound in the warm Indian rivers.

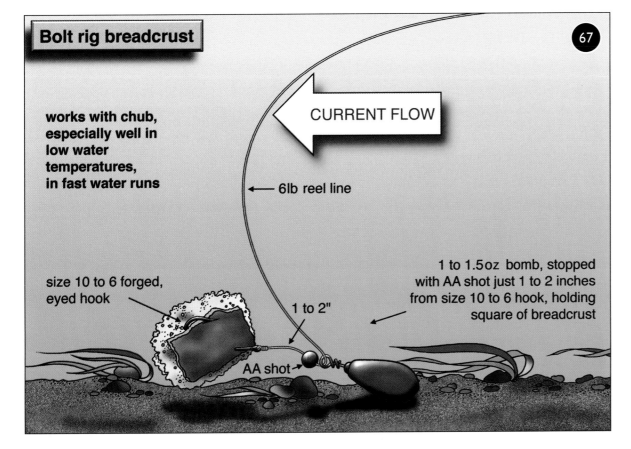

FREELINING

Sadly for the majority of modern carp and tench fishermen who choose only to bolt-rig fish much of the time, freelining the bait has become a method option they now rarely consider.

STILL WATERS

It is so very easy to stay in the rut, albeit a most successful one, of putting two or three baits out on buzzers and sitting back to await events. Yet equally there will be numerous occasions even on the hardest-fished waters, such as during those early couple of hours around dawn when most are still nodding in their bivvies, that creeping about stalking fashion with just one rod and the absolute minimum of tackle not only permits close visual contact with tench and carp (bream too) it also allows you to experience thrilling battles using all-through action outfits (an Avon rod coupled to a 5–6lb reel line for tench and a soft 1½–1¾lb test curve rod matched with 8lb test for carp) and simple freelining techniques. But it does however require the ultimate in watercraft of stealth, concealment and constant observation of marginal territories through Polaroid glasses of fish bubbling away or moving through lily pads, reed lines and sedges, plus a high level of opportunism. May I also suggest a wonderful aid to freelining in particular, Polaroid binoculars, which I have mentioned earlier. They're simply invaluable.

You see the truth is that species like tench, even bream and especially carp, are naturally attracted to the warmer, invariably weedier, more habitat-rich band of water along the margins, particularly where trees overhang and shallow bays or inlets exist, due to a much increased larder of natural food items, in comparison say with extremely deep and colder parts of the same fishery. Put in simple terms there's more food close in and that's a fact.

Naturally this will change as the weed growth diminishes during the approach of autumn when fish move out into the protection of deeper water. But during the warm, sunny summer months, providing they have not been scared away from this marginal richness (and of course those who camp out within feet of the surface with racks of rods hanging out in stark silhouette to margin patrollers are not exactly helping themselves) both tench and carp can be induced to suck in a freelined offering quite literally within seconds of it being flicked out using a gentle underarm swing. Sounds too easy? Well, I guess once

The simplicity of freelining allows you to extract sizeable fish from the most overgrown marginal habitats, like this mirror carp being returned by Ron Smith.

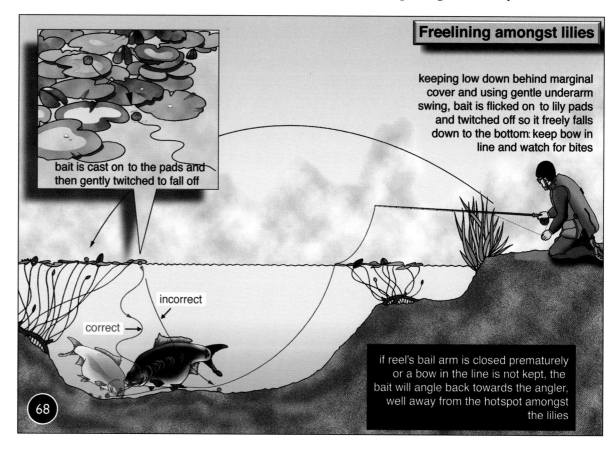

Freelining amongst lilies

bait is cast on to the pads and then gently twitched to fall off

keeping low down behind marginal cover and using gentle underarm swing, bait is flicked on to lily pads and twitched off so it freely falls down to the bottom: keep bow in line and watch for bites

incorrect

correct →

if reel's bail arm is closed prematurely or a bow in the line is not kept, the bait will angle back towards the angler, well away from the hotspot amongst the lilies

68

*Armed with just net and organizer
bucket, John stalked this superbly shaped
5½ lb summer chub on freelined lobworm
from Suffolk's River Waveney.*

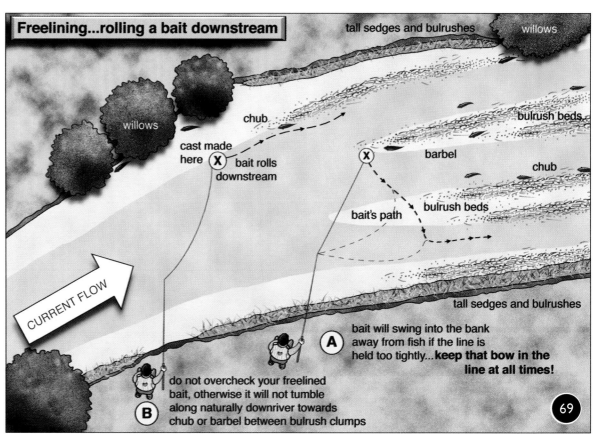

Freelining...rolling a bait downstream

tall sedges and bulrushes

willows

willows

chub

cast made here **X** bait rolls downstream

X

barbel

bulrush beds

chub

bait's path

bulrush beds

CURRENT FLOW

tall sedges and bulrushes

A bait will swing into the bank away from fish if the line is held too tightly...**keep that bow in the line at all times!**

B do not overcheck your freelined bait, otherwise it will not tumble along naturally downriver towards chub or barbel between bulrush clumps

69

you have done your homework in creeping about and spending more time observing than actually fishing, in essence freelining really is that instantly successful.

I do know that it is unbelievably exciting and fulfilling when, from a standing start, all hell breaks loose as a fish feels cold steel and goes charging off in a cloud of surface spray, bottom silt and a bow wave that would do a speedboat justice. Here I have to admit that I'd much rather crash about in a hit-and-haul struggle with a low double, through an obstacle course of marginal swims, than predictably put the

net under a 20 hooked 90 yards out. And of course by adopting the freelining method you can even winkle out carp from those ridiculously shallow and deeply silted areas where they gorge on bloodworm, heads completely buried and their hump backs sticking out above the surface. And worm incidentally is the bait for carp feeding in this mode – the largest, longest, heaviest lobworm you can lay your hands on.

The second you put the hook into any one of a group of carp all deep feeding in silty shallows the rest instantly disperse and are not liable to return for some time. But it's all wonderful fun. You simply move on and, through binoculars, locate some more action by observing bubblers, areas of discoloured water, tail patterns or backs humping through silty shallows.

BAITS

Remember freelining is exactly what the term implies: a hook tied direct to the reel line with no other hindrance except the bait. This is why fish accepting such a bait do so with hitherto unknown confidence (compared to most other forms of presentation) because without shots, tubing, weighted floats, heavy leads or feeders, they have little reason to suspect skulduggery until it is too late. And because baits need to be large and weighty enough for casting, the method allows you to enjoy concocting or catching your own, from flavoured pastes (trout or carp pellet paste is my favourite) to torching lobworms from the lawn at night or raking mussels from the lake bed around the margins.

Mussels are perhaps the most deadly yet underused

and underrated natural bait of all those used to lure tench and carp. Old hat you say? Don't you believe it. And yes, everything you have read in old books about offering the entire insides of a medium-sized (4–5-inch) mussel implanted on a size 2 or 4 hook is sound advice indeed. Even a modest-sized tench can suck it down without batting an eyelid. If using mussel does have a drawback it is that eels simply adore them and usually belt off on such a fast run that the line quite literally blurs from the spool.

Another great eel bait, which carp incidentally and especially catfish simply love, is squid, the nicest to use being those lovely little baby calamari of about 4–6 inches long which any accommodating wet-fish shop owner should be able to supply. Cockles from the sea (ready boiled out of their shells) are another great natural bait for freelining although they need to be presented two or three up on a size 6 hook, say, for sufficient casting weight.

Personally I never go anywhere without at least two or three tins of luncheon meat in the back of the car or my tackle bag. Cut into cubes or oblongs of desirable size, as an instantly available bait (compared to obtaining, collecting or concocting all others) meat is priceless. You can even munch away on a cube every so often whilst waiting for the fish to do likewise! Don't try this with flavoured luncheon meat, however, as most brands of these excellent alternatives are unfit for human consumption. Prawns are just as useful, although I invariably end up eating more than I ever put on the hook. They can in fact be freelined whole (with a few pieces scattered as loose feed attractor) or two up once boiled and peeled. The choice is yours. For tench and carp I prefer them ready peeled; for chub and barbel in their raw uncooked state prawns are so much like crayfish.

Of course there is absolutely nothing to stop you side hooking or hair rigging a large boilie or a couple of large weighty particles – two butter beans for instance – for freelining. But do beware that tench or carp in the particular water being fished are not regularly bombarded with the same baits presented on bolt rigs. Bites could then, I am afraid, prove very few and far between. It's all common sense really.

Freelining, remember, relies on there being no association between bait which the fish is about to suck down and any nasty past experiences. If there is no association and you have done everything to ensure it is not spooked by the line (always allow plenty of slack by not tightening up once the bait comes to settle on the bottom) the fish will wolf the bait down greedily with complete confidence and provide you with an unmissable bite, the line suddenly tightening like a bow string, often after a few preliminary twitches. This is why you should be holding the rod throughout. Only when seeking eels, catfish and carp from low fish density waters when bites are not liable to materialize immediately do I rest the rod and fix on a simple, lightweight indicator such as a roll of silver kitchen foil.

By no means last amongst bait options, don't let's forget good old-fashioned breadflake. It has tremendous all-round attraction and pulling power, although maybe not for carp in fisheries which have become pressurized by anglers occupying swims 365 days a year. But even then there are always areas which receive little attention due to the difficult factors of either approach, weeds, or the presence of snags and submerged trees. In a fair proportion of tench and carp waters, where the simplicity of freelining breadflake pinched on with just enough pressure so it sinks ever so slowly, the results will surprise you.

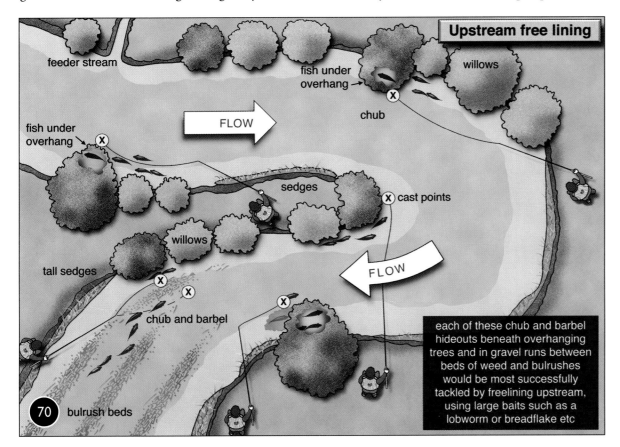

feeder stream

Upstream free lining

willows

fish under overhang

chub

FLOW

fish under overhang

sedges

X cast points

willows

FLOW

tall sedges

chub and barbel

each of these chub and barbel hideouts beneath overhanging trees and in gravel runs between beds of weed and bulrushes would be most successfully tackled by freelining upstream, using large baits such as a lobworm or breadflake etc

70 bulrush beds

PLACING THE BAIT AND STRIKING

For the benefit of those who have difficulty in placing their bait with consistent accuracy, allow me to chew over a few key points. For starters, how you hold the rod handle around the reel stem is of paramount importance, because all other problems arise from your grip. Having laid your elbow along the top of the rod handle, divide your four fingers (two each side) around the reel's stem. Do not place three fingers on one side and one on the other; it must be two fingers on each side of the stem. If you do this (try it right now if you can) your forefinger will then be perfectly placed for applying pressure to the spool's rim. Remember, the sense of touch provided by your forefinger is second to none, so use it to good effect not only for feathering the line down and playing fish, but also for casting.

Some anglers prefer to trap the line against either the spool's rim or the rod handle once they have opened the bale arm ready for casting. Doing this, however, means that the actual weight of the bait cannot be felt and so the cast cannot be gauged accurately. The answer is simply to hook the line around the ball of your forefinger. You'll then find a new sense of awareness within your casting technique. It takes a little practice, that's all.

As always when freelining, the line itself is your visual bite indicator. Be on guard and ready to strike in an instant, whilst simultaneously hauling hard on the rod into a full bend – even walking backwards if need be, in order to bounce and wallow the hooked fish away and out of danger from lily roots.

So keep your eyes on the line at all times while the bait is descending and strike not only at those accentuated bites where the line slowly or speedily zings tight but at those barely perceptible movements when it simply stops and you know the bait hasn't touched bottom. This means a fish has obviously intercepted the bait on the drop but is actually chewing it on the spot and not moving off. So strike anyway – and fast.

Be careful not to cast your freelined bait directly at or on top of confidently feeding fish. Where tench or carp are moving through lily beds, cast the bait beyond their movements directly on top of the pads (feathering it down lightly with your forefinger on the spool so it lands gently) and then ease or flip it back gently into the feeding zone before allowing it to free fall down between the pads. Keep a distinct bow in the line from bait to rod as in Diag. 68, so it falls naturally and not an an unnatural angle slanting backwards (if the bale arm is closed prematurely) towards the rod as in Fig. B and away from the lilies.

Ensure the slipping clutch on your reel has been set for these hit-and-hold tussles, and will only give line begrudgingly at the very last second, in order to avoid a certain crack off. Playing fish by backwinding is not recommended as you cannot possibly evaluate the situation and critical degree of pressure that needs to be applied by backwinding through the gears. It is just far too insensitive. However, index-finger pressure and control upon the spool's rim against a preset clutch, used in harmony with an all-through action and a well-bent rod comes as near as you can get to giving the bare minimum of line on

With his rod literally poked through branches, a summer carp stalker displays the epitome of concealment – a goal to which everyone must aspire in order to catch carp at close range on freelined baits.

demand. It can prove to be the all-important difference between extracting a good fish from lilies or submerged branches or snapping off and leaving a hooked fish tangled up amongst snags.

This is a distinctly different kind of skill from most other methods of presentation, which is why it is so compulsively exciting. You are not only presenting a bait into areas that other methods cannot, you are hoping to extract fish and sometimes even specimen-sized fish from jungle-type habitats, where the vast majority of fishermen would never dream of casting. This is why fish will gulp in your freelined bait without hesitation.

RUNNING WATER

Much of what I have said relating to tench and carp, and to some extent bream, in still waters also applies to river fishing and particularly to species such as roach, chub and barbel – perch too. An avon-action rod of 11–12 feet with a 1¼lb test curve, coupled to a 5–6lb reel line should suit most situations, except perhaps for the sensitivity of roach fishing, when a step down to a 2½lb reel line and still lighter rod makes for more pleasurable sport. Tie hooks direct and don't worry about the point and barb being visible, when using slugs and worms, because for optimum penetration they need to be. Providing the bait behaves naturally fish won't spook regardless of how much of the hook is actually showing.

The main difference in running water is that you need to take the river's speed of flow into account. Otherwise, if the freelined bait is held too tightly, as in Diag. 69, Fig. A where insufficient line is allowed to peel freely from a nicely filled spool (you cannot freeline successfully if the line is not filled to the spool's rim) as the bait is taken downstream by the flow, it will hang back or swing across the current instead of going down with it like Fig. B. Thus it

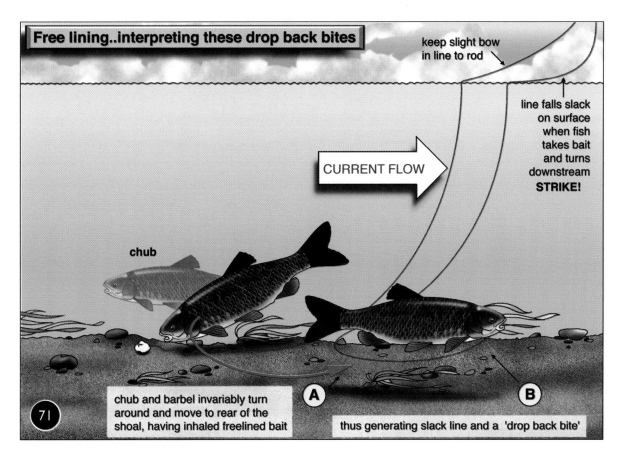

Free lining..interpreting these drop back bites

keep slight bow in line to rod

line falls slack on surface when fish takes bait and turns downstream **STRIKE!**

CURRENT FLOW

chub

71

chub and barbel invariably turn around and move to rear of the shoal, having inhaled freelined bait

Ⓐ

Ⓑ

thus generating slack line and a 'drop back bite'

could easily be refused even by modest-sized fish. So with decent-sized specimens, which over the years have seen all the rigs, you won't stand an earthly.

The skill element is allowing the bait, such as a lob, cube of meat, cheesepaste or large piece of breadflake, a completely free-falling passage on its way downstream just like other items of natural food that are tumbled along unhindered by the current. Every so often use gentle forefinger control against the rim of the spool, especially when the line looks to be peeling off too fast. It should be checked momentarily but never so firmly that the bait swings unnaturally upwards or away from the line of flow. Remember always to lay the line down directly above the bait when it hits the surface (using an exaggerated flick of the rod) if a strong wind is blowing downstream, before closing the bale arm. Otherwise

the wind will create a bow in the line and drag the bait downriver at an unnaturally fast speed.

Upstream Freelining

You can of course cast upstream and across the current just ahead of choice lies on both banks, such as beds of rushes, overhanging trees or bushes, or weed rafts, and immediately keep in touch by winding gently as the bait trundles back towards you with the rod tip held high and a distinct bow in the line. Freelining upstream often allows you to approach swims which cannot possibly be fished in the traditional downstream manner, as Diag. 70 illustrates. As always the secret is to keep your eyes glued to the line at all times. It is your float and your bite indicator all rolled into one.

Bites vary tremendously when freelining

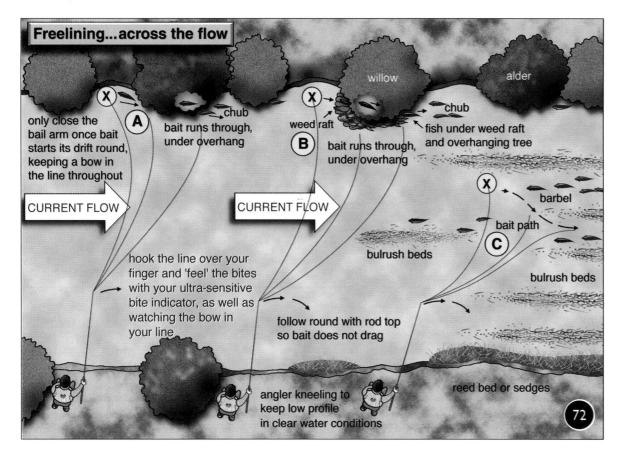

Freelining...across the flow

only close the bail arm once bait starts its drift round, keeping a bow in the line throughout

CURRENT FLOW

hook the line over your finger and 'feel' the bites with your ultra-sensitive bite indicator, as well as watching the bow in your line

A

chub
bait runs through, under overhang

weed raft

CURRENT FLOW

follow round with rod top so bait does not drag

B

willow

chub
fish under weed raft and overhanging tree

bait runs through, under overhang

bulrush beds

alder

X

barbel

bait path

C

bulrush beds

angler kneeling to keep low profile in clear water conditions

reed bed or sedges

72

It has been said many times but is still perfectly true, bites from barbel often start with a gentle, rustling sandpapery-like feeling of the line across the pad or ball of the forefinger. This is caused by the fish's whiskers which do a plink-plonk against the line as it agitatedly swings its head from side to side whilst centralizing the bait beneath its undershot mouth. Furnished with a long snout, the barbel literally loses sight of the bait at the last moment and must rely totally on the feeling from its sensory whiskers which are equipped at the tips with taste pads.

Even the gentle bites from modest-sized roach, perch or small chub can be detected across the forefinger sufficient to induce an immediate strike, even when you are not watching the line. And when a sizeable chub hits an animal bait like a big lobworm or especially a fat juicy slug, it does so with such force that the line tightens firmly across the forefinger. Watching the rod tip bend round seconds later is academic.

Those who deliberately set out to freeline for species like roach, chub and barbel during the hours of darkness when they are at their least wary, enjoy a whole new set of values based entirely on touch. And there is nothing to match the sensitivity of touch as a sensory indication. In darkness everything is heightened to fever pitch so that when the pull from a chub tightens the line across the ball of your forefinger it feels like the pull of a shark and an immediate reflex action results in a strike and a hooked fish.

Actually I'll go even further and suggest that unless you are freelining the bait directly downstream in fast water and are waiting for a rod-tip indication, once the bait has settled on the bottom strikes should be made on the feel from line indications alone, and not by rod-tip registrations. Because by the time the fish bends the tip round it will have felt resistance and might even eject the bait. Makes sense, doesn't it?

upstream. Sometimes the line will quite suddenly fall completely slack as a chub grabs the bait and rushes off several yards downstream with it to the rear of the shoal. Sometimes it falls noticeably slack following a preliminary twitch or two. And occasionally it will suddenly zing tight should a fish immediately swim upstream with the bait. Gentle but noticeable drop-backs of several inches are perhaps the most common bite indications when freelining upstream. These are a result of the fish inhaling the bait (as in Diag. 71, Fig. A) and turning around with it (Fig. B). And of course, as the bale arm should already be closed, for taking up slack an instant sweeping back strike should be made.

When freelining across the flow to key lies in mid stream such as to between the gaps in beds of bullrushes or to hide-out habitats fringing the opposite bank (naturally we are not talking huge rivers here) like lapping willow or alder branches, weed rafts and the like (see Diag. 72), once the bait has started to drift downstream close the bale arm and follow round with the rod tip so the bait does not drag (as Figs A, B and C). Learn to feel for bites in addition to watching the bow in the line by hooking the line around your forefinger, your ultra-sensitive built-in bite indicator. This can only be achieved by gripping the rod handle with two fingers on each side of the reel stem, as I've mentioned earlier. Try it and see and you'll find that for holding the line upon the ball of your forefinger for casting, for feathering the line down at the end of the cast, for applying pressure to the rim of the spool during the fight, and for feeling bites transmitted down the line there is no more effective way of controlling your bait.

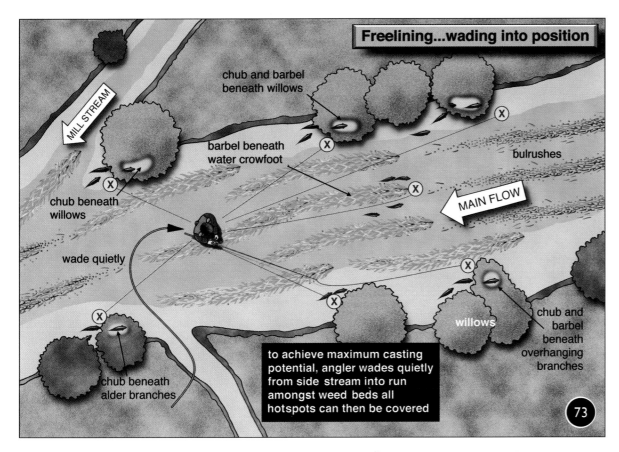

Freelining...wading into position

MILL STREAM

chub and barbel beneath willows

barbel beneath water crowfoot

chub beneath willows

wade quietly

bulrushes

MAIN FLOW

willows

chub and barbel beneath overhanging branches

chub beneath alder branches

to achieve maximum casting potential, angler wades quietly from side stream into run amongst weed beds all hotspots can then be covered

73

Wading

In medium to wide rivers that contain lots of weedy shallows interspersed with gravel beds from which onion-like bullrushes sprout in tall, thick beds, their pointed tops quivering to current strength, don't be afraid of actually getting into the water wearing thigh waders and stealthily creeping into positions which cannot be reached from the bank. Fish in these secure hideouts are usually most obliging, as long as your casting is accurate, as in Diag. 73, for instance.

The presence of thick and long flowing beds of potomogeton or water crowfoot (which has those lovely little white flowers on top) between angler and fish, ensures that frightening sound waves are kept to an absolute minimum. But, by the same token, be prepared for some awkward hit-and-haul tussles with barbel and large chub that have to be carefully steered across the flow over and even through thick weed beds. But then with waders on you can always physically extract a heavily weeded fish at the risk of scaring others in the shoal.

Lastly, and this applies to freelining directly downstream during daylight, do not wind baits like cheesepaste or breadflake back upstream when bites do not materialize. They look most unnatural swimming against the current, except that is to pike which sometimes grab hold. So if you don't want a pike active in the swim always jerk them off prior to retrieving which helps to bait the swim too. With worms however chub, perch, trout, and of course pike, will all go for a fluttering worm tantalizingly making its way upstream in a series of twitches. Try it and see!

Having freelined his bait through a shallow, fast-water run along an overgrown stretch of the River Lea, Dave Wilson is rewarded with a fat chub.

QUIVERTIPPING FOR CHUB AND BARBEL

Summer or winter, in the heat or in the severest of weather conditions, even when rivers are running close to the surface freezing over, or in a raging flood, if there is one species guaranteed still to bite it's got to be the chub. And above all others, quivertipping stands out as the most successful method for several very good reasons.

First, by opting to ledger, the bait is presented completely static on the bottom which is so important during February and March, particularly if subzero temperatures prevail. Chub, together with species like barbel and roach, hate chasing their food in really cold water and need time both to approach and eventually suck the bait in. So a fair wait after casting, say between five and ten minutes at least, should be allowed in cold water. In mild air streams and especially during prolonged bouts of mild weather, however, bites often come literally within seconds of the ledger settling on the bottom, even before the tip has taken on its slight curve from current pressure. This means the bait is still probably rolling across the river bed, and you have the potential of really bagging up with chub in such conditions, believe me. Barbel, however, are rarely aggressive during the cold months of winter and I would put their prime period for being active between June and November.

WHICH ROD?

The secret in quivertipping for chub and barbel, as when tipping specifically for other species like bream for instance, is using the correct tool for the job. That is to say you must have a rod with sensitivity in its quivertip compatible with the majority of river situations you are likely to encounter. Should you regularly fish wide, fast and powerful rivers, like the Wye or the Severn for instance, you'll benefit from using a 12-foot rod (to keep most of the line above current force) which has a fairly rigid action and an

In search of chub and barbel inhabiting this turbulent pool, the angler is well equipped for any eventuality using John's own Ryobi Avon quivertip rod and a 6lb reel line.

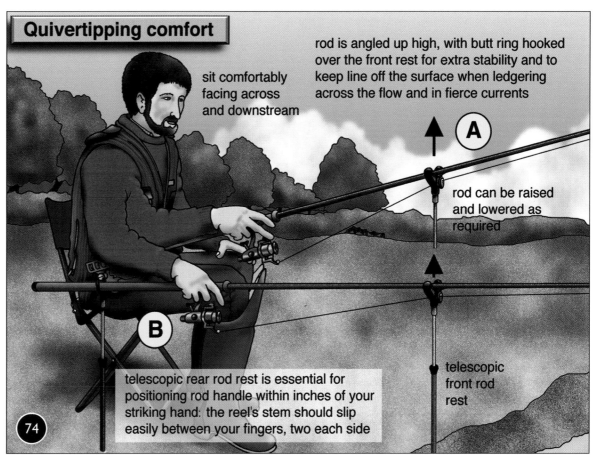

Quivertipping comfort

sit comfortably facing across and downstream

rod is angled up high, with butt ring hooked over the front rest for extra stability and to keep line off the surface when ledgering across the flow and in fierce currents

A

rod can be raised and lowered as required

B

74

telescopic rear rod rest is essential for positioning rod handle within inches of your striking hand: the reel's stem should slip easily between your fingers, two each side

telescopic front rod rest

Brian Ward tempted this 12lb 2oz barbel from Norfolk's River Wensum on quivertipped sweetcorn.

integral, powerful, tapered quivertip. If your ledger rod only accepts screw-in tips then models in the 3–4oz range should suit these same heavy water conditions.

Then again, at the other end of the scale, your fishing might be concentrated within much smaller, slower river systems, where a lightweight multi-tip rod (which usually has a choice of two or three tips of varying tapers stored in the handle) of 9–11 feet covers most situations admirably. As with all locations in freshwater fishing, it's horses for courses.

As I tend to fish around some, from my local Norfolk hotspots along the upper reaches of the Wensum, Yare and Waveney, to the Kennet in Berkshire and Hampshire's fabulous rivers Avon and Stour, my overall preference is for an 11–12 foot rod with a medium action and built-in tip of around 2oz which, in addition to picking up sufficient line on the strike with 20–35-yard casts, is more than sensitive for registering the tiny trembles of specimen, over-suspicious chub inhabiting the more popular fisheries.

For those who are not already equipped with a specialist quivertip rod and are unsure about choice, may I be totally presumptuous and suggest that my own 11-foot Ryobi JW Avon Quivertip rod, which has a 1¼lb test curve standard tip for use with 3–7lb lines, and an integral quivertip with a 2oz test curve, will cover an extremely wide spectrum of ledgering situations, not only in running water but with its additional standard tip in still water also.

REELS AND LINES

I admit to a complete preference for small-format reels when quivertipping, models within the 2000 size range which have decidedly smoother slipping clutches than larger models. As long as the clutch is silky smooth I am not worried whether it has a front or a rear drag system. In my experience feathering the line down to gain the utmost accuracy at the end of the cast is also more pleasurable with small reels and if no more than a 100 yards of, say, 5 or 6lb line is needed why

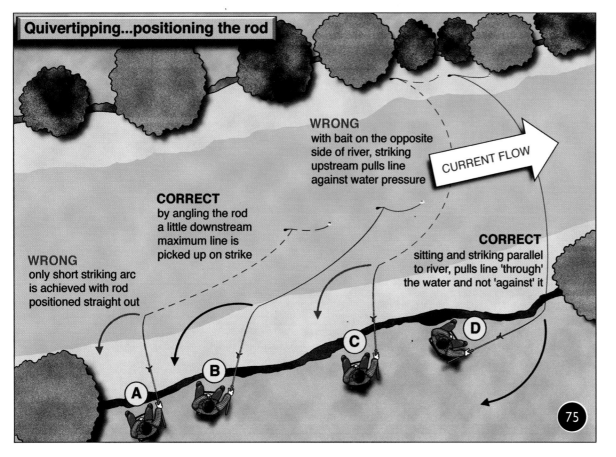

Quivertipping...positioning the rod

WRONG
with bait on the opposite side of river, striking upstream pulls line against water pressure

CURRENT FLOW

CORRECT
by angling the rod a little downstream maximum line is picked up on strike

CORRECT
sitting and striking parallel to river, pulls line 'through' the water and not 'against' it

WRONG
only short striking arc is achieved with rod positioned straight out

A

B

C

D

75

should you put up with the increased weight of larger reels and that overall clunkier feeling? Occasionally I may step down to a 4lb reel line when taking chub and barbel from really tiny rivers and streams but generally I prefer the safety factor in reserve of 6lb test. Besides, constantly heaving out large block-end feeders demands such a line as do the very much stronger currents of all rivers during the winter months. Don't fish lighter just for the sake of it.

ROD RESTS

Some dialogue about rod rests is in order at this point because I see so many anglers fishing at a distinct disadvantage when quivertipping, not because they have over-invested with their rod and reel set-up, but because they have simply not given the slightest importance to using the correct rod rests for the job at hand. This often is hitting small movements of the quivertip indicator quickly, with chub especially.

Leaning the rod against just one rest with the butt cap on the ground is perhaps the best example of how to do it all wrong. Those valuable split seconds that elapse between hittable bites registering on the quivertip and your hand clamping around the reel stem and forearm along the handle for striking can cost you many a good fish. Rarely fished-for chub, for instance, may well hang on for you to hit a proportion of bites but generally speaking unless you are sitting comfortably alert with your striking hand at the ready mere inches from the reel stem, if not

With Norfolk's River Wensum full of ice and midday temperatures below zero, chub bites will be mere tremors on the quivertip. Terry Houseago therefore is poised to hit them.

already gently positioned around it ready for a bite, you won't regularly watch chub sliding over the net during the cold winter months. You have gathered by now that just one rod rest is not enough. You need two and both should be telescopic and of good quality with strong, pointed ends for pushing into frozen bank sides. My front rod rest telescopes from 5 to 9 feet; the back rest from 3 to 5 feet.

The butt rest should have a simple screw-in U-shaped head, unless you fish distant swims along the far bank in big rivers where it is essential that the rod is positioned as high as possible to keep as much line as possible above the surface. Then I suggest the Drennan butt rest which, due to its solid end, completely supports the rod butt, is a worthy addition to your kit.

Another way out is to ensure that either the butt ring or second ring is hooked over the U of the front rod rest after casting (Diag. 74, Fig. A), something I instinctively do anyway whenever the rod is angled up high, because it also helps to stabilize the rod in windy conditions. This is so simple yet so effective, believe me. It is also a useful ruse for night fishing if like me you prefer a narrow beam torch to illuminate a white-painted tip because once the torch has been set the tip always comes to rest in exactly the same position (see page 161, Diag. 82). Remember always to point the torch from a downstream position so it shines out and up at the tip. There is then no reason for it spooking fish or impairing your natural night vision for doing things like baiting up or netting and unhooking fish without additional light.

I have a ritual for setting up my rod rests when winter quivertipping and for much of my summer fishing for that matter, and that is first to get myself comfortably seated facing downstream and across. Then I push in both rod rests so that my right striking hand is within inches of the reel stem grip

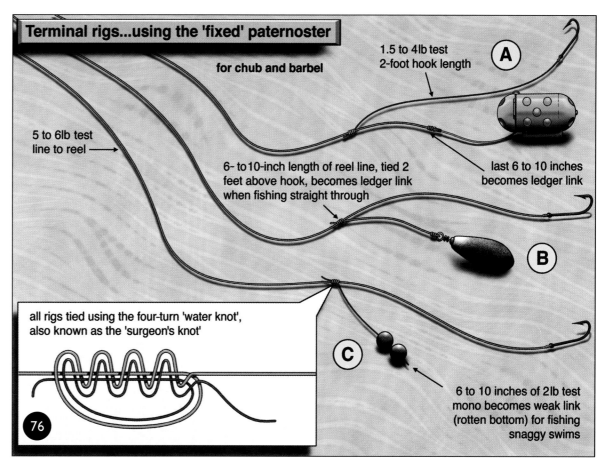

Terminal rigs...using the 'fixed' paternoster

for chub and barbel

1.5 to 4lb test 2-foot hook length — **A**

5 to 6lb test line to reel →

6- to 10-inch length of reel line, tied 2 feet above hook, becomes ledger link when fishing straight through

last 6 to 10 inches becomes ledger link

B

all rigs tied using the four-turn 'water knot', also known as the 'surgeon's knot'

76

C

6 to 10 inches of 2lb test mono becomes weak link (rotten bottom) for fishing snaggy swims

and can actually rest there if I so wish, without my having to lean too far forward (see Diag. 74, Figs A and B).

STRIKING

You will find that line pick-up and subsequent striking the hook home, particularly on those long casts downstream, is greatly improved if the rod is not positioned out at right angles to the bank (as in Diag. 75, Fig. A), but actually angled downstream (as in Fig. B). An upstream sweep of the rod then follows through a long striking arc for maximum effect, the only exception to striking in this way being the situation in Fig. C where a long cast has been made over to a swim on the other side of a wide river, the

flow of which bows the line downstream beneath the surface. So sitting (as in Diag. 75, Fig. B and striking upstream in the same way would prove most ineffective and pull the line through an unnecessary arc against water pressure. Sitting parallel to the bank and striking sideways (as in Fig. D), on the other hand, ensures the line is pulled *through* the water on the strike and not *against* it.

While many barbel actually hook themselves, with chub I cannot stress enough the importance of line pick-up on the strike, especially on large, slow-moving rivers where the flow cannot help you. I suppose the acid test is always feeling contact with the bomb, feeder or ledger shots, even if you miss the bite. If you don't feel any sensation of the ledger rig on the strike then something is amiss and you could never have connected with the fish anyway, because you are simply not picking up sufficient line to bang the hook point home. So study Diag. 75 carefully.

TERMINAL RIGS

Let's consider the most effective end rigs for catching chub and barbel when quivertipping. Unless there is next to no flow and you can get away with just a single AA or swan shot pinched on the line 12–15 inches above the hook, for really close-range swims there is no finer or more simple rig than the fixed paternoster ledger.

As you can see from Diag. 76 it can be made up in three ways, each benefiting from the reliability of a four-turn water knot as the junction between reel line and ledger/hook link. Look at Fig. A, where a

lighter hook length may be required, the end of the reel line actually becomes the ledger link to which shots, bomb or feeder are attached. This link is at its workable best if 6–10 inches long. In Fig. B a length of 6lb reel line is cut off and simply tied 2 feet up the line which permits you to fish straight through. Fig. C shows a rig I rarely need but it is occasionally very useful when fishing tight in amongst really snagging tree swims where submerged branches can prove troublesome. A much lighter (2lb test) link is tied 2 feet up the 6lb reel line with a four-turn water knot effectively to become the rotten bottom, or weak link which easily breaks and ditches the shots or small bomb, should it become snagged, thus allowing you to land a hooked fish or simply to retrieve the hook without pulling for a complete break.

In Figs A, B and C, I have illustrated a hook length of around 2 feet long which is a good starting point for general fishing. This of course may be drastically reduced to just 6–8 inches long for producing a hittable indication on the tip when water temperatures are at rock bottom. Conversely, to promote a bite from really hard-fished-for, super-spooky chub for instance, inhabiting slow-moving, gin-clear water, it can be increased to between 4 and 6 feet long, stepping down to just 1½lb test, size 18–20 hook and a single caster which could even initiate bites on the drop. So be alert and keep your eyes glued to the quivertip from the second the ledger link touches bottom. And if the tip won't take on its usual, gentle bend after the customary two or three turns of the handle, strike at once. A chub will have inhaled the semi-buoyant caster on the drop.

LOOSE FEEDING AND FEEDERS

When fishing fast-flowing small- to medium-sized rivers during the winter months for chub, loose feed such as maggots, casters and liquidized bread can be introduced regularly throughout the day by using a small block-end feeder on the ledger link, or it can be fed in by hand in slow currents. My favourite technique is to make up a batch of mashed bread on the evening before fishing (by soaking and then squeezing out the excess water from old bread scraps – so it sinks quickly in a kaleidoscope of a million particles) and then right at the beginning of the session the following morning, usually whilst walking to the most upstream swim on the particular stretch being fished, introduce half a dozen golf balls of mashed bread into the head of each likely looking chub run. I can then work my way back downstream throughout the day in a leisurely fashion trying each run with the knowledge

four-turn 'water knot'

Quivertipping..terminal options

77

juggling about with 'AA', swan shots or various bombs and feeders on the paternoster ledger link (depending upon current strength) so that it only just holds, encourages drop back bites

A

alternative ledger link terminal options

'Feeder link' with keel weight

E

D

B

C

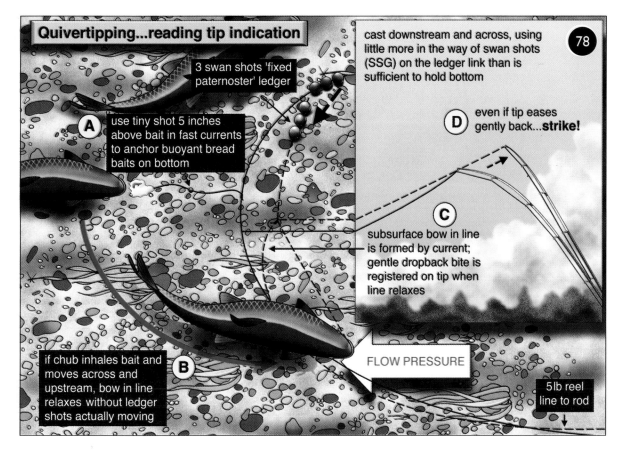

Quivertipping...reading tip indication

3 swan shots 'fixed paternoster' ledger

A use tiny shot 5 inches above bait in fast currents to anchor buoyant bread baits on bottom

B if chub inhales bait and moves across and upstream, bow in line relaxes without ledger shots actually moving

cast downstream and across, using little more in the way of swan shots (SSG) on the ledger link than is sufficient to hold bottom

78

D even if tip eases gently back...**strike!**

C subsurface bow in line is formed by current; gentle dropback bite is registered on tip when line relaxes

FLOW PRESSURE

5lb reel line to rod

BALANCING THE RIG

Holding out in the flow with sufficient weight (or feeder) on the link to hold bottom, yet not so much that a fish cannot dislodge it and so register a drop-back bite easily, is the key to good quivertipping. In gentle currents it is often the difference between success and failure or several chub in the net and nothing, especially in subzero weather conditions. In mild conditions a bite on the tip, especially in fast water, may be so severe it looks as though the rod is going in. Yet a week later when the thermometer drops sharply, learn to expect no more from chub especially than a mere ¼-inch tip movement, either a forward pull or a drop-back so gentle it could well be mistaken (as most in fact are by many anglers) for the ledger moving position slightly or rubbish hitting the line.

These ever so gentle drop-back bites occur far more often during the cold winter months when chub pack tightly together. One fish inhales the bait but merely moves across the flow or even upstream a little – sometimes dislodging the ledger, sometimes not – as opposed to that classic warm-water antic of grabbing hold and instantly belting off downstream with it to the rear of the shoal, providing an unmissable pull round on the tip. Part of the secret to winter chubbing tactics therefore is encouraging these drop-backs by fine tuning of the rig and juggling about with a BB, AA or a swan shot (see Diag. 77, Fig. A) or various bombs (Fig. C) on the link (depending upon current strength) or by selecting exactly the correct block-end feeder for holding bottom, but one that will dislodge easily to the pull of a fish. There is absolutely no point in fishing heavier than you need to, quite apart from all the obvious advantages of bite indication. When seeking chub in really slow-moving rivers a cage feeder (Fig. E) holding a lightly dampened white

that the inhabitants of each will have had time enough to locate the free nosh and possibly be on the lookout for more. And it works time and time again, not only with mashed bread but also with maggots and especially chopped works. But you do need a good supply of lobworms.

For the chub and barbel of big rivers, particularly those flowing powerfully, nothing concentrates loose food items more accurately than a block-end feeder. And in rivers like the Severn for instance the most effective way of selecting a barbel swim is by observing current speed and patterns. Look for really fast turbulent water on the outside of a wide bend and then plan to offer the barbel your bait within that filter lane, a slightly slower area of the river between turbulence and the slack on the inside of the bend. Great spots for barbel these.

Drennan oval blockends (see Diag. 77, Fig. B) which come in a choice of flat weights of between ¾ and 2½oz are highly recommended for these really strong currents. There is nothing worse than using a feeder that dislodges too easily and spreads your loose feed all the way across the river as it prematurely bumps round in the current. For standard use the Drennan twin-weight blockend (Fig. D) which has both flat and removable end weights is excellent and comes in sizes from ⅛–1¼oz. As I mentioned earlier whilst considering rod rests, the secret in keeping that feeder well out static on the bottom of the swim where the fish are situated is to keep as much line out of the water as possible, by positioning the rod tip up high. Remember to cast downstream and across instead of straight out as this creates more pressure against the line.

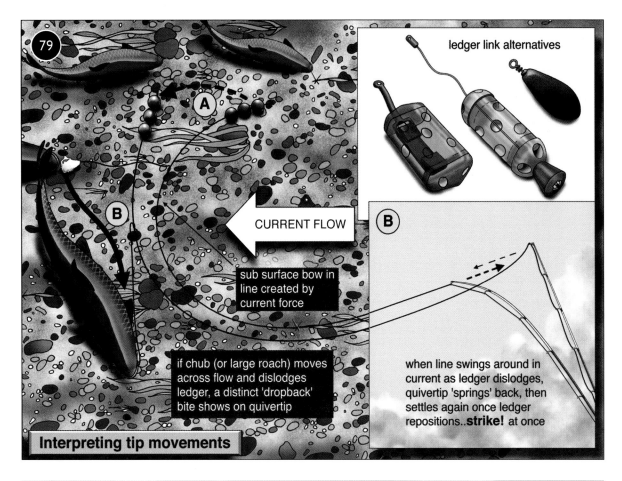

ledger link alternatives

CURRENT FLOW

sub surface bow in line created by current force

if chub (or large roach) moves across flow and dislodges ledger, a distinct 'dropback' bite shows on quivertip

Interpreting tip movements

when line swings around in current as ledger dislodges, quivertip 'springs' back, then settles again once ledger repositions..**strike!** at once

breadcrumb mix works nicely with breadcrust or breadflake hookbaits.

INTERPRETING MOVEMENTS (BITES)

You can perhaps best interpret what actually happens down there on the bottom of a cold fast-flowing river by looking at Diag. 78 showing my simple fixed paternoster ledger with three swan shots on the link which, let's assume for argument's sake, are just right for the current pace and depth of swim being fished.

The cast has been made downstream and across and the line has taken on a slight bow which reduces pressure on the quivertip. Note that in really fast, cold water I pinch on a small shot 5 inches above the bait to ensure it remains static on the river bed and does not flutter over the fishes' heads too far off bottom. Now should a chub move across and upstream with the bait (as in Figs A and B) the bow in the line relaxes slightly (as in Fig. C) while the tip eases back accordingly (as in Fig. D).

Should the chub only move across the river bed (as in Diag. 79) it will eventually dislodge the swan shots/feeder bomb ledger (as Fig. A) which registers as an obvious drop-back on the quivertip because the bow in the line swings around (as in Fig. B) until the ledger repositions and holds steady once more. Obviously a strike should be made instantly. Do not wait for the tip to pull round. Drop-backs are equally as positive an indication as the tip pulling right round. Or, looked at another way, a flat or lift bite where the float rises out of the water, as when fishing

Famous Throop Mill fishery on the Dorset Stour provides fabulous habitats for both chub and barbel in fast streamy runs beside beds of bullrushes — quivertipping heaven!

Interpreting those tiny drop-back bites when quivertipping has resulted in many a good haul of barbel and fat winter chub from John's local River Wensum.

the lift method is just as positive an indication of a fish having taken the bait as if it had completely disappeared from sight.

Barbel Bites

With nine out of ten barbel bites the rod tip suddenly arches over with great force, due to the aggressive manner in which the species characteristically vacuums up the bait and turns across the current and the fish quite literally hooks itself in the process. But barbel inhabiting rivers which are regularly fished can learn to wise up. You may then experience short, sharp drop-backs that simply do nothing more, so an instant strike is required. Educated barbel also learn to suck up and

spit out the most commonly used baits without hooking themselves.

Regardless of baits used, the barbel angler should always remember that they feed most aggressively when there is a sudden increase in river flow and also in subdued light conditions, either coloured water or during the hours of darkness, dusk being the prime time for expecting immediate response to a ledgered bait.

BEST BAITS

Most barbel enthusiasts would argue that the most effective bait combination is a cube of luncheon meat, or a bunch of maggots or casters ledgered over a carpet of hempseed. Hemp seems to have magical qualities as far as barbel are concerned and soon has them rooting about through sand and gravel for the tiny seeds. For close-range swims incidentally use a large frying-pan-type bait dropper to deposit a carpet along the bottom, then quivertip your bait over it. When bites simply do not happen give the barbel added confidence by presenting a small cube of meat or cheese for instance on a short hair rig.

Tares also work well as both attractor and hook bait but sweetcorn is probably better. Other particle-type baits such as maple peas, maize, stewed wheat, tick beans, peanuts and tiger nuts also work well either side hooked or presented on a short hair. Boilies are also a fine bait for barbel, especially where small nuisance species continually peck at corn, maggots or casters. Small (10-12mm) boilies presented two up on a short hair (tight up to a size 8 hook) are fantastic. Chop up a handful of boilies into quarters and mix in with an attractor such as hempseed or tares. When barbel do not respond to boilies, simply thread just one on to the hair and cover with paste of the same mix from which the boilies were made. Paste releases the smell of the bait

far quicker, often resulting in an immediate response. Progressing further along the aroma theme, do give prawns and shrimps a try, either cooked or uncooked, in their natural state or ready peeled. They are the closest crustaceans to two of the barbel's favourite foods, namely crayfish and the tiny freshwater shrimp.

Never discount plain old breadflake or breadcrust as barbel hook baits or a lump of either sausagemeat or cheese paste. But perhaps the most attractive large offering of all is a great big lobworm. Barbel simply adore worms. For free baiting in medium-paced swims, break several lobs into fragments and throw into the head of the swim at regular intervals. The same of course goes for other single baits like cheese paste, sausage paste, trout pellet paste and meat cubes.

Lastly, and especially during the early season, don't be afraid of quivertipping a small, freshly-killed fish. Minnows are simply ideal and a food item that barbel will quickly snuff up. Trouble is, chub also love small fishes!

When planning an early morning winter chubbing trip, soak those old bread scraps and squeeze into a mash the night before.

QUIVERTIPPING FOR ROACH AND BREAM

U tilizing the supersensitive finely tapered quivertip to interpret bites from roach and bream, which at times can both prove frustratingly shy, must rate as the deadliest method of all. It is as if the quivertip was invented for these species, which of course it more or less was. The late Ken Smith of Norwich for instance actually won the National Championship way back in 1960 with a 50lb catch of bream from the tidal River Bure below Thurne mouth using a finely tapered solid glass quivertip spliced into a ledger rod of his own design, geared specifically to the strong tidal pull of the lower Bure. And from that point onwards quivertipping has grown in popularity to the extent that compared to twenty years ago, when swing tipping was the favoured indicator for the bream of slow-moving rivers and still-water fisheries, the vast majority of anglers today favour the quivertip even in lakes and pits.

Let's face it, the quivertip is so much nicer to use (not clanging around the rod tip like the swing tip) when designed as an integral and fixed part of the rod. Casting is not impaired in any way and, providing you use the correct tool for the job, the biggest fish can be landed even on the most finely tapered tip. So a word about various rod options is I think in order before we progress any further.

WHICH ROD?

Rods with a built in quivertip head the list, being designed for a specific purpose, with multi-tip rods coming second. These usually have a choice of two or three varying tapered tips stored in the rod's handle, to combat a variety of conditions, from close-range still-water work to fast river currents. Generally these tips push into the rod's top joint (some rods are three jointed) and are rated in test curves of ½oz divisions by most manufacturers. For example, a 1oz tip has a really soft action, best suited to roach and canal work or still waters when close-range fishing, and to really delicate bites. At the other end of the scale a 3½oz tip has a stiffer, more progressive action which is not going to double up under current pressure alone, as would lighter tips. It is therefore geared to really deep, fast currents and weir pool bream, for example.

Thirdly, and at the bottom of the options list, far behind those already mentioned come general-purpose ledger rods into which quivertips fit via a screw tip ring. Inevitably there will be a dead spot at this connecting junction which seems to dampen sensitivity. But screw-in tips are nevertheless still far more sensitive than straight-rod ledgering.

Now let's consider actual rod length. My overall preference is for an 11–11½ even a 12-foot rod, because line pick-up on the strike (particularly for those slack liners or drop-backs) is always of

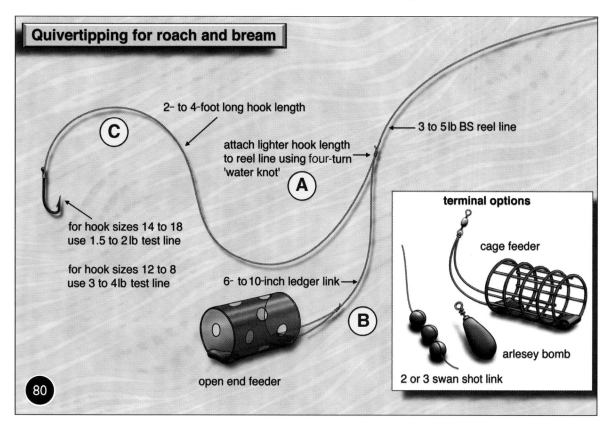

Quivertipping for roach and bream

2- to 4-foot long hook length

C

3 to 5lb BS reel line

attach lighter hook length to reel line using four-turn 'water knot'

A

for hook sizes 14 to 18 use 1.5 to 2lb test line

for hook sizes 12 to 8 use 3 to 4lb test line

6- to 10-inch ledger link

B

open end feeder

terminal options

cage feeder

arlesey bomb

2 or 3 swan shot link

paramount importance, though obviously when canal or small river fishing a 10–10½-foot model is quite adequate. As with everything else it boils down to horses for courses.

If I had to select just one tool to combat a multitude of situations in both still and running water it would be an 11½-foot rod with a built-in tip of around 1¾–2oz test curve. I'd insist on the last 14–16 inches of the tip being painted matt white, as this makes it so much easier to see against a variety of backgrounds.

As I live in Norfolk and catch both roach and bream from deep and fast tidal rivers and occasionally pop over to Ireland to fish vast loughs and 20–30-foot deep rivers such as the Shannon, where picking up sufficient line on the strike in order to set the hook is imperative, I require a rod on the meaty side to accompany reel lines of up to 5–6lb test. I find I use my own Ryobi JW Avon Quivertip rod for the majority of roach and bream fishing situations. Anglers who only ever fish the Grand Union canal however and other similar slow-flowing fisheries need to step down accordingly and use an extremely finely tapered and supersensitive quivertip for registering the tiniest bites. So choose a set-up which suits the bulk of your specific fishing requirements.

REELS AND LINES

As far as reels and lines go I admit to a preference for small-format reels in the 2000 size range which invariably come equipped with a smoother slipping clutch than larger models. And while I may very well scale down to a 1½lb hook link to tempt bites from

About to lift a quivertip/feeder-caught roach from the lakes at Moycullen in Ireland, there is no mistaking the famous white cap of triple world match-fishing champion, Bob Nudd.

When quivertipping for specimen river roach, John steps down to a 1½–2lb hook length for presenting casters or maggots on size 14–18 hooks.

tangle booms or this and that – all of which do nothing but get in the way and actually hinder bite registration, quite apart from gathering blanket weed or other suspended loose rubbish. As in Fig. B, the end of the reel line actually becomes the bomb or feeder link, which I prefer 6–10 inches long, depending upon bottom debris. If the bottom is covered with filamentous algae or soft-rooted weeds, 10–12 inches is not too long. But for general use around 8 inches is the ideal link length.

As a general rule I tend to use much longer hook lengths for the bream say of still water. I find this aids natural presentation of small baits and thus promotes more positive bites. Bites on the drop for instance are commonplace with roach and bream during the warmer months particularly with small, semi-buoyant, slow-falling baits like casters or a maggot and caster cocktail presented on a 1½–2lb test, long hook length and a small, light hook, say 18s to 14s (Fig. C). These bites are often registered on the tip by the fact that you cannot always tighten after casting out. The tip simply stays straight, so strike instantly because the bait has been sucked in whilst falling. In fact strike whenever the quivertip behaves in an odd manner: when it doesn't take on a gentle bend as you wind up to the rig; when it suddenly eases or springs back for no apparent reason, denoting drop-back bites – but above all beware of liners.

LINE BITES

These line bites often occur when bream (I have never experienced line bites with roach) are tightly

wary, clear-water fish, I never step below a 3lb reel line. In most cases I prefer the safety margin provided by 4–5lb test which is imperative anyway if whacking out medium- to large-size block-end, open-end, cage or grip-mesh feeders as part of the terminal rig for quality bream.

I also find that feathering the line down during the latter part of the cast to obtain accuracy with the bomb or feeder is so much easier when using small-format reels. Besides if no more than 100 yards of 5–6lb is

required, why bother with the excess weight, larger bale arms and limited finger control of a larger reel?

TERMINAL RIGS

Whether quivertipping in running or still water, I use a fixed paternoster rig which is quick and easy to construct simply by joining a 2–4-foot hook link to the main line using a four-turn water knot as in Diag. 80 (Fig. A). I do not use swivels, beads, anti-

(Opposite): *To overcome the strong subsurface tow on Ireland's massive Lough Ree, Dave Batten and Martin Whitehouse use their quivertip rods angled parallel to the shoreline to enjoy this bream feast.*

packed or are feeding in earnest. As their tall bodies brush against your line, the quivertip naturally indicates numerous tiny plinks and plonks which in most cases look exactly like the real thing. Careful observation of the tip however will reveal that most of these are rather abrupt indications, whether tiny, sharp tip movements, or lightning pull rounds which spring back just as violently.

What you must look for in between is the genuine bites which are usually of a noticeably slower nature. It is impossible always to get it right and no doubt there will be many strikes completely missed at what appears to be unmistakable bites, plus the occasional unavoidable foul hooked fish. At certain times, particularly in the early season immediately after the spawning ritual, line bites are commonplace when ledgering for bream and it is fair to say that there isn't an angler living who has not at some time or another been frustrated by them.

HOOKS AND HOOK LENGTHS

Hook length, strength and actual hook sizes are of course always dictated by bait size and the size of roach and bream expected. I would for instance, if seeking bream only, opt for 5lb straight through to a size 10 or 8 hook if offering lobworms or breadflake to specimen-sized still-water fish, those living on the bottom of fast deep rivers like the Shannon or my local River Yare. Also when fishing for the inhabitants of weir pools, trying to bring a slab-sided bream upstream against the flow, you are just asking for a small hook to pull out, or a light hook length to break. For roach a 2½–3lb test reel line is ideal, scaling down to a 1½lb hook link and size 16–18 hooks when necessary.

For the bream of fast-running water there is also little point in using an overlong hook link, 20–24

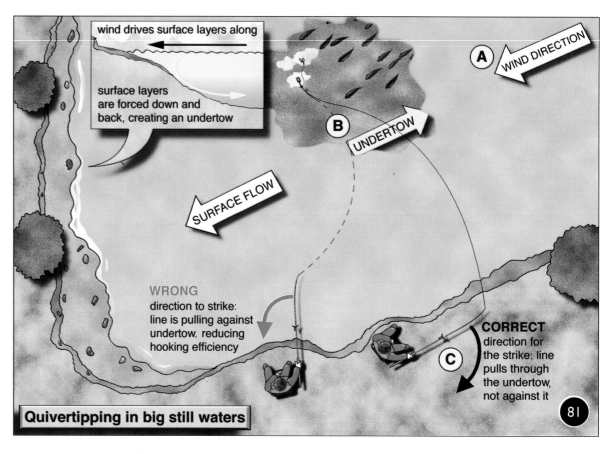

wind drives surface layers along

surface layers are forced down and back, creating an undertow

A WIND DIRECTION

B UNDERTOW

SURFACE FLOW

WRONG
direction to strike: line is pulling against undertow, reducing hooking efficiency

CORRECT
direction for the strike: line pulls through the undertow, not against it

C

Quivertipping in big still waters

81

inches being quite sufficient. I like to pinch on a small shot 6–8 inches above the bait to be sure that it stays anchored to the bottom. Buoyant baits, particularly breadflake, can all too easily flutter up and down above the bottom in a good push of water when presented on a fixed paternoster rig. This small shot is imperative for quivertipping in low temperatures when bream and roach are loath to chase their food.

BALANCING THE RIG

In clear flowing rivers which contain small shoals of quality bream you can visually choose a suitable swim with the help of Polaroid glasses. But don't make the mistake of using too much groundbait. Very often a couple of handfuls of loose feed, such as

sweetcorn or chopped worms, is all that is required to start the shoal feeding. Don't sit right on top of them – clear water bream can scare easily. Remember simply to add sufficient swan shot to the ledger link so that it only just holds bottom. And believe me, juggling about with a BB or an AAA shot to get this right is really worth the trouble as the most gentle bites will dislodge a balanced shot link and indicate a drop-back on the tip. Such fine tuning with swim feeders is not so easy to do, taking into account the varying weights of a full feeder compared to an empty one. But where possible, endeavour to balance the rig so drop-backs are instantly indicated which will put many more fish in your net.

After casting in deep flowing water, angle the rod upwards set on a pair of rod rests to keep as much line as possible above the surface. Learn to respond to those drop-back bites, bites that are indicated by the quivertip suddenly springing back because the roach or bream dislodged the feeder when it sucked up the bait. Fish which simply turn away downstream with the bait will of course pull the tip around in a positive manner. But many more bites will be drop-backs of some sort or another due to the manner in which most bream, especially, vacuum up the bait and consequently move to one side or another with it. When tightly packed in huge shoals they simply haven't the room to turn around with the bait. So learn to interpret these bites and you'll catch many more bream.

FEEDER CHOICE

As for the best types of feeders when quivertipping, everything depends on the type of water being fished. For instance in really deep rivers which flow strongly I prefer blockends loaded with casters and maggots or a plastic open-ended feeder filled with dampened breadcrumbs to which hook bait samples have been added. Both types will not release bait until they hit bottom so aim to cast downstream and across the flow almost directly to where you wish the swim to be fed. Don't cast straight out so the current pulls the rig around and your bait is scattered diagonally across the river bed.

Obviously grip-mesh and wire-cage-type feeders are not recommended for deep, running water, due to their instant release of cereal feed which makes them perfect for use in still waters, the crumb exploding around the hook bait as the feeder hits bottom. A word of warning here. Do not hold the line tight when the feeder hits the surface or it will angle back towards you scattering feed everywhere. Allow it to touch down in a vertical line by feathering the line against the rim of the spool before tightening up to the tip.

To make an effective groundbait for deep rivers, soak and then squeeze the water from two old loaves into a mash. To this add either maize meal or brown crumb to stiffen plus hook bait fragments. And to ensure it goes straight down to the bottom before breaking up, add a packet of pearl barley or several cupfuls of cornflakes. Flaked maize works even better. Obviously such a dense groundbait will not release from a feeder. It should only be used for baiting up by hand.

CASTING ACCURACY

Casting accurately, cast after cast after cast, is perhaps the most important single factor in quivertipping, for bream especially. So learn to concentrate your feed within a tight area and bites will not be long in coming. What helps is casting directly overhead aiming at a tree or landmark on the opposite bank, followed by gentle feathering against the spool with your forefinger to bring the feeder down at the desired distance. To this end simply slip a small slim elastic band over the spool when bites start to materialize and you will consistently hit the target area. Whether bites are happening or not, keep casting and depositing that feed on a regular basis, building up a carpet of nosh within the swim. If you lose interest because bites are not forthcoming you will not be giving a shoal of bream much reason for moving into your swim. And of course whenever possible take out an insurance policy by prebaiting the night before you intend fishing and make an early start at dawn when bream are feeding naturally at their hardest.

Quivertipping..before and after dark

butt ring hooked over front rod rest, ensures quivertip comes to rest in torch beam and exactly same position every cast without fail

white painted tip illuminated in centre of torch beam

torch with narrow beam is positioned downstream to shine outwards and upstream, thus illuminating only the quivertip

telescopic front rod rest

telescopic rear rod rest

CURRENT FLOW

82

How you sit and at what angle the rod is rested to the water are also most important factors when quivertipping for bream.

STRIKING

Consider Diag. 75 on page 150, for instance: a 100-yard wide and 15–25-foot deep river with a good push of water. Now if ledgering fairly close in, say up to 15 yards out, as in Fig. B, then angling the quivertip rod out and pointing slightly downstream provides an ideal position for bite detection and striking. You will note that an upstream and upwards strike will then easily set the hook through a straight line with minimal power loss. But just consider what would happen in Fig. C with the rod similarly positioned and the bait placed over halfway out across the river. Due to current pressure against the line, an enormous subsurface bow is created (despite keeping the rod tip high) so that upon striking most of the power is not transmitted to the hook. It would be far better to sit facing directly downstream with the rod set parallel to the bank as in Fig. D, so that upon striking the line is not pulled up *against* current pressure but cuts *through* it, thus banging the hook home. As a general guideline if you cannot feel the ledger when striking, then the chances of setting the hook are minimal.

SUB-SURFACE TOW

A similar situation occurs in really large, windswept still waters. Remember to angle the rod tip low down (to minimize wind) and almost parallel to the shoreline. This achieves two things: it makes bites very much easier to see and, when you strike sideways, the line is pulled *through* the water as opposed to being lifted up *against* it. Far more bites

are thus converted into hooked bream. The Irish loughs spring to mind here and mighty Lough Ree in particular because I have enjoyed some wonderful bream fishing there on the quivertip. In calm conditions use binoculars to search for small clusters of feeding bubbles which regularly rise to the surface of a large still water in only a comparatively small area. Down below on the bottom a shoal of bream will be feeding in earnest on natural food items. Patches of distinctly coloured water where bream have stirred the bottom up also provide an instant clue to the swim you should be fishing.

On my last trip, however, a strong wind was blowing right to left across the lough, as in Diag. 81 (Fig. A), and it would have been tempting to have the wind on my back and point the rod downward. Trouble was, due to a strong undertow which is all too common when large sheets of still water rough up, the line beneath the surface was actually bowed in the opposite direction to the wind, as in Fig. B. So facing the wind and striking across it (Fig. C) immediately converted a large proportion of bites into fish in the net. And on the day, a worm tipped with maggot proved to be the most effective bait for those Irish bream. Come to think of it, this combination scores wherever you quivertip for bream.

Incidentally, for small baits like casters and maggots use hooks in sizes 14–18 and for corn or brandlings sizes 14–12. Larger baits like worm and breadflake are best presented on hooks in sizes 10–8.

When bites prove spasmodic moving the bait just a few inches simply by winding the reel handle half a turn sometimes results in an immediate response, especially when baiting with worm or maggots. If the bottom is covered in dense weed, use buoyant baits like breadflake or breadcrust/maggot or breadcrust/caster cocktails.

Another excellent hook bait, particularly in still-water fisheries where carp and tench anglers loose feed trout or carp pellets, is a paste made from the same. Simply use a coffee grinder to reduce pellets to a fine dust, then knead in sufficient raw eggs until the mixture is the consistency of marzipan. A couple of pints of ground pellets can then be mixed in with your cereal feed as an inducer. But at the end of the day a thumbnail-sized piece of flake taken from the inside of a new loaf and squeezed firmly around the shank of a

For really deep, fast-moving rivers the ideal feeder choice is a plastic open end which won't release the casters and corn-laced breadcrumbs until it hits bottom.

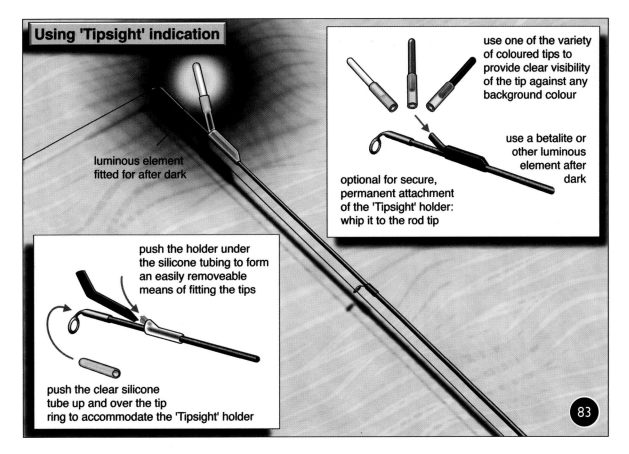

Using 'Tipsight' indication

luminous element
fitted for after dark

push the holder under
the silicone tubing to form
an easily removeable
means of fitting the tips

push the clear silicone
tube up and over the tip
ring to accommodate the 'Tipsight' holder

use one of the variety
of coloured tips to
provide clear visibility
of the tip against any
background colour

optional for secure,
permanent attachment
of the 'Tipsight' holder:
whip it to the rod tip

use a betalite or
other luminous
element after
dark

83

size 10–8 hook (leaving the point and barb clear for easy penetration) usually takes you straight through the pain barrier to those quality roach and bream.

RIVER SPECIMENS AT NIGHT

The very best opportunity for latching on to real specimens in running water, especially a jumbo-sized roach, even in clear-water small-river conditions, is by quivertipping during the hours of darkness. It makes sense to arrive while there is still sufficient light to set up and familiarize yourself with the swim and current strength and to introduce some mashed bread feed. Use a size 8 hook (yes, an 8) direct to a 3lb hook length/fixed paternoster rig and put your faith in a thumbnail sized piece of fresh white breadflake.

Set up the rod with the quivertip high, pointing out and slightly downstream on two rod rests, locking the butt or second ring over the front rod rest to ensure the white-painted quivertip comes to rest in exactly the same position each cast. Then position a narrow beam torch a few feet downstream, ensuring that it shines outwards and upstream illuminating only your quivertip (see Diag. 82).

Alternatively, use a luminous tip sight which fits easily on to the end of your quivertip. The plastic holder (see Diag. 83) is held tight to the extreme tip just before the end ring by a silicone tube which accommodates a starlight micro SL9 green chemical light or similar luminous light source. The tip sight holder can in fact be left in position on the rod and for a permanent fixture it is best whipped on.

THE POLARIS SIDEWINDER II INDICATOR

Lastly let me describe this extremely effective indicator which although not technically a quivertip in the true sense (because it fits two-thirds of the way up the rod) does register the tiniest of bites via a rapid tapered solid glass tip and therefore fits into this method. It is particularly good for fishing in choppy conditions, because unlike the quivertip it is unaffected by wind or wave action. It can in fact be employed in situations that would prove impossible for a quivertip; fishing with the rod tip pointing directly at the ledgered bait for instance.

The sidewinder is pushed into a plastic collar which sits on top of your rod about two-thirds of the way up so you are looking straight out at the indicator tip. There is no detackling, the line simply passes through the worm-eye-type top ring, so you cast out and feather down the ledger rig (sinking the rod tip) and tighten up until the sidewinder tip is tight alongside the rod. Then back wind slightly until the tip is just off straight. By having a slight tension on the tip, both forward and drop-back bites can be seen easily. To ensure that you have tightened right up to the ledger rig, keep winding gently until the tip stops dropping back. Important for detecting shy bites, this.

The sidewinder comes with a choice of two tips. A soft one for still water and a medium taper tip for slowly moving rivers or whenever there is a strong undertow in still waters. The sidewinder really works superbly well for bream in large, open and windswept still waters and was in fact invented by Terry Smith of Sheffield to overcome fishing in adverse conditions in the huge loughs of Ireland where he has accounted for numerous huge hauls to over 300lb in a single sitting.

PREDATOR METHODS

Wels catfish are among the most voracious of predators. John hooked this 22½-pounder on a ledgered deadbait from Jimmy's lake in Fobbing, Essex.

DOWNRIGGER TROLLING FOR PIKE

On the basis that even in mild weather pike will not always leave the sanctuary of really deep water to hunt in search of food and especially during the winter months when water temperatures are at an all-time low and pike lie dormant on the bottom, there is undoubtedly a time and a place for downrigger trolling.

It is not a method I regularly use in English freshwater because most of the fisheries where I catch pike are less than 15 feet deep. Indeed I cannot think of any area within my local Norfolk Broads complex that even exceeds 12 feet, although the tidal rivers which feed them do have depths in excess of 20 feet. However, reservoir fisheries, deep river reaches like those found along Ireland's mighty River Shannon, not forgetting the Irish loughs, the Lake District and numerous Scottish lochs, are all simply crying out to be downrigger trolled.

To pinpoint a depth at which using a downrigger becomes profitable is not easy, but for argument's sake let's say anywhere deeper than 15–20 feet is worth giving the method a try. There is of course no magical quality to downrigger fishing. It is simply that your lure or mounted deadbait is trolled behind the boat at between one and two knots all the way down there just a few feet above bottom where the pike are actually situated and not several water layers above them. So the method is particularly suited to very deep water, and very cold deep water – there is a difference.

The obvious advantage of downrigger trolling, quite apart from bait presentation at the correct tasking depth band, is that you can subsequently enjoy the fight on relatively light tackle once the line has pulled from the adjustable line clip on the heavy downrigger ball without any additional weight on the line, not even a swan shot. The only other method of keeping a lure or bait down deep is to load the trace up with a heavy trolling lead of several ounces, and this is rather like going to bed with your socks on.

Downrigger fishing is most comfortably and effectively achieved with two anglers sharing a boat using preferably one or at most two rods each. One angler concentrates upon steering, engine speed and depth readings from the fish finder/sonar unit, while the other also keeps an eye on the finder and services the rods. You can then switch over every hour or whenever you please.

Electric motors, such as those in the American Minn Kota range will, if fed by a really heavy duty battery, provide you with a most pleasant and silent day's downrigger fishing (see also Method 27, 'Float Trailing for Pike'). For this mode of deep-water fishing, however, a silent motor is not imperative, so any reliable outboard engine that can propel your boat along at up to a steady three knots against a headwind will suffice.

THE IDEAL OUTFIT

Before I go any further let's talk about an ideal downrigger trolling outfit. For starters really long rods are out and a real pain in a small boat. I suggest a snappy 10–11-foot carbon pike or carp rod with a medium-fast action and a test curve of somewhere around 2¼–2½lb A heavy salmon spinning rod would do at a pinch.

There is nothing in the rule book to stop you downrigger trolling with a large-sized fixed-spool reel, but I advise against it, and recommend a good quality multiplier that has a smooth clutch and holds say 200 yards of 15lb monofilament. Multipliers are far more direct and well suited to this method of trolling – models produced by ABU, Ryobi and Shimano in the 6500–7000 size range being absolutely ideal – and instead of monofilament I would recommend you use either dacron or braid of around 20lb test. In fact as the new breed of gel spun polyethylene braided lines have such a low diameter compared to monofilament of equivalent test, you can increase the safety factor by stepping up to 25–28lb. It will still be thinner than 10lb mono.

I first became impressed with downrigger trolling when out after landlocked salmon and pike on massive Lake Vanern in Sweden and then a few years later in the province of Manitoba, in Canada. Within those cold, clear, sweet water lakes unless you trolled at depths between 50 and over 100 feet where the giant lake trout were holding station you didn't catch any. So a downrigger was imperative. It was as simple as that.

Big open, wild and often windy still waters which average over 15–20 feet deep are prime locations for downrigger trolling.

An inexpensive, portable downrigger unit like the Cannon Mini Troll holds a 4–6lb lead ball, lowered at 1 foot of depth for each turn of the handle. Note the Down East rod holders.

There are now several American-type downriggers available in the UK and, at the more portable end of the range, units such as the Roberts Downrigger and the Cannon Mini Troll, which both clamp easily on to the boat's gunnel, are ideal for situations where ascertaining the exact depth is not so much of a problem as neither comes with a depth counter. It is however a simple matter to mark off with narrow strips of different coloured insulation tape, say in 10-foot divisions, on the stainless steel lowering cable. Actually with the Cannon Mini Troll one turn of the spool handle equals 1 foot of depth. So even these basic inexpensive units are easy to use.

The 4–6lb lead trolling ball is connected to the cable via a snap link swivel and lowered via a pulley at the end of the built-in boom. You have the option of holding the rod throughout the troll once the lure or bait has been lowered down to the desired depth (not recommended) or only when runs are expected as the boat passes over a known hotspot. Between times it is best to have the rod in a rod holder, either an adjustable rest of the shepherd's crook type mounted on a G clamp which fits over the gunnel, or a specialized trolling rest made of lightweight black, polycarbonate which has a side mounting bracket for screwing permanently on to the gunnel. The rod rest is then easily removed from the bracket when the boat is not in use.

If you really get heavily into downrigger trolling I suggest one of the larger Cannon units such as the Easi Troll which, in addition to a depth counter, also has a built-in tube-type rod holder. It comes with 150 feet of 150lb test stainless steel cable, retrievable on a single-handed control clutch and

brake system for a smooth and controlled descent of the lead downrigger ball. The unit is easily fitted to the gunnel at either corner of your boat via a mounting bracket which remains a permanent fixture. So the downrigger is removed in seconds for transportation home when leaving the boat unattended. Incidentally double rod holders are available for most Cannon downriggers. These fit into the rear mount and are specifically designed for stacker fishing where the lines of two rods can be used on just one downrigger. You simply attach a double (stacker) release clip on to the downrigger ball which permits, for instance, a deadbait to be trolled 10 feet directly behind and a diving plug top work 3 feet above and 25 feet behind. In North America, where the concept originated, stacker fishing with multiple set-ups is commonplace when downrigger fishing for pike and muskellunge.

Another excellent range of American downriggers manufactured by the Big Jon Trolling Systems Company is available in the UK direct from the importers Bob Carolgees, PO Box 224, Northwich, Cheshire, CW8 2AW. Of the Big Jon manual downriggers (there are several models) I rate the Runabout most suitable for pike fishing within the British Isles. This compact model has a built-in rod holder, footage counter, adjustable disc clutch and clamp for gunnel mounting with 2¼-inch jaws. For those demanding a fully automatic system, Big Jon also manufacture an entire range of electric downriggers. The Little Jon unit is ideal and similar to the Runabout already mentioned except for the powerful low-amp sealed motor which, through the flick of a switch, instantly lowers or raises the lead downrigger ball. Instead of a gunnel clamp, the Little Jon has a 4 x 4-inch mounting plate with four screw knobs. A quick slide-mounting base unit and an installation wiring kit for hooking up to a 12-volt battery are also available as optional extras.

LURES AND BAITS

The lures and mounted deadbaits employed when downrigger trolling are largely no different from those used for casting. So a 12-inch wire spinning trace of 20lb test or a snap tackle comprising two size 6 trebles on a 16-inch 20lb wire trace complete the end rig department. I prefer to use firm-bodied deadbaits for this trolling technique and it goes without saying that for optimum presentation they should be fresh. In sea baits, I rate mullet, Joey mackerel, scad and small calamari squid (yes, squid) very highly indeed. Of the enormous choice in freshwater fish, I like small rainbow and brown trout (particularly when exploring reservoir trout fisheries for pike), roach and smallish eels of say 10–12 inches long.

To mount the majority of these deadbaits, work two prongs of the top treble into an eye socket with just one prong of the bottom treble midway along the flank (as in Diag. 84). Turn the bait around and reposition the hooks once the flesh around the eye socket starts to break up. This offset mounting ensures that the bait will simultaneously slowly rotate and wobble in a most attractive manner. Mount squid so they are trolled tentacles at the rear, with the top treble in the very front of the body and the lowest nicked into the eye. Adding a third treble between these two will provide better hooking potential.

Large spoons in the 20–35g range such as Landa Pikko, ABU's Atom UTO, and Toby Salmar, Copper Vincent and Kuusamo Suomi all work really well, but make sure the points of the treble have been sharpened well. Both sinking and shallow diving plugs also score heavily. I have tremendous faith in Rapalas Slither and Sinking Magnum range which are actually all produced for saltwater work so both trebles and fittings are extra strong. Yo Zun's Ark Minnow, Creek Chub Pikie, Dixie Minnow and Big Dixie work well too.

Large-bladed, especially double-bladed (extra vibration), spinner baits are also very much worth a try, and I find it's worth twisting a size 6 or 4 treble on a short wire link to the bend of the large single hook. Bonus fish which would otherwise come adrift will undoubtedly come your way as a result.

An oddball artificial also worth trying particularly in coloured water, is Landa's Trikk which in the 24g size has no fewer than three vibratory blades ahead of a soft-bodied imitation fish concealing a strong double hook. Or what about a 28g in-line buzz bait such as the Mean Hornet which sports a huge front propeller and hair skirt at the rear hiding a large treble! Then there is the Arbogast AC plug, really a floating diver, but its hyperactive motion and soft rubber tail make it perfect for downrigger fishing. And you just can't resist clipping on the ridiculous, four-segment Luhr Jensen Beno Eel if only to watch it slither down behind the lead ball. I could go on and no doubt so could you; indeed I hope you do, for in truth there are few artificial lures which won't work at some time or another when being trolled behind a downrigger.

A little ruse I picked up in Canada whilst trolling for lake trout but which I have since found can also induce more aggressive takes from pike when working large artificials, particularly plugs and spoons, is to swap the rear treble for a large single hook and bait it with fish strip. It makes a predator hang on just that much longer (while you're taking up the slack) thus greatly increasing the chances of setting the hook. Try it and see. Use long, tapered

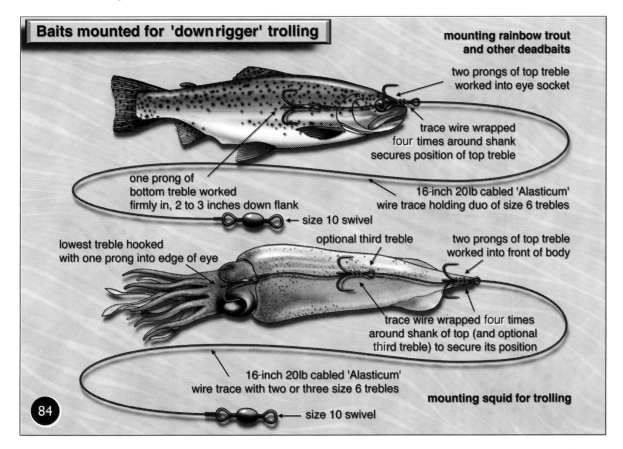

Baits mounted for 'downrigger' trolling

mounting rainbow trout and other deadbaits

two prongs of top treble worked into eye socket

trace wire wrapped four times around shank secures position of top treble

one prong of bottom treble worked firmly in, 2 to 3 inches down flank

16-inch 20lb cabled 'Alasticum' wire trace holding duo of size 6 trebles

← size 10 swivel

lowest treble hooked with one prong into edge of eye

optional third treble

two prongs of top treble worked into front of body

trace wire wrapped four times around shank of top (and optional third treble) to secure its position

16-inch 20lb cabled 'Alasticum' wire trace with two or three size 6 trebles

mounting squid for trolling

← size 10 swivel

84

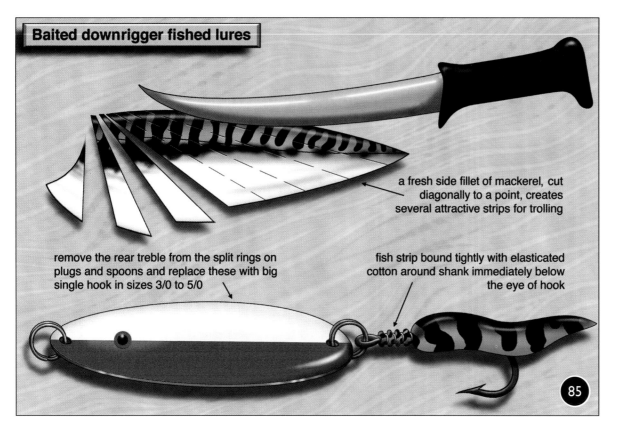

Baited downrigger fished lures

a fresh side fillet of mackerel, cut diagonally to a point, creates several attractive strips for trolling

remove the rear treble from the split rings on plugs and spoons and replace these with big single hook in sizes 3/0 to 5/0

fish strip bound tightly with elasticated cotton around shank immediately below the eye of hook

85

diagonal strips cut from the side of a fresh deadbait with a really sharp knife for the hook. I find mackerel by far the best fish for this – its coloration and markings along the flanks can only enhance the attraction of your lure. The best way of attaching fish strip, incidentally, is to bind it on tightly around the shank immediately below the eye with elasticated cotton (as in Diag. 85).

WORKING THE DOWNRIGGER

As can be seen from Diag. 86, the reel line goes almost vertically down to the lead trolling ball which has been lowered to a predetermined depth, usually several feet above the river or lake bed. When set too low over an irregular bottom, both bait and downrigger ball will hang up every so often, so it

pays to keep a watchful eye on the electronic finder (you cannot seriously downrigger troll without one) and raise the rigs smartly whenever depth shallows up. Conversely the ball then needs to be lowered again so the lures or baits fish within the desired depth band once the bottom has shelved down deep again. Hence the reason, particularly when trolling over irregular-bottomed waters, for using just one rod apiece. Otherwise someone will be doing nothing but raising and lowering rods all day long.

It pays to concentrate on those fish-holding features which clearly show up on the sonar screen. These include deep gullies, drop-offs or sudden peaks rising from what is basically a uniform bottom. Troughs between islands, massive concentrations of bait fish and rock formations all attract pike and when one has been located others could follow. In man-made reservoirs created by flooding farmland,

look for old tree stumps, bushes, fences, cottages and other sunken buildings. All attract small bait fish and thus pike, just as reefs do in the sea.

The reel line is retained by the adjustable clip attached (via a short nylon-covered link) to the trolling ball some 10–20 feet above the lure or deadbait and gently lowered to the selected depth whilst line is payed out from the multiplier (in free spool with the ratchet on) with one hand on the cable reel handle. Don't, whatever you do, let go of the handle when lowering the downrigger weight. Once the lure or bait arrives at the correct depth the downrigger weight is locked and the rod tip wound right over into a tight curve (don't wind it up too tight or the line will pull out) so that when a pike grabs hold and rips the line from the downrigger clip the rod tip springs back and picks up the inevitable slack. It is unfortunately at this point when the main downside of downrigging occurs, no pun intended. The pike can all too easily spit out the lure or bait before you have managed to wind like the clappers and heave the rod back in order to tighten up to it. This is one very good reason indeed for using dacron or one of the new low-diameter minimal-stretch braided lines. Where stretch becomes a problem, as it does when taking up that right angle of line between rod tip and lure during trolling with a downrigger, monofilament simply cannot live with the new breed of braided fishing lines. But don't just take my word for it.

Alternatively you might like to try accelerating the engine by several knots when working really deep water and you see a rod suddenly spring back. It has worked for me on numerous occasions in an effort to straighten and get some torque on the line quickly. But be careful; it is just as easy to rip the hooks out if using braid and a big pike sets off smartly in the opposite direction as you simultaneously hit the throttle.

Either way, endeavour to crank the downrigger ball up quickly as soon as the pike is hooked. If using

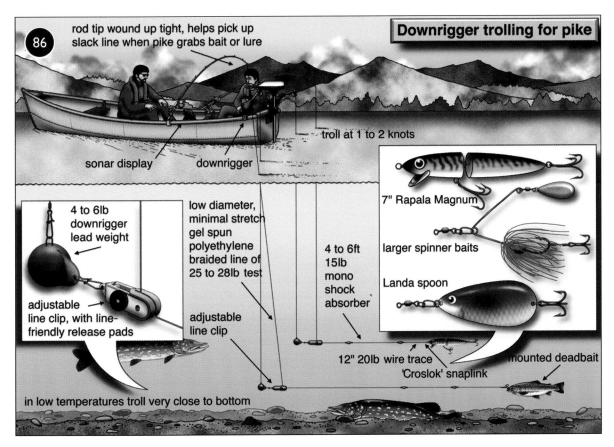

John hoists the rewards for choosing to troll a mounted dead roach downrigger style in deep water – a superbly shaped 25-pounder.

two units (one from each corner of the boat) the second may need to be lifted and the bait or lure wound in to avoid a nasty tangle, should a pike veer over to that side of the boat. But this is all quickly and easily achieved, and sounds like much more hassle than it is in practice.

As the pike nears the surface in readiness for netting, particularly in specimen-sized pike, it is all too easy to rip the hooks out or even snap up should it make one last-ditch dive for freedom when held on a short braided or dacron line. To obviate this a 15lb test monofilament shock absorber or up trace of 4–6 feet is used between the wire trace and your braided reel line joined by a small size 10 swivel (as in Diag. 86).

The lure or bait is not necessarily always pulled from the line clip when a fish hits. You see the rod tip knocking and tapping in a distinct manner but for any one of a number of reasons, usually because the pike is either really small or actually swims with the boat, the line does not pull from the adjustable line clip. You may of course have it clipped in far too tightly but trial and error will strike a balance here. Either way, start winding quickly so the rod helps to spring the line and carry on winding until the rod really arches over and a powerful strike can be made. Don't for goodness sake strike into thin air without the line being tight, or the hooks cannot be set. This, of course, is only amplified when downrigger trolling in excessive depths.

When takes are missed repeatedly, try shortening the distance between downrigger clip and your mounted bait or lure, to just over 6 or 8 feet. Conversely, really spooky pike inhabiting well-flogged crystal-clear reservoir venues may not respond unless the artificial or bait is set well away from the downrigger ball – 20–30 feet. This of course results in extra problems with hook setting but then without any takes you won't catch much anyway.

Downrigger trolling often proves to be a fabulous game of cat-and-mouse whereby those who continually look for the best feature lies, who are continually altering and adjusting tackle set-ups or try varying lures and mounted baits, who try differing trolling speeds in order to instigate a take, will eventually succeed.

DRIFT FLOAT FISHING FOR PIKE AND ZANDER

Making full use of a gentle wind, Jason Davies employs a vaned drift float to work a livebait across the wide bay of a Norfolk gravel pit.

This specialized technique is most effective when bank fishing large, windswept still waters like broads, meres, reservoirs, loughs or huge gravel pits and wide slow-moving Fenland-type rivers where, due to the sheer distances involved in trying to cast out a bait, particularly livebaits, all other methods are impracticable. Drift fishing can also prove deadly if predator fishing from a boat anchored in really clear water and those crafty spooky fish keep beyond normal casting range. For shallow-water fish in particular, again drifting a bait to them beneath a sail-type drift float creates minimum suspicion and as a consequence means it is more likely to be taken.

Naturally you require a reasonable wind from either directly behind or a crosswind blowing over your right or left shoulder to get the very best from drift float fishing, especially from the bank, so select your target areas carefully. Even plan an assault around known hotspots or potentially rich areas well in advance, so you are aware exactly in which direction the wind needs to be blowing in order to reach certain lies.

Drift fishing opens up a whole new exciting way of exploring the largest sheets of water in search of pike and zander using both live and deadbaits. Even huge reservoirs and 50-acre-plus gravel-pit complexes won't seem so daunting once you start to cover them systematically with a drift float.

TACKLE COMBOS

First let's consider the tackle required. You do of course need a long rod for keeping control of your drift float and for picking up line over great distances and I suggest a 12-foot medium-fast taper carbon pike rod with a test curve of around 2½lb. Obviously with purely zander in mind an overall reduction in power will promote maximum enjoyment from a species which, let's face it, is not the greatest of fighters.

I suggest a fixed-spool reel in the 3000–3500 format with a wide spool (ensuring the line peels off in large coils) that holds at least 250 yards of 12lb monofilament. As there is no amount of casting involved, a smallish multiplier in the 6000–6500 range is arguably a more efficient tool for the job. But the choice is yours.

MONOFILAMENT REEL LINES

If using monofilament it needs to be treated well with a silicone floatant such as mucilin so that it floats well. The ET Auto Greaser, a foam insert

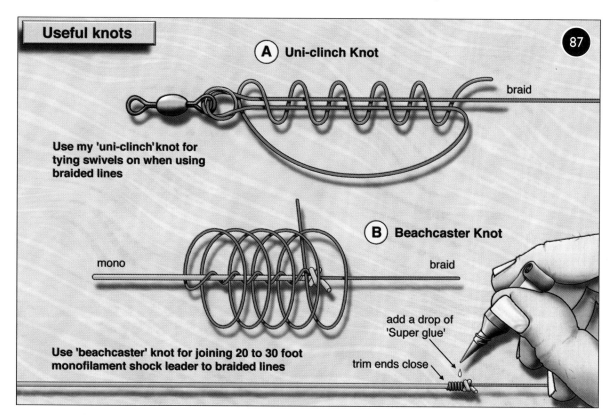

Useful knots

(87)

(A) Uni-clinch Knot

braid

Use my 'uni-clinch' knot for tying swivels on when using braided lines

(B) Beachcaster Knot

mono

braid

add a drop of 'Super glue'

trim ends close

Use 'beachcaster' knot for joining 20 to 30 foot monofilament shock leader to braided lines

Note how the drift float folds (just like a waggler) during the retrieve and whilst playing fish.

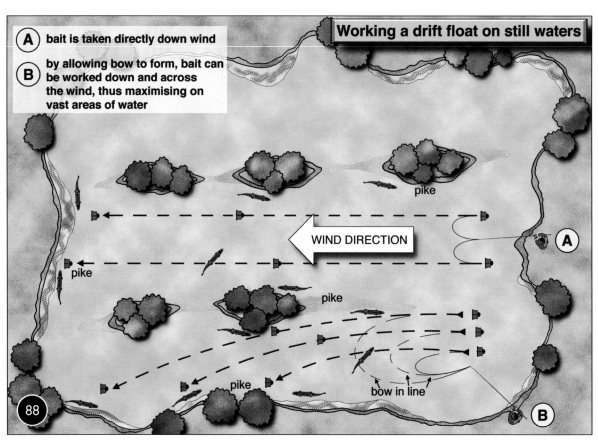

A bait is taken directly down wind

B by allowing bow to form, bait can be worked down and across the wind, thus maximising on vast areas of water

Working a drift float on still waters

WIND DIRECTION

pike

pike

pike

pike

pike

bow in line

88

A

B

which fits firmly into the butt ring, automatically does the job when filled with the ET special floatant.

The problem with monofilament however, even low-stretch brands, is that when talking distances in excess of 80–90 yards the amount of stretch that still has to be taken up for the hooks to be successfully set is enormous. The only way of achieving a hook-up using monofilament at distance is to point the rod at the fish, tighten up the clutch on your reel so it cannot possibly slip under pressure, and keep winding like a maniac until the weight of the fish is felt. Continue winding with the rod bent in a full arc keeping torque on the whole time. Don't worry, with as much as 25 per cent stretch in monofilament, there is no way you can snap up at long distances. Only when the pike senses danger, having been towed in for several yards, and eventually opens its

jaws to eject the drifted bait will the hooks actually find purchase and at this point your monofilament reel line must be stretched like a bow string.

OK, monsters might swim off in the opposite direction to assist in hook penetration but most are quite happy to be wound in until they start to sense danger. So remember to keep that rod well bent because if it straightens when the pike opens its chops and flares its gills and starts head shaking to get the bait out, it will come off. As the distance between pike and rod shortens, readjust the reel's clutch to a firm playing mode and, as an extra precaution, slacken off a bit more immediately prior to netting, in case it makes a last-ditch bid for freedom. Some pike allow you to wind them all the way in from over 100 yards out and then go berserk when just a few yards from the net. So beware.

BRAIDED REEL LINES

Recent years have seen wonderful advances in fishing line development and the new breed of low-diameter, extra-limp, gel spun braided polyethylene lines which have next to no stretch are simply marvellous for the drift-fishing method. They tend to hang in the surface film due to a specific gravity of slightly less than water and so working a bait downwind and being able to straighten the line without it sinking using just a gentle arm movement is an absolute joy. Fish are felt immediately on the wind down and the strike is instant. And while by comparison to monofilament braid is several times the price, its performance is that much greater too. For drift float fishing at extreme range and for working heavy pirks in saltwater over wrecks lying 100–200 feet deep, I now use braid exclusively. Its advantages over monofilament are unbelievable, but do remember it lacks stretch when that big fish decides to thrash away on a short line.

Incidentally brands of braid which are oval in cross section as opposed to round tend to float better and so aid presentation. What you do need to be careful about however is using a knot suitable for these new lines when tying on swivels, and my clinch-uni combination in Diag. 87 Fig. A is perfect for the job. Should you wish to add a 20–30-foot monofilament leader to the braided reel line as either a cushion or in order that a power-gum stop knot can be tied on for fishing really deep water (although the stop knot can be tied over braid) use the beachcaster's knot (Fig. B) and add a drop of superglue to finish.

One last piece of advice about non-stretch braided lines: do not simply use braid of the same test as you would monofilament. Because there is no stretch you need a safety margin, so to replace 12–14lb mono, for instance, use a braided line of 20–25lb test which is actually thinner anyway. And wind it on to the reel really tightly otherwise it tends to bed in.

ABOUT DRIFT FLOATS

There are now numerous sail-like drift floats on the market and all came as a result of the original ET drifter shown in Diag. 90, Fig. A which is attached both top and bottom throughout the drift. But when you strike, a tiny release eye sleeved on to the line pulls free from the top of the float so it folds (now connected through the bottom ring only) like a waggler for an easy retrieve and whilst playing fish. However, there are problems associated with the top ring attachment in that tangles may occur when the float spins in strong winds, plus there is a degree of resistance on striking when the float submerges.

Certain floats like the Fox drifter (which comes with a choice of two bodies that each fit a moulded shaft) are fitted with a domed peak that houses an additional spigot for the release eye. This means the line can be attached at either the top of the stem when the wind is light to moderate (Fig. B) or at the body (Fig. C) for really strong winds, thus reducing chances of the float lifting out of the water.

Of course there is nothing to stop you from fishing the drift float with the line through the bottom ring only with bead and stop knot above – just like a true waggler. But the line (if using monofilament) must be regreased close to the float virtually on every case. This of course is where a self-floating braided line really helps.

There is another excellent and most advanced set-up shown in Diag. 91, namely the Dave Batten Super Drifter, and I shall be covering this in depth later on. For the present, however, let's continue rigging up a standard drift float. As can be seen from Diag. 90, top insert, once stop knot, bead and float are on the line the next consideration is using the right type of weight to cock it.

You can simply pinch on sufficient swan shots at the top of the wire trace (Fig. D) or concentrate the weight required in a single bullet on the line immediately above the trace swivel (Fig. E). I particularly like the Fox Egg Sinkers (Fig. F) which have a ½-inch length of silicone rubber fitted over the inner tubing at one end. This fits tightly over the trace swivel, ensuring the oval-shaped weight does not slip up the line during the cast or, and more importantly, if a pike swims upwards with the bait, thus preventing the float from lying flat and

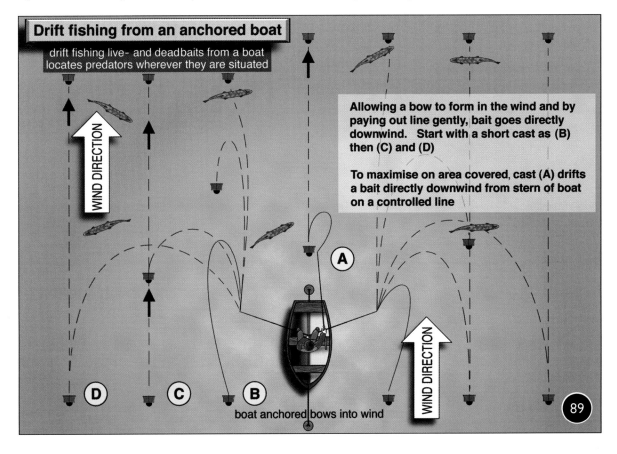

Drift fishing from an anchored boat

drift fishing live- and deadbaits from a boat locates predators wherever they are situated

WIND DIRECTION

Allowing a bow to form in the wind and by paying out line gently, bait goes directly downwind. Start with a short cast as (B) then (C) and (D)

To maximise on area covered, cast (A) drifts a bait directly downwind from stern of boat on a controlled line

(A)

WIND DIRECTION

(D) (C) (B)

boat anchored bows into wind

89

registering a lift bite. Large, lively baits will also do this of course but you soon get used to their registrations via the sail-like vane.

BAIT PRESENTATION

There is little difference between fishing live and deadbaits on the drift except that some might prefer a livebait mounted with the barbed prong of the top treble through the livebait's top lip and the barbed prong of the bottom treble nicked into its pelvic fin root (Fig. G). Alternatively use exactly the same arrangement for both live and deadbaits with the barbed prong of the top treble nicked in just below the dorsal fin and the barbed prong of the bottom treble in the bait's pectoral fin root (Fig. H). With sea deadbaits lacking a central dorsal fin, ensure the top hook is more or less in the middle of the fish's back so it is presented lifelike in a horizontal position.

Use a duo of size 8 semi-barbless trebles to an 18-inch trace of 15–20lb wire, unless your bait exceeds 6–7 inches in which case a duo of size 6s is recommended. For zander step down to size 10s and 4–5-inch baits.

WORKING A DRIFT FLOAT

Drifting a bait along any old how won't necessarily catch you any bonus pike. It still needs to be worked in order to reach known drop-offs, deep gullies, channels between islands and so on. You therefore need to hold the rod for much of the time to steer your rig along the particular line you wish to take.

At the end of each drift you can put the rod down and let a livebait chug around for a few minutes. And I have an elastic band around the rod handle opposite the reel so a loop of line can be retained with the bale arm open, in case a fish grabs hold when I'm not looking. But really the excitement of drift fishing comes from continually working that float and the level of anticipation which escalates each time a livebait starts moving erratically or the rig approaches a known hotspot where big fish have been previously taken. Drift fishing is a probing, searching, exploring, 'I want to know what's down there' method of catching predators, so treat it as such.

If fishing an irregular-bottomed pit for instance, or a shallow lake that suddenly deepens into an extreme hole, you need to be aware of these sudden depth changes. So exhaustive plummeting (where possible) of any new location is imperative if optimum results are to be achieved.

You can allow the float to be taken directly downwind in more or less a straight line by slowly feeding out line, (as in Diag. 88, Fig. A), or you can work down and across to reach various spots by allowing a bow to form between rod tip and float, giving line freely in order to maintain that bow whilst searching out a particular line (as in Fig. B). Start with a short cast to drift the bait along marginal features, tightening up so it swings into the lee of the wind for a few minutes before slowly retrieving and systematically working a longer line on successive casts. An enormous area can be covered using this simple technique. If your float is set both top and bottom or top and middle, remember to tighten up and give a controlled pull at the end of each drift in order to release the eye so the float folds waggler style for an effortless retrieve. It's then a simple matter of resetting the release eye at the start of each new cast.

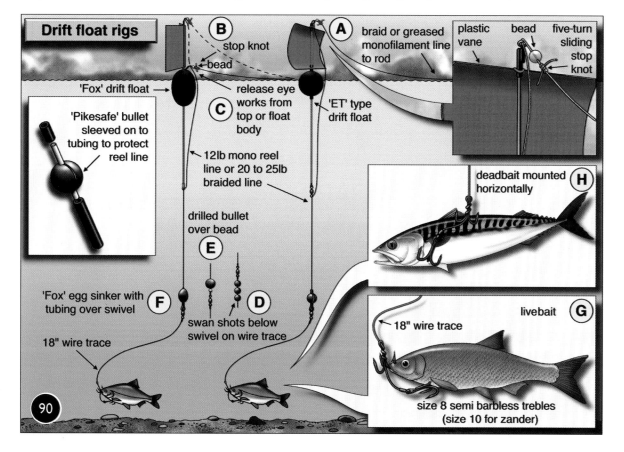

Drift float rigs

(B) stop knot
bead

(A) braid or greased monofilament line to rod

plastic vane — bead — five-turn sliding stop knot

'Fox' drift float →

release eye works from top or float body (C)

'ET' type drift float

'Pikesafe' bullet sleeved on to tubing to protect reel line

12lb mono reel line or 20 to 25lb braided line

drilled bullet over bead (E)

deadbait mounted horizontally (H)

'Fox' egg sinker with tubing over swivel (F)

(D)

swan shots below swivel on wire trace

livebait (G)

18" wire trace

18" wire trace

size 8 semi barbless trebles (size 10 for zander)

90

BOAT FISHING

As can be seen from Diag. 89 using the drift float from a boat anchored either side on or bows into the wind allows for an enormous amount of water to be covered accurately – particularly large, even-depthed broads, meres, estate lakes and some reservoirs.

When drifting downwind from the boat, pay line out gradually allowing the float to tighten the slack before playing out more line, (as in Fig. A). When fishing across the wind, however, out each side of the boat (Fig. B) start with a short cast and pay out several yards of freeline so that a bow develops between float and rod tip. By paying out just enough line to keep the bow working, the bait will then continue drifting directly downwind. And by casting slightly further on each successive cast (Fig. C) and (Fig. D), (just as in Diag. 88 when working from the bank) an enormous amount of water can be covered. Predators are rarely spread out evenly like currants in a well-baked cake, so you need to locate them – one by one. Endeavour to set the bait to fish within 2 to 3 feet of the bottom (hence the need for careful plummeting) wherever it maintains a consistent depth. If, however, you know the bottom fluctuates between, say, 8 and 16 feet during a particular drift, as is often the case when searching gravel pits (see Diag. 92), you have no alternative but to set the sliding stop knot to 7 feet deep. There is, however, a way of overcoming this problem by having two power-gum depth-setting stop knots and beads, as illustrated in the excellent Dave Batten Super Drifter float rig, Diag. 91. One is set below the super controller at the shallowest depth allowing for length

Illustrator Dave Batten is not only good at designing predator rigs like his own super drifter float set-up, he catches effectively with it too.

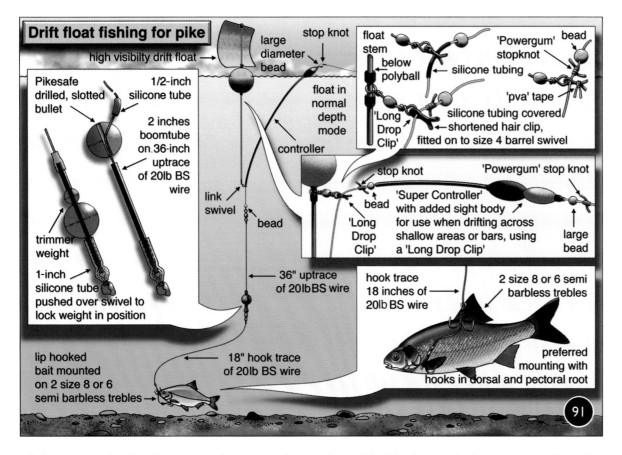

Drift float fishing for pike

high visibilty drift float →

large diameter bead

stop knot

Pikesafe drilled, slotted bullet

1/2-inch silicone tube

2 inches boomtube on 36-inch uptrace of 20lb BS wire

float in normal depth mode

controller

float stem

below polyball

'Powergum' stopknot

bead

silicone tubing

'pva' tape

'Long Drop Clip'

silicone tubing covered shortened hair clip, fitted on to size 4 barrel swivel

trimmer weight

1-inch silicone tube pushed over swivel to lock weight in position

link swivel

bead

36" uptrace of 20lbBS wire

stop knot

'Powergum' stop knot

bead

'Long Drop Clip'

'Super Controller' with added sight body for use when drifting across shallow areas or bars, using a 'Long Drop Clip'

large bead

hook trace 18 inches of 20lb BS wire

2 size 8 or 6 semi barbless trebles

lip hooked bait mounted on 2 size 8 or 6 semi barbless trebles →

18" hook trace of 20lb BS wire

preferred mounting with hooks in dorsal and pectoral root

91

of the trace and 36-inch uptrace of course and a second power-gum stop knot is set for the deeper area of water you wish to fish when you release the line from the clip.

The clip itself is made from a standard hair grip, shortened to gain the full benefit of the natural spring action, with ends just flared out and filed smooth to allow entry of the line. There are two ways of securing the line: you can put 0.5mm or 1mm silicone tubing on the clip itself, or place a 1-inch length of 0.5mm silicone tubing on the reel line for trapping in the clip. Line placed directly in the bare clip pulls out too easily on the cast and risks damage on the clip itself.

With the various makes of line clip now available on the market, it is possible that one of these may work equally well or even better. The clip is set below

the polyball body specifically so that it allows the float to spin in turbulent, variable direction winds.

Moving down the float we reach the bottom fixing. There are two options for use here: the float can be loose with no direct connection to the super controller or it can be attached and retained with silicone rings so that they move as one. The latter is achieved by sliding the large swivel on to the controller tubing, trapping it between two short lengths of thick-wall silicone tubing. This ensures that the controller always maintains a safe distance from the float; should the bait hold the drift back and the line pass the float the controller pivots with the line.

The controller is made of a stiff plastic boom tubing and not the soft flexible type. Above the water line are fitted preferably two controller bodies with

the upper one flourescent red or orange for increased buoyancy and visibility respectively, particularly when using the float with the double depth option. The controller lies flat in the shallow setting and stands up when confirming that the depth has reset, once the line is clear of the long drop clip. Having covered the float and the controller, now is a good time to look at the set-up and release of the long drop clip (see Diag. 92).

Once you have decided that you need this option you first need to identify your shallowest depth to be drifted over by plumming (Fig. A), and also your deepest setting in a similar fashion (Fig. C). You may have to adjust up trace and hook trace lengths to accommodate the really shallow depths that are sometimes experienced on some gravel bars and shallow areas, but keep them safe.

Having found where the water gets deeper then you should note the distance at which you can release your line by casting to the approximate spot with a bomb attached to your drift reel line and make a mark on the line with a build-up of Tippex or nail varnish to indicate where and when you can effect the release. This will also allow you to coat the line with grease as you reel in (though obviously not if choosing to fish with braid).

Tie the stop knots in power-gum at the appropriate position with a bead below the deeper one to stop the float. Set the line into the clip below your shallowest stop knot, using the rubbered clip or the tubing on the line – your choice. You will need to experiment here with how firmly or lightly you set this depth in the clip as you need a balance in holding the line secure during the cast and the ability to release the line, once you are over the release point (Fig. B). If there is any problem of unclipping on the cast you can use PVA thread to hold the clip closed and your line in position; the PVA will normally have dissolved by the time the float gets into position.

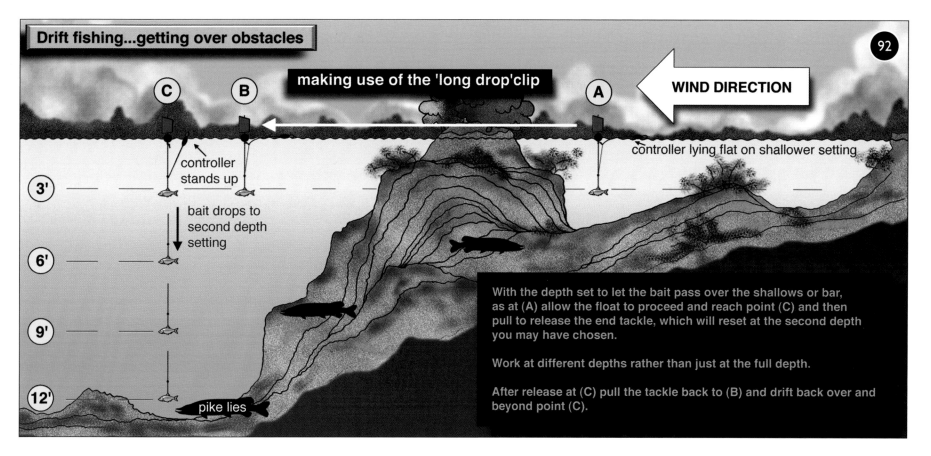

Drift fishing...getting over obstacles

92

making use of the 'long drop'clip

WIND DIRECTION

controller lying flat on shallower setting

A

B

C

controller stands up

bait drops to second depth setting

3'

6'

9'

12'

pike lies

With the depth set to let the bait pass over the shallows or bar, as at (A) allow the float to proceed and reach point (C) and then pull to release the end tackle, which will reset at the second depth you may have chosen.

Work at different depths rather than just at the full depth.

After release at (C) pull the tackle back to (B) and drift back over and beyond point (C).

The way to release the line is to allow the float to go beyond the mark on your line by a few yards and then wind down tight to the float and apply a very firm, sustained pull (strike). If you don't succeed first time, repeat the drift to a greater distance and try again. It can take some experimenting to get the clip setting just right, in the balance between casting and release, but it is worth trying. All this may seem rather complex but if you wish to overcome the depth barrier of shallow water and gravel bars then it is worth giving a try.

Moving down the line below Dave Batten's Super Drift float, we come to a 30–36-inch wire uptrace (to avert bite-offs should the bait tangle above the hook trace swivel) to which is attached a split and drilled bullet (or two) sleeved on to 2 inches of brown tube. This is secured to the trace swivel via silicone tubing in a fixed mode should a pike rise with the bait, giving a slack line bite and the risk of deep hooking – the float registering a classic lift bite by falling over flat.

So when the float lies flat, be ready to tighten up to your bait in case it is a take. If you are in doubt, strike. With the controller behind the float, the line will reset at the surface and not sink, allowing you to continue drifting. This is unlike floats which have the top ring attached via a silicone link fixing, which may pull free, leaving the line free to sink slowly, slowing or halting the drift settings with all the consequences if a pike should take the bait at this point.

FLOAT FISHING STATIC DEADBAITS FOR PIKE AND ZANDER

Quite apart from the enjoyment to be gained from watching a float suddenly bob and jerk crazily across the surface before sliding positively under, float fishing static deadbaits creates the absolute minimum of resistance to an interested predator. And although the reference throughout this method is geared towards the capture of pike, the technique is equally effective for zander; you simply step down in hook and bait size accordingly. I would also step down in overall power to an Avon-style rod combination with a 6–8lb reel line where zander only are expected. With pike in mind, however, let's talk about the tackle required.

RODS AND REELS

For optimum control of the float and line pick-up over great distances my preference is for a 12-foot rod of around 2–2¼lb test curve which makes a reel line of around 10–11lb an ideal choice. Incidentally if you are not sure about which breaking strain line a particular rod is capable of handling, there is an extremely simple formula to use. We have the late Dick Walker to thank for the fact that most of the specialist-type carbon-fibre Avon, carp or pike rods produced today all have one thing in common – they are rated in test curves – with a figure of somewhere

between 1 and 3lb clearly marked together with the rod's length and manufacturer's logo immediately above the handle.

Dick applied a basic rule of thumb during the early days of carp fishing way back in the 1950s, when designing his specialist-built cane rods, such as the famous MK4 carp and Avon rods, and as yet no one has improved upon the test curve principle. Incidentally the term 'test curve' simply relates to the strain (in lb) required to pull the rod's tip round into a quarter circle using a spring balance. To ascertain the rod's ideal line strength, you then simply multiply that figure (its test curve rating) by five. Therefore a test curve of say 2¼lb will result in an ideal line strength of approximately 11¼lb. To find the rod's safe lower limit, multiply by four, which gives a line strength of 9¼lb and for its safe upper limit by six, which allows lines of up to 13½lb to be used. So in short, a 2¼lb test curve rod is best matched with lines of 9¼–13½lb breaking strain. But I must stress that such figures offer only a general guideline, because far lighter and heavier lines may be used with the same rod in experienced hands. Remember that the test curve rating method was designed for rods constructed of built cane which had a parabolic action, and did not have the versatility of today's carbon-fibre equivalents. But it

is still an extremely useful way of instantly gauging the power of a particular rod and calculating a strength line so that both rod and line stretch simultaneously like one gigantic elastic band. There is no safer, more enjoyable way of subduing the biggest adversaries.

Now what about reels? I must admit to having a pet aversion towards oversize fixed-spool reels and in my opinion many of the top-notch, large-format designer reels sold today for both carp and pike fishing are, in addition to being overpriced, probably better suited to beach casting. I see little point in forking out a fortune on a superlight, state-of-the-art carbon-fibre rod, only to load it up with an outsize and overweight fixed-spool reel. Only when line capacity is the deciding factor (as it is when drift float fishing for instance) would I ever consider using a format larger than the 3000 size for anything that swims in British freshwaters.

OK, I've got that off my chest. You'll gather that as long as your reel holds 200 yards of 10–12lb monofilament and is equipped with a smooth slipping clutch, it is perfectly suited to the technique of float fishing static deadbaits.

WHY A STATIC BAIT?

Now what about this word 'static'? Why is it so important? Well in the majority of still-water fisheries, big, old, fat female pike especially, certainly a higher than average size of pike anyway (taking into account all other methods of bait presentation) are more likely to suck up a static deadbait from the

Static deadbaits and an early morning start go hand in hand for capturing big pike from the Norfolk Broads. John favours 2¼lb test curve 12-foot rods for this method.

Using a sliding predator float rig set well over depth, Terry Hazlewood enjoys the heavy lunges of a big still-water pike.

bottom than go chasing about after spinners or livebaits, particularly in heavily coloured water. There is no doubt whatsoever that in turbid water with minimal visibility pike concentrate on smelling out their food by scavenging along the bottom rather than chasing after a moving bait using their vision.

Take my local waters, the Norfolk Broads, for instance, during the winter months which for week upon week, particularly during prolonged windy weather, often colour up to such an extent that sight of a herring's head is lost before the tail is lowered in. Now in water this thick – like brown Windsor soup, for the most part – lures and livebaits, even slowly wobbled deadbaits, are all overwhelmingly outfished by a static deadbait.

This is not to say that static deadbaits won't be

effective in crystal-clear lakes and pits, for example. To catch a really big fish I would be quite happy with my money on a well-presented static. Indeed presenting static deads has virtually become the accepted big-fish method in the majority of still-water fisheries. It is simply that in densely coloured water statics reign supreme. And whenever possible, short of gale-force conditions, presentation beneath a float is preferred for both its sensitivity and, as I said earlier, for the angler's enjoyment.

FLOAT RIGS

For close-range situations whilst bank fishing, and when presenting the bait directly downwind from an anchored boat, my preferred rig is to use a sliding float with the line passing through its middle and stopped in the usual manner with bead and sliding stop knot above (tied with power gum) at least twice the swim depth (Diag. 93, Fig. A). This may seem excessive but I feel it is so important for the last few feet of line at least to lie along the bottom (as in Fig. B). This is why the two swan shots used to keep the bait down and against which the float rests prior to casting are pinched on the reel line 20 inches above the 20-inch wire trace (Fig. C). There is therefore no way a big, old, suspicious pike can bump into the line and trace swivel (carp spook and give liners remember, so give pike the same respect) as it sidles up to engulf its free meal from the bottom. To ensure the reel line above the sliding float sits upon the surface it is covered well with mucilin. You are then treated to the most glorious uninhibited bites on the float (as it slides across the surface like a scene from Jaws) without the slightest resistance being felt by the pike until it has moved some considerable distance directly away from the rod, when the float will finally submerge. But by then of course you will have struck.

You see, the pike feels absolutely no resistance because the float is merely being pulled along as opposed to under. The same principle applies to even a four-year-old child being able to pull a dinghy along which is floating upon the surface. Yet the strongest man could not pull that dinghy beneath the surface! From all this you have, I hope, gathered that a pike will subsequently not sense any degree of buoyancy from the flat float as it engulfs the static deadbait in its jaws and moves off. This is why if presenting static baits correctly you will experience

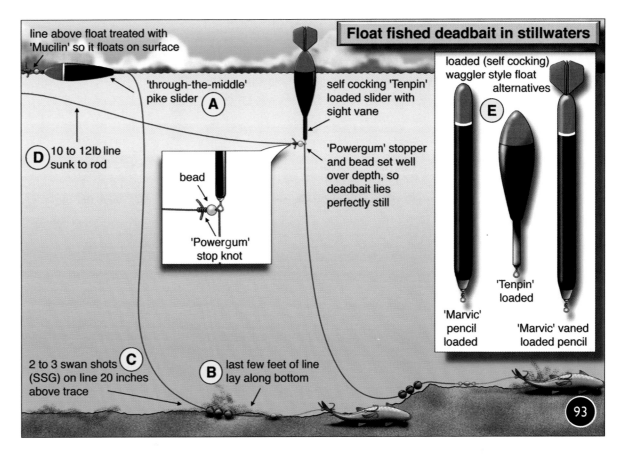

Float fished deadbait in stillwaters

- line above float treated with 'Mucilin' so it floats on surface
- 'through-the-middle' pike slider **A**
- self cocking 'Tenpin' loaded slider with sight vane
- loaded (self cocking) waggler style float alternatives **E**
- **D** 10 to 12lb line sunk to rod
- bead
- 'Powergum' stop knot
- 'Powergum' stopper and bead set well over depth, so deadbait lies perfectly still
- 2 to 3 swan shots **C** (SSG) on line 20 inches above trace
- **B** last few feet of line lay along bottom
- 'Marvic' pencil loaded
- 'Tenpin' loaded
- 'Marvic' vaned loaded pencil
- 93

very few dropped runs, and an immediate strike can be made. I use a similar rig for offering deadbaits to river pike. This is exhaustively explained in Method 11, 'Stret Pegging'.

When float fishing at greater distances however, especially across the wind when a floating line would quickly drag the (flat) float-fished static away from the position to which it was cast, it is essential that a cocked float (bottom end only slider) be used and the line between float and rod tip sunk beneath the surface (as in Fig. D). Think of this technique if you will as simply scaled-up waggler fishing in still water, which it more or less is. Cast several yards beyond the intended swim and immediately dunk your rod tip beneath the surface (just like fishing a peacock waggler – see Method 13, 'Waggler Fishing'). Crank the reel's handle a few turns in order to get the line

below the surface quickly, while the deadbait is sinking and not afterwards or you may unintentionally drag it through bottom debris and hamper presentation. In really choppy conditions, ensure the rod tip is set low to the water (even beneath the surface) on two rod rests pointing directly at the float.

As long as you effectively sink your line (splodge some liquid leader sink or neat washing-up liquid around the spool before casting), the bottom end only float will remain in any position despite surface chop, even when cast across or up into the wind to ensure the deadbait remains perfectly static. To this end I prefer to set the stop knot so the float fishes well over depth, encouraging those last few feet of line to lie along the bottom. Again pinch two swan shots on 20 inches above the trace as described for

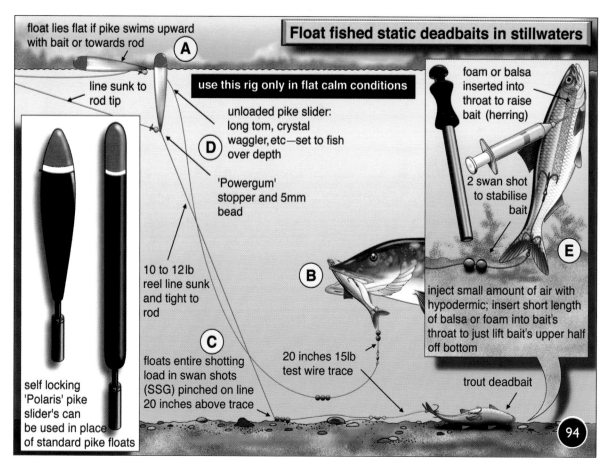

float lies flat if pike swims upward
with bait or towards rod
(A)

line sunk to
rod tip

Float fished static deadbaits in stillwaters

use this rig only in flat calm conditions

unloaded pike slider:
long tom, crystal
waggler, etc—set to fish
over depth
(D)

'Powergum'
stopper and 5mm
bead

10 to 12lb
reel line sunk
and tight to
rod

(C)

floats entire shotting
load in swan shots
(SSG) pinched on line
20 inches above trace

self locking
'Polaris' pike
slider's can
be used in place
of standard pike floats

(B)

20 inches 15lb
test wire trace

foam or balsa
inserted into
throat to raise
bait (herring)

2 swan shot
to stabilise
bait
(E)

inject small amount of air with
hypodermic; insert short length
of balsa or foam into bait's
throat to just lift bait's upper half
off bottom

trout deadbait

94

the close-range flat float rig. By far the best sliding floats to use here are self-cocking loaded models such as longtoms, tenpin drifters, or the Marvic vaned loaded pencil (as shown in Diag. 93, Fig. E). So the only weight down the line is the two (or three) swan shots pinched on the line 20 inches above the trace.

If you are worried about a pike becoming deeply hooked through fishing well over depth and decide to set the float at little more than swim depth, every wave that raises the float will also raise the tail of your (supposedly) static deadbait off the bottom in a most suspicious up-down, up-down motion. In addition, the bait has every chance of being bounced away from its intended position by wave action and subsurface tow. This will not be the case if the self-cocking float is set well over depth where, incidentally, it offers no

more risk of a pike becoming deeply hooked than if set exactly to swim depth. If the float was set (let's be silly here to prove the point) 50 feet over depth, and a pike ran 4 feet in the opposite direction away from the rod, the float would still go under. And if the pike moved 4 feet towards the rod so would the float. Exactly the same principle prevails regardless of how far over depth the float is set.

When fishing in flat-calm conditions and crystal-clear water, for educated pike (that is to say pike which are regularly caught and are therefore suspicious of deadbaits) you may like to try a more sensitive approach by using a normal (unloaded) float which will then lift and fall over flat, as in Diag. 94, Fig. A (just like a peacock quill float does when tench fishing – see Method 12, 'The Lift Method')

should a pike merely suck the bait off the bottom but go nowhere (as in Fig. B). Once again it matters not how far over depth you set an unloaded float providing the entire shotting load is concentrated (in swan shots) 20 inches above the trace (as Fig. C). After casting out and sinking the line, simply tighten up until the float cocks nicely and can be clearly seen (Fig. D). Once again be sure to set the rod on two rests pointing directly at the float with the rod tip only a couple of inches above the surface. Incidentally the self-cocking (no need for bead and stop knot) Polaris pike and zander floats can be used here. See Method 6, 'Float Ledgering', for a full rundown on how they work.

The reason you cannot tighten up to the same degree and use an unloaded float in windy conditions or when a strong subsurface flow prevails, is because sooner or later a tight rig will be pulled downwind and the bait dragged into bottom debris. A useful trick for presenting statics over a really mucky or silty bottom is to raise the bait's upper half by injecting air into the shoulder region or inserting foam strip or a short length of balsa dowel into its throat (as Fig. E). Pike which learn to become wary of statics just lying on the bottom wolf raised baits up eagerly. Try it and see.

Incidentally (and this applies to all float rigs mentioned in this method) after casting out, whether boat or bank fishing, I like to open the bale arm and clip a small loop of line beneath an elastic band or use a run clip positioned around the rod handle above the reel. It is a justifiable precaution against the occasional zonking run which might otherwise pull the rod in. Much of my serious deadbaiting for pike takes place during long dawn-until-dusk sessions on the Norfolk Broads where, due to surface chop, runs are not always immediately seen. Reels which have free spool or a bait runner facility, eliminate this necessity of course.

TRACES AND BAITS

Now let's talk about traces and baits. As can be seen from Diag. 95 I prefer to use a reasonably long (20-inch) 15lb test wire trace of either braided alasticum or the extremely supple and low-diameter Wonder Wire marketed through Caliber Tackle, which is made from no fewer than forty-nine strands. Even 25lb Wonder Wire is no thicker than 15lb alasticum and so provides an excellent safety margin coupled to sensitivity. One word of warning however: it cannot be twisted like alasticum and seven-strand type wires. Either use mini crimps or simply tie a two-turn half blood knot, pulling on the short end only, otherwise you will create kinks in front of the treble hook or swivel. Also called the figure-of-eight knot (in the US) the two-turn half blood would seem ridiculous if using monofilaments because it would of course instantly slip. But this is not so when using Wonder Wire which really works. Do not, however, trim the ends too close.

Unless presenting really large baits when size 6 trebles suit, I use a duo of semi-barbless size 8 trebles for both whole and half baits. As can be seen from Fig. A the top treble (held in position by wrapping the wire four times around its shank) nicks firmly into the whole bait's tail root using the barbed prong, while the bottom treble's barbed prong goes into the flank 2–3 inches away depending upon bait size (as Fig. B). This actually permits the pike to swallow a good half of the bait before the hooks enter its throat so few deeply hooked fish should result (Fig. C). When using tiny fish like sprats or small smelt, set the trebles only 1–1½ inches apart (Fig. D). The same goes for small half baits such as a herring or large smelt heads (as Fig. E). Half baits are particularly effective for the static method of presentation on account of their attractive juices permeating quickly through still water. Cutting the

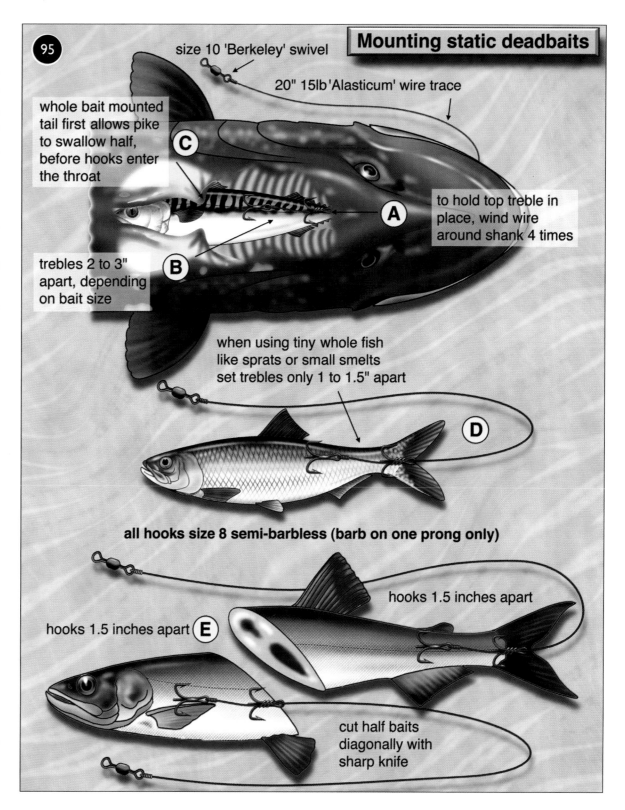

95

size 10 'Berkeley' swivel

Mounting static deadbaits

20" 15lb 'Alasticum' wire trace

whole bait mounted tail first allows pike to swallow half, before hooks enter the throat

C

A

to hold top treble in place, wind wire around shank 4 times

trebles 2 to 3" apart, depending on bait size

B

when using tiny whole fish like sprats or small smelts set trebles only 1 to 1.5" apart

D

all hooks size 8 semi-barbless (barb on one prong only)

hooks 1.5 inches apart

hooks 1.5 inches apart **E**

cut half baits diagonally with sharp knife

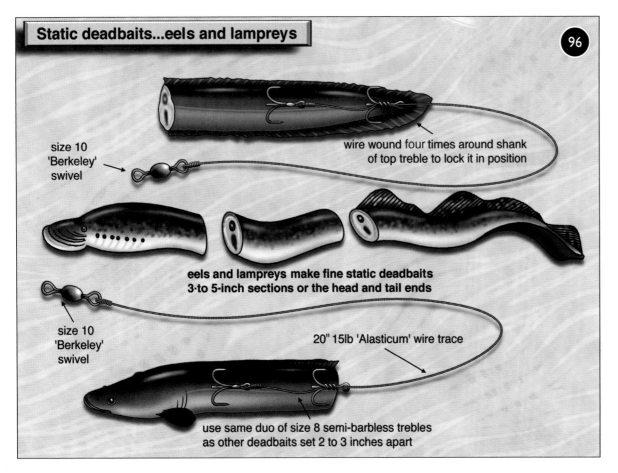

Static deadbaits...eels and lampreys

96

size 10 'Berkeley' swivel

wire wound four times around shank of top treble to lock it in position

eels and lampreys make fine static deadbaits 3-to 5-inch sections or the head and tail ends

size 10 'Berkeley' swivel

20" 15lb 'Alasticum' wire trace

use same duo of size 8 semi-barbless trebles as other deadbaits set 2 to 3 inches apart

bait diagonally across with a sharp knife provides greater length on both halves for hook positioning.

I use all kinds of fish when static deadbait fishing (see Diag. 96) including sea fish like grey mullet, sand eels, scad, red mullet and garfish, plus faithful standbys such as herrings, mackerel and smelt. Oddities such as lampreys, squid and cuttlefish also score well. Actually, as long as it is fresh or freshly blast frozen and appears appetizing with a nice aroma I cannot think of a species of fish which will not be readily wolfed down by pike. On some fisheries, especially heavily coloured waters, baits from the sea may appear to have a distinct edge over freshwater deadbaits due to their very much higher levels of oil and attractive juices. But in truth I doubt that pike are as selective as we

think. There is no doubt however that they will shy away from baits upon which they have been repeatedly caught in the past, so offering a different bait to educated pike in hard-fished waters will invariably produce more runs. All freshly killed freshwater fishes (and I must emphasize freshly killed) are in my opinion equal to any sea bait. I particularly like dace, roach, rudd, chub, grayling, bream hybrids and trout in the 6–8-inch size bracket which can be used either as whole or half baits. The head end, the tail end, or indeed simply a 4–6-inch chunk of freshwater eel (see Diag. 96) also make magnificent pike baits and a trip during the warmer months spent catching eels, to be frozen down specifically for use during the winter, is time well spent indeed. Eel section is also a

fabulous bait for zander when used in 2–4-inch lengths. Gudgeon, bleak, plus small dace, roach and rudd of up to 4–5 inches are also favoured.

FREEZING DOWN BAITS

Many of the baits already mentioned are of course available prepacked from specialist tackle shops but the cost compared to obtaining and freezing down your own is quite considerable, quite apart from the freshness aspect. The secret is to keep a sharp eye out on the wet-fish stalls at your local market for recent landings, and to buy up those sprats, herrings, smelt and mackerel as they come in. Another excellent source comes from trout farmers, some of whom are only too pleased to sell off small disfigured fish that will never be required for stocking. And as trout are reared by the thousand all of a particular size you can sometimes even obtain baits of exactly the length required.

Pike fishermen who also enjoy the occasional sea trip can also think well ahead by taking home all the small fresh mackerel caught on feathers. And don't throw away those bony horse mackerel better known as scad. They make great pike baits.

If you cannot bring yourself to kill small freshwater species like dace, roach and skimmer bream which other anglers enjoy catching, then capitalize on collecting eels for deadbaits wherever you see a dredger working. As the bottom mud is piled up beside the river bank, walk along with a bucket and collect them as they wriggle out.

With all the baits I've mentioned here don't simply bung them into the freezer in one big lump. Spare a few minutes to wrap each individually in cling film before popping into the freezer in batches of so many fish.

Invest in a sizeable freezer bag or, better still, a mini coolbox which will take a couple of freezer which is most important. This tiny sardine is readily obtainable from many wet-fish shops, delicatessens and from supermarkets in large frozen packs. So it is always available throughout the winter months, whereas small natural fish sources may dry up.

A handful of whitebait can be scattered into a couple of preselected swims every other day for a week or two prior to fishing. Or they can be mashed, liquidized or minced and simply mixed with brown breadcrumbs to form a groundbait which can be thrown in around the float up to distances of 30 yards while you are actually fishing. A word of warning however: plan to execute your prebaiting as dusk falls or you could attract diving birds and all your efforts will be in vain.

You can't stop the Wilson Brothers – Dave and John teamed up for a haul of gravel-pit doubles caught on static deadbaits during a 'Go Fishing' TV programme.

A float-presented static deadbait accountsed for this nicely marked twenty. Note how effectively John grips it using a chainmail glove on his left hand.

blocks in addition to your batch of deadbaits. Then they will remain in tiptop condition all day through.

PREBAITING

As a general rule freshwater predator fishermen do not groundbait for pike and zander, yet there are circumstances when it really pays dividends. Take a huge windswept, featureless gravel pit or reservoir, for instance, with few visible features around which predatory fish can be expected. In this scenario you can't easily go to the fish, so get them to come to you. Or put another way, attract them to a particular area by regularly prebaiting with small dead fishes.

For this job I find that whitebait really do the business, creating a hotspot without overfeeding

FLOAT FISHING ROAMING LIVEBAITS FOR PIKE AND ZANDER

Using a livebait to explore beside predator-holding structures and features on a free line controlled only by rod-tip movement and the use of a small float, is one of the most exciting methods of catching pike and zander. Although the following text is geared to pike fishing, everything applies equally to catching zander on float-fished livebaits, as they often occupy the same swims. When targeting zander specifically, and there is little chance of a pike, tackle strength may be reduced accordingly to obtain maximum enjoyment. So first let's consider a suitable outfit to work this method effectively.

RODS AND REELS

Because I prefer to hold the rod throughout and be continually working the livebait in the direction where I expect a pike to be lying, a long light-weight rod is preferred. For both still and running water I use a 12-foot carbon-fibre model of around 2lb test curve which has a medium tip action and is nicely matched to a line strength of 11–12lb. When considering reels I feel that a fixed spool is preferable to a multiplier in that gentler casts can be made in order to preserve the bait's condition. And again because the outfit is going to be held for long periods I see no reason (as seems the vogue these days unfortunately) of fixing a heavy, outsize fixed-spool reel on to a superlightweight, state-of-the-art carbon-fibre rod. So any smooth-running fixed spool in the 2500–3000 size format (certainly no larger) which holds 200 yards of 11–12lb monofilament and has a sensitive slipping clutch should fit the bill admirably. Whether it has a front or stem drag system is quite academic.

For catching zander only, an ideal combination would be a 12-foot Avon rod of around 1¼lb test curve, coupled to a 2000 size format fixed-spool reel holding 6–7lb test monofilament. But where both pike and zander are on the cards it would be safer to stick with the pike outfit already suggested.

FLOATS AND TRACES

Equipped with a suitably lightweight combination, I feel sure you will then be more inclined to hold it throughout and will consequently catch more pike. In fact in waters of fair visibility, where an attractively presented livebait is going to be snapped up quickly because the pike homes in on it with visual ease, there

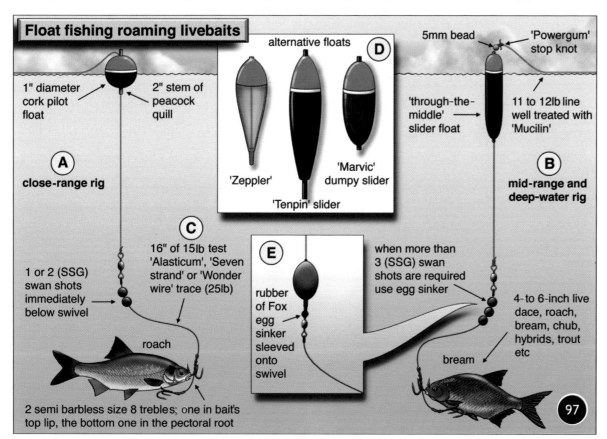

Float fishing roaming livebaits

1" diameter cork pilot float

2" stem of peacock quill

A close-range rig

1 or 2 (SSG) swan shots immediately below swivel

roach

2 semi barbless size 8 trebles; one in bait's top lip, the bottom one in the pectoral root

alternative floats **D**

'Zeppler'

'Tenpin' slider

'Marvic' dumpy slider

C 16" of 15lb test 'Alasticum', 'Seven strand' or 'Wonder wire' trace (25lb)

E rubber of Fox egg sinker sleeved onto swivel

5mm bead

'Powergum' stop knot

'through-the-middle' slider float

11 to 12lb line well treated with 'Mucilin'

B mid-range and deep-water rig

when more than 3 (SSG) swan shots are required use egg sinker

bream

4- to 6-inch live dace, roach, bream, chub, hybrids, trout etc

97

is nothing to beat this technique. That is not to say that artificial lures and deadbaits won't work; it is simply that because you are offering the pike part of its daily diet which consists mainly of live fish, actual presentation with regard to line, float, trace diameter and hooks will arouse far less suspicion prior to and upon the livebait being engulfed. Thereafter, of course, should you tighten up prematurely so the pike feels undue resistance, it might then eject the bait. The same could happen as a result of using too large a float, because each time the pike opens its mouth to turn the bait around for swallowing head first, the excessive buoyancy attempts to pull the bait back up to the surface. Once again suspicious resistance felt by the pile could result in the bait being spat out. You perhaps now understand why I choose to use such small floats when presenting free-roaming livebaits, as can be seen from Diag. 97. Provided the line between float and rod tip has been treated well with mucilin floatant, maximizing on the bait's movement (a sunken line won't allow it to travel far), not only will it last longer and cover more areas, but when a pike does grab hold, the bait will not be pulled away by such a small float during the killing and turning process.

As can be seen from Fig. A, for all close-range work in both still and running waters and in depths down to 10–11 feet, I use a 1-inch diameter cork pilot float, fixed to the line through the middle with a thin, 2-inch length of peacock quill. It must seem strange to the younger angler of today when reading old angling books, that such a float was once used free running on the heavy reel line (to keep it up) merely as a pilot float above one of those monstrous duck-egg-sized Gazette-type pike floats, plugged to the line with wooden

A small sliding float and free-roaming livebait on a greased line were the downfall of this nice pike about to be lifted out by Dick Brigham.

John uses small baits and size 10 trebles for zander, scaling down to a 6–7lb reel line coupled to an Avon-style rod for maximum enjoyment.

To avoid deep hooking, endeavour to strike early rather than later. Even small pike can quickly engulf recommended 4–6-inch livebaits.

dowel. But then as a youngster who first became enthralled by the chance of catching pike during the early 1950s I can only ever recall being able to purchase those Gazette floats, designer pike sliders not having been conceived at that time. Indeed like most of the aids to angling which we all now accept as standard and consequently take for granted, contemporary float design has been developed to overcome various problems. And the main problem

with the old Gazette 'pike bungs', as they were affectionately called, was their overpowering size and consequent buoyancy which literally pulled baits from the mouths of small pike during the turning process. In addition the wooden dowel plug had the habit of swelling following long hours in the water, resulting in the line suddenly and inexplicably fracturing due to strangulation. And don't forget the fact that unless an equally large livebait was used capable of towing the

Gazette along, most pike within the immediate vicinity would rarely get to see a free-roaming offering.

These days of course most of us would be disgusted by the use of a ½lb roach and larger for livebaits. Such breeding stock fish which are a joy to catch on light tackle would be ill afforded from the majority of our river systems, yet to recover from the ravages of predation by cormorants, chronic water abstraction and the continuing over eutrification through farming chemicals. So thinking anglers now use small livebaits – dace, roach, rudd and bream – in the 4–6-inch size bracket presented on equally diminutive, supersensitive predator floats. There are numerous alternatives in mini-sliding through-the-middle and bottom end only predator floats on the market (Fig. D) to my suggested pilot float set up. The choice is yours. I prefer the fixed pilot float, because whenever the one to two swan shots pinched on to the trace immediately below the swivel are lifted by the bait swimming upwards or by a pike having grabbed the bait and swum upwards with it, the pilot float lays flat. So it is ultra-sensitive, just like any fixed float used to catch smaller species. You may of course present any small, bottom end only slider similarly, simply by pinching a small shot on the line each side of the end ring. You will find however that

when irregular-bottomed fisheries necessitate constant changes in depth between float and bait, it is much easier simply to pull the pilot float either up or down the desired distance. So the peacock stem insert should not fit too tightly.

There is of course no best depth at which to set the livebait. But on the assumption that a large proportion of a fishery's pike population are at any one time actually lying on or very close to the bottom, it seems logical to offer the bait at 1–2 feet above bottom. In the cold winter months once water temperatures have dropped and remained only a few degrees above zero for long periods, few runs will materialize unless the bait is virtually touching bottom and actually bumps pike on the nose. This applies to whatever float rig is employed.

For mid-range work in large still waters, for trotting the livebait long distances in deep, strongly flowing rivers and anywhere deeper than rod length, I recommend a through-the-middle sliding float rig (as in Fig. B). Try and keep its size (and thus buoyancy) restricted to how many swan shots are required on the trace for casting or for keeping the bait down in strong currents. When a float demands in excess of three swan shots concentrate the weight by using an egg sinker made by Fox Pike Systems, which threads on the line above the trace (Fig. E) and is fixed rigid by pushing a rubber sleeve over the trace swivel. Egg sinkers come in various sizes and are a great way of ensuring that lift bites (should the pike or bait swim upward) are registered. As Fig. C illustrates, the 16-inch 15lb test trace holds a pair of size 8 semi-barbless trebles (size 10 for zander) with the top one hooked into the bait's top lip with one (the barbed) prong only, and in the same way at the root of the pectoral fin with the bottom treble. This ensures extremely free movement of small livebaits and good hooking potential even when the strike is made more or less instantly. This is assuming the bait's head is actually inside the jaws, which a small fish should be with any reasonable-sized pike.

Tiny jacks which hang on to the bait across the middle for ages before even attempting the turning process are bound to come off, but who cares. Most pike of worthwhile fighting proportions, say fish of 7–8lb and upwards, have the capacity to engulf 4–6-inch livebaits and be struck instantly, with the hooks finding purchase in a high per centage of takers. I am of the view that to miss a relatively small pike through premature striking is infinitely better than to hook deeply a big pike that has gorged the livebait. And as there is never (unless you saw the pike grab hold) any way of knowing what size predator has taken the bait, adopt the attitude that if it comes off, it was probably not worth catching anyway. Being philosophical about it all will, I am certain, result in

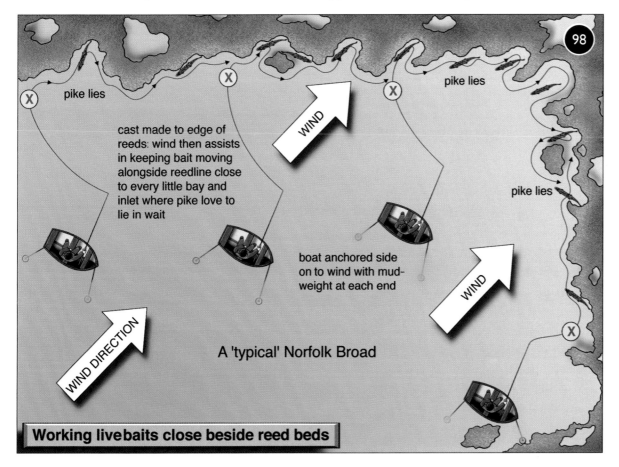

pike lies
cast made to edge of reeds: wind then assists in keeping bait moving alongside reedline close to every little bay and inlet where pike love to lie in wait
WIND
pike lies
pike lies
WIND DIRECTION
boat anchored side on to wind with mud-weight at each end
A 'typical' Norfolk Broad
WIND
98

Working livebaits close beside reed beds

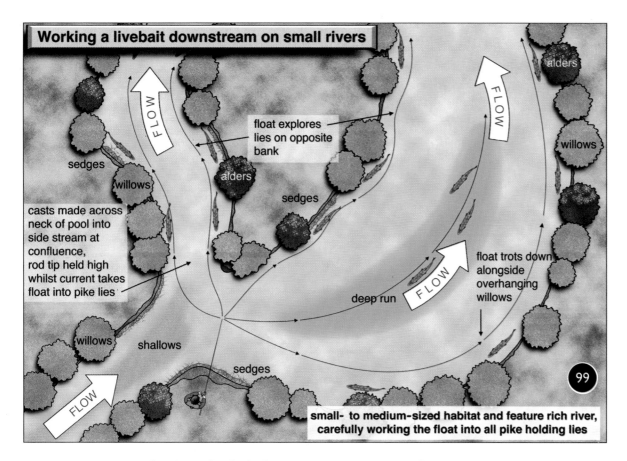

Working a livebait downstream on small rivers

FLOW

float explores lies on opposite bank

alders

willows

sedges

willows

alders

sedges

casts made across neck of pool into side stream at confluence, rod tip held high whilst current takes float into pike lies

FLOW

FLOW

willows

deep run

float trots down alongside overhanging willows

willows

FLOW

shallows

sedges

FLOW

99

small- to medium-sized habitat and feature rich river, carefully working the float into all pike holding lies

your experiencing very few deeply hooked pike.

Incidentally, an alternative wire for making the most supple of traces is the Wonder Wire, marketed in the UK through Caliber Tackle (see page 185).

WORKING THE BAIT

As I have already mentioned, regardless of whether the float is fixed or a slider, it is imperative to keep the line between float and rod well treated with mucilin floatant. Not only does a sinking line hamper the bait's movements through drag, and render it much less attractive and lifelike to a pike that fancies a chase, it makes control of the float extremely difficult. Whenever the wind blows the line into a huge bow, for instance, it is a simple matter (with a floating line) to lift the rod tip high and flip the line over straight

again without affecting the bait's direction. Gentle pressure against the float will invariably encourage the bait to move in the opposite direction, so fish with the bale arm open throughout and, after casting, simply apply gentle forefinger pressure against the spool when directing the livebait's movement.

Remember that continual haphazard casting only saps the livebait's strength and its will to swim. So think before every cast as to exactly where the bait needs to be placed. Consider Diag. 98, for instance, of a typical reed line found in the shallow waters of the Norfolk Broads where, by using the wind to your advantage, the livebait may be continually worked along the pike-holding gaps in the reed beds. The boat is anchored side on to the wind with a mudweight at each end, say 30 yards from the reeds. You then need only make one cast up to the edge of the reeds and let

both livebait and wind do the rest, with the absolute minimum control. This technique is especially deadly where the reeds sprout from depths of 3 and 4 feet, with holding pockets for pike to hide amongst behind the leading stalks forming bays and inlets.

When river fishing and the livebait is on target heading towards or beside potential pike-holding features such as reed beds, confluences, overhanging trees or bridge arches it is so satisfying when there is a plop and the float suddenly zooms under – exactly where you envisaged a fish might be lying. This is the attraction for me in working roaming livebaits beneath a float. Consider Diag. 99 depicting a typical river scene, where searching the choice target areas is bound to produce pike given reasonable conditions. Keep forever working the bait through gentle control, to explore each and every nook and cranny.

Whilst wandering the river bank, be sure to tread as stealthily as though chub fishing. In small clear-flowing river systems especially, the largest pike are often lying within mere feet of the bank. A heavy footfall or your shadow cast upon the skyline prior to the first cast along a tempting run might well preclude any action from that particular spot. In fact I rate the occurrence as no coincidence that many a big pike taken from clear-flowing, overgrown rivers, has taken the bait on that very first trot down.

The answer is to travel light with just one outfit plus net and all sundry items in your waistcoat or jacket pockets, making full use of bankside cover in the way of tall reed beds or overhanging trees. To ensure the baits remain fresh, clip a small battery-operated aeration pump to the side of the bucket and do not fill it with water. You need just a few inches slopping about and this helps aerate it naturally.

Unfortunately the majority of anglers seem to credit pike with less intelligence or at the very least a lower degree of natural caution than most other species. Whether it is because they have teeth and do occasionally make suicidal attacks of gay abandon, such as grabbing a fish hooked on the way in whilst ledgering or float fishing, I don't really know. But you can be sure that throughout most of their lives pike are extremely wary predators (otherwise they get eaten), so treat them with the respect they deserve.

STRIKING

Lastly let me say a few words on the art of striking pike because, having watched countless anglers pike fishing over the years, I would hazard a guess that a fair proportion of fish are lost due to the fact that the hooks were never driven in on the strike in the first place. The secret is winding tightly down to the fish once the float has gone and those knocking trembles have been transmitted up the line (a lovely feeling) until its weight can actually be felt with the rod tip pointing directly at the pike. Then, and only then, drive the rod back overhead in a powerful sweeping strike so it curves into a full bend. Keep winding and don't allow the rod tip to straighten at any time whilst pumping, so that when the pike eventually senses danger and opens its jaws in that head-shaking, gill-flaring routine in an effort to rid itself of the bait, the bait moves under considerable torque and the hooks will find purchase. Remember that until the pike opens its chops it is actually impossible for the hooks to dig in. Proof that the bait is clamped so tightly is occasionally experienced when at no time throughout the fight does the pike open its jaws, except when it's a few feet away from the net, whereupon just when you've slackened off as a landing precaution, it promptly opens its jaws and flings the bait clear.

Marketing Manager of Ryobi Masterline, Chris Liebbrant, long trots a float-fished livebait down a deep run along Hampshire's River Test.

FLOAT PATERNOSTERING FOR PREDATORS

By employing this immensely versatile method of float fishing, using a large slider (usually a through-the-middle predator float) numerous problems can be instantly overcome whilst seeking predators like perch, zander, pike and even chub. You may wish for instance, simply to present a livebait above bottom weed and snags, or within a small gap in dense weed beds, or indeed at any depth between bottom and the surface of extremely deep water, whether float fishing or ledgering in still water. Or you might want to place a livebait close to a particular lie or feature in either still or running water, without having to reposition it every few minutes or whenever it succeeds in outrunning interested predators.

RODS AND REELS

A general pike-fishing outfit comprising 11–12-foot, 2–2¼lb test curve rod and a 3000 size format reel well filled with 10–12lb test should suffice for all heavy work. It can prove more enjoyable to scale down for zander and especially when after perch or chub, where an 11–12-foot, 1¼lb test curve Avon-action rod and small fixed-spool reel coupled to a 6lb line is the perfect combo.

RUNNING PATERNOSTER SURFACE FLOAT RIGS

Pike and Zander

In really coloured water when free-roaming livebaits can easily outrun predators and particularly in extremely cold water conditions when predators slow right down and are not always even willing to pursue a lively bait, positioning that bait in a chosen area allows the predator more time to home in on its vibratory pulses, making some immediate action far more likely. There are occasions when this method decidedly outfishes all others by a mile, proving devastatingly effective. This is especially so where pike and specimen zander are hotspotted in confined areas. Consider Diag. 100, Fig. A, for example, which although basic in design is most effective for supporting a livebait at any given depth from 2 feet above bottom upwards.

As Dave Batten is obviously well aware, float paternostering is one of the most successful methods of catching zander. But scale down to an Avon outfit for enjoying their fight.

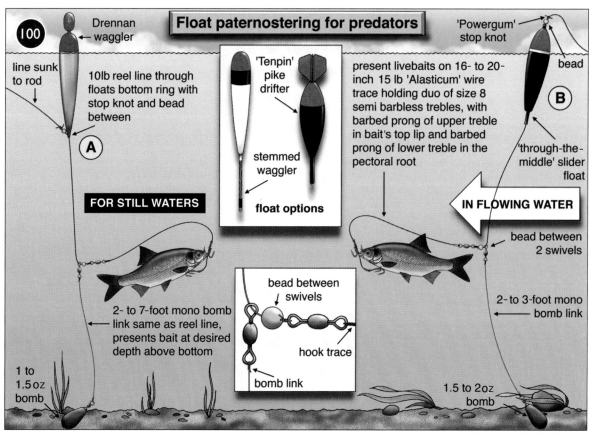

John dispenses with wire when purely seeking chub or perch, like this bristling 2½ pounder, and uses small livebaits on a size 6–4 hook tied to a 16-inch mono trace.

When distance fishing for pike and zander in still water, or whenever conditions are extremely rough and there is a subsurface tow, a bottom end sliding float is preferable (to a through-the-middle float) because the line needs to be sunk between float and rod tip. Otherwise wind movement will continually drag the rig out of position. However, for close-range work in still waters when fishing immediately downwind and particularly when river fishing, whether from a boat or the bank, a through-the-middle slider is imperative, (as shown in Fig. B) to keep the line on or actually above the surface. Give it a good treatment of mucilin at the start of the session.

Note how the livebait is mounted on a 16–20-inch, 15lb wire trace holding a pair of size 8 semi-barbless trebles, with one barbed point of the bottom hook in the pectoral root and the barbed point of the

upper hook carefully nicked into the bait's top lip. This provides for maximum movement of the livebait allowing it to swim freely about within the radius of the trace. To maximize on covering any given area, wind the rig in 2 or 3 yards every ten to fifteen minutes – always at the ready for an instant take upon repositioning.

As for bait, I like 5–7-inch roach, dace or chub for pike, and dace or large gudgeon when zander are the target species. Whatever the predator, don't be tempted into using rudd when float paternostering because they have a nasty habit of spiralling upwards and are past masters at tangling the rig.

Perch and Chub

Perch enthusiasts can happily use a scaled-down version but exactly the same running paternoster float

rig (as in Diag. 101, Fig. A), virtually regardless of swim depth, except that the wire trace is replaced by a 16-inch monofilament (same as reel line) trace holding a single size 6–4 hook nicked through the bait's top lip only for maximum manoeuvrability and consistent hooking. If you are worried about the single hook working itself out once the bait is on, simply push a ¼-inch length of wide elastic band over the point so it lodges behind the barb (as in Fig. B).

The small ¾–1oz bomb used on the link may be replaced by sufficient 2 x SSG or 3 x SSG shots for fine tuning the rig. These jumbo-sized shots have an added benefit when fishing over dense bottom weed or amongst snags, old tree roots and the like, in that they easily slide off the link if not pinched on too tightly, allowing a snagged rig or even a hooked fish to be retrieved with minimal loss. It is

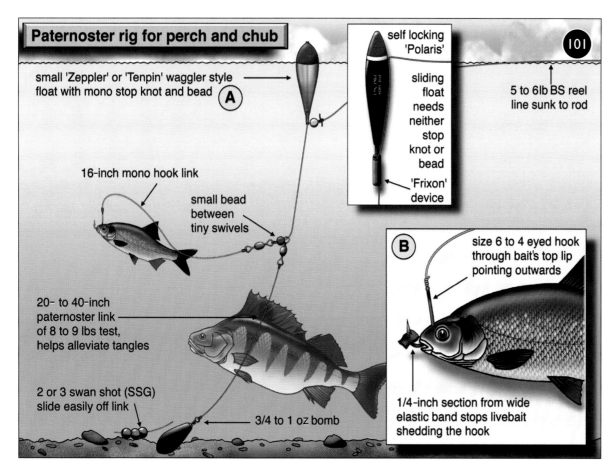

Paternoster rig for perch and chub

small 'Zeppler' or 'Tenpin' waggler style float with mono stop knot and bead (A)

16-inch mono hook link

small bead between tiny swivels

20- to 40-inch paternoster link of 8 to 9 lbs test, helps alleviate tangles

2 or 3 swan shot (SSG) slide easily off link

3/4 to 1 oz bomb

self locking 'Polaris'

sliding float needs neither stop knot or bead

'Frixon' device

101

5 to 6lb BS reel line sunk to rod

(B) size 6 to 4 eyed hook through bait's top lip pointing outwards

1/4-inch section from wide elastic band stops livebait shedding the hook

worthwhile making the link heavier (say 8–9lb test mono) which helps to avoid tangles associated with the thinner 5–6lb reel line. (Lines of the same diameter always tangle more easily.) Incidentally, for coming to grips with big perch and chub inhabiting deep and fast mill or weir pools this rig really is the business.

To combat fast currents, use a fairly heavy bomb and a medium-sized through-the-middle slider with the rod tip supported high up on two rod rests so that the line stays clear of the surface from rod to float. Otherwise, swirling currents will drag the rig (if a bottom end slider is used) uncontrollably around, possibly into snags. Finally, remember that with chub it is imperative to strike immediately the float shoots under, or the bait will be ejected quickly either minus

its rear end or minced to pieces by the chub's powerful pharyngeal teeth situated in the back of its throat.

Line Retention

May I suggest here that you make it a practice never to fish this method with a closed bale arm or you could witness an expensive rod and reel combo go for a dive never to be seen again. After casting open the bale arm and simply slip a loop of reel line beneath a plastic run clip on the rod handle opposite the spool, or beneath an elastic band, enabling the float to be pulled under and a fish to take a few feet on line without resistance before the strike is made. Obviously baitrunner-type reels are particularly suited to this form of presentation,

because even with the bale arm closed a fish is allowed to run and take line under the very lightest spool tension which is not going to make it drop the bait.

Built-in Plummet

The beauty of float paternostering is that finding the correct depth is never a problem because the rig has a built-in plummet in the way of the link bomb. As a general guide the float's sliding stop knot needs to be set at 1–3 feet over depth to allow for the angle the rig takes on once you have tightened up and retained a loop of line after opening the bale arm. Whenever the float is set too shallow and goes zooming under on the cast, simply reposition the sliding stop knot further up the line, remembering to wet the line first with saliva to minimize the chances of line fracture due to heat caused by excessive friction.

I find it pays to make a few exploratory casts (obviously without bait) when tackling previously unfished waters in order to gain an idea of depth fluctuations. Due for instance to the way in which mineral deposits are excavated from gravel pits, depth can vary enormously as much as several feet over very short distances. So learn to use the float paternoster's built-in plummet facility to your advantage right from the start, because it will help you build up a mental picture of bottom topography.

Subfloat Paternoster Ledgering

Whenever float fishing in still water with the running paternoster proves impossible due to the excessive distances involved, dense bottom weed, or nasty snags, or when gale-force winds preclude any kind of surface float being seen, incorporating a subfloat with a standard running paternoster rig is the answer. Simply slide a clear plastic Drennan subfloat (or a black-painted through-the-middle slider) on to the

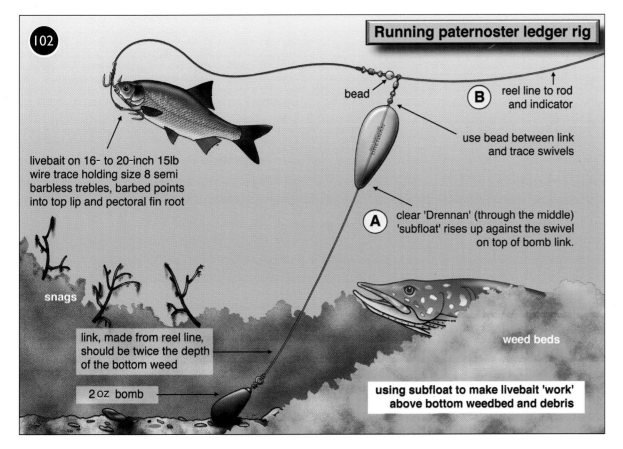

102

Running paternoster ledger rig

livebait on 16- to 20-inch 15lb wire trace holding size 8 semi barbless trebles, barbed points into top lip and pectoral fin root

bead

reel line to rod and indicator

B

use bead between link and trace swivels

A clear 'Drennan' (through the middle) 'subfloat' rises up against the swivel on top of bomb link.

snags

link, made from reel line, should be twice the depth of the bottom weed

weed beds

2 oz bomb

using subfloat to make livebait 'work' above bottom weedbed and debris

Tackle designer and perch fishing fanatic, Alan Pierce, used a sub-float paternoster rig to good effect for this big still-water stripey.

link before tying on to the running swivel (as in Diag. 102, Fig. A). This of course will rise and ensure the bait works well above bottom debris. Actual bomb link length depends entirely on the distance above bottom at which you want the livebait to work. And as the link will lie at around a 45-degree angle once you have tightened up to the rig and clipped on an indicator (as in Diag. 102, Fig. B) I suggest it should be at least twice that of bottom weed or debris height.

Indicators

After casting, quickly sink the rod tip (to alleviate any kind of subsurface bow) and gently tighten up without pulling the bomb into snags or weed. Open the bale arm before slipping a loop of line beneath an elastic band, or a run clip positioned on the rod

handle directly opposite the reel if using an electronic bite alarm and bobbin or monkey climber set-up.

Although clipping a simple drop-arm-type indicator on to the line and opening the bale arm is far more sensitive, particularly when using units incorporating an LED buzzer alarm, actual bait movement can prove to be immensely irritating. So you may also need to clip up a loop of line as already mentioned. An excellent all-round electronic bite indicator for subfloat paternoster ledgering is the Fox Micron PS bite indicator which has a pressure release that instantly switches off the alarm when the rod is lifted from the unit. It operates on a mercury tilt action which lights up both the LED in the buzzer unit (screwed into the rear bank stick) and the indicator head, on a

forward take or a drop-back bite. The high visibility red head incorporates a betalight slot for night fishing and a fully adjustable line clip which goes on to the line immediately below the spool with the bale arm open.

If a run does not materialize after, say, ten to fifteen minutes, ease the rig up by raising the rod tip high and wind in gently for several yards before resetting the indicator. This can be repeated several times during the one cast, to ensure a wide area is covered by the bait, unless dense weed beds or known bottom snags restrict its passage.

FLOAT TRAILING FOR PIKE

This devastatingly effective method for pike fishing from a boat in both slow-moving river systems and large still waters, particularly reservoirs and lochs or loughs, is also referred to as slow-mode trailing. This term is perhaps more apt because there are situations where a float is in fact not used. The technique can also be put to good use when in search of predators like perch and zander so, while the following text is geared specifically to catching pike, simply scale down your tackle and bait size accordingly.

Trailing, which means exactly that, consists of drifting, motoring (using an electric outboard) or rowing along whilst trailing the baits 10–30 yards (or further) behind the boat. As trolling under power is illegal on many of our English inland waterways,

trailing is the next best thing and some would even say a more versatile and deadly method for producing the whoppers because, by careful manipulation of the oars or electric motor, baits can be slowly trailed really close up beside feature hotspots like overhanging trees, piled banking, weir sills and the like and over bottom structures to which pike are attracted. Sudden drop-offs in still waters immediately come to mind here as do troughs and gullies between islands or running parallel to a shoreline. Such feature areas are also commonly found in many of our really large gravel-pit complexes. So if the local club permits the use of a boat, get out there and make full use of all these potential pike hotspots.

For this you really do need to invest some dosh in a sonar/fish-finder unit, if only for the instant bottom read-out it provides as you row or motor along. To plumb and mark in depth contours on a makeshift map manually or, worse still, to rely on memory alone as to what the depth was and where even a comparatively small area, is not very practicable. You can be many yards out when guessing and for trailing the bait really close to feature lies, or bottom-hugging structures, this is simply too inaccurate.

In very thick soupy water, for instance, the bait can be worked really slowly whilst trailing whether by oar or electric motor. The method has enormous potential and is extremely versatile, allowing you to work a pair of rods quite comfortably when fishing alone, even when rowing, while two anglers sharing a boat can easily work a pair of rods apiece – but I would suggest no more. Before we go any further, however, let's run over the tackle required.

John can't fathom why Dave Batten is looking so happy during a trailing-for-pike trip out on Ardleigh Reservoir in Essex. They both blanked.

RODS, REELS, LINES AND TERMINAL SET-UPS

In order to angle the lines away from the boat I prefer to use long rods when trailing, and 12-foot carbon-fibre, medium tip actioned models with a 2–2¼lb test curve fit the bill admirably. Fixed-spool reels in the 3000 format, particularly those incorporating a free spool/baitrunner facility, are ideal for trailing in that line can be instantly taken by a pike without feeling undue resistance provided spool tension in the free spool mode is adjusted accordingly. For this very reason my personal preference is for a multiplying reel in the 6000–6500 format which is simply left in free spool with the ratchet on during trailing or in gear but on a light clutch setting. Pike can then grab hold and even belt off with only the minimum of resistance, and the ratchet's squeal relates to how fast and how far it is running. You might almost say the sound is music to your ears! The choice between fixed spool and multiplying reels is, I admit, based purely on personal preference. Indeed those who enjoy the simplicity of using a centre pin will find trailing from a boat a most enjoyable method because there is no casting involved. The centre pin's ratchet is engaged throughout the trail and so it indicates a run by squealing like a stuck pig, just like a multiplier. Should the pressure or the movements of a lively bait repeatedly make the ratchet click over, simply retain a loop of line beneath an elastic band on the rod handle immediately above the centre pin. Any sudden or really fast run will then instantly pull the loop out and allow the reel to give line freely without resistance other than the audible ratchet.

An ideal line strength to match the 2–2¼lb test curve rods recommend is around 10–13lb test. When big water trailing however in Irish loughs or trout reservoirs where monster pike are on the

A float-trailed rainbow trout livebait set to work near the bottom over 20 feet down produced this reservoir twenty.

cards, as a safeguard line strength may be increased to 15lb test – monofilament and not braid. Although I have recommended the latter for trolling, downrigger trolling and drift float fishing, for the comparatively short-range method of trailing, a monofilament line provides just the right amount of elasticity.

If you are equipped with a standard fixed-spool reel, don't despair. Simply slacken off the clutch with the bale arm and anti-reverse lever both engaged, until a pike can pull off line freely. But do not have it so loose that the spool rotates as the oars or motor trail the bait along. When a run occurs you simply need to readjust the slipping clutch quickly before striking, that's all.

TERMINAL RIGS

Now for terminal rigs of which there are two completely different set-ups: one with a float; one without. The most popular and most enjoyable, because we all love to watch a float, is the sliding float rig shown in Diag. 103, Fig. A. It is a simple set-up really with a through-the-middle sliding float set a few feet deeper than swim (to allow for the angle at which the line is trailed behind the boat) with a bead and power-gum stopper. As can be seen from Fig. B, to keep the bait down close to the bottom and cock the float, a bullet, egg or barrel lead is fixed on the line over a protective sleeve of fine-diameter silicone tubing immediately above the trace swivel. To ensure the lead does not slide up the line (which could minimize a flat float bite should a pike swim upwards with the bait), push the end of the silicone tubing over the trace swivel (as Fig. C). For this reason I particularly like the Fox Pike Systems egg sinkers which are not in fact lead, but made from precision-turned brass finished in black zinc, because they incorporate an internal protective sleeve with a silicone rubber tube at the bottom end for pushing over the trace swivel.

The trace itself should be 20 inches long and made from 15lb test braided alasticum or seven-strand wire holding a duo of size 8 or 6 (depending upon bait size) semibarbless trebles. To mount livebaits simply push the barbed prong of the upper treble into the bait's top lip, with the barbed prong of the bottom hook nicked into its pectoral roof (as in Fig. D). Should pike be repeatedly missed due to the bait being aborted quickly (educated whoppers can do this on popular reservoir fisheries with frustrating regularity), set the lowest hook into the bait's pelvic, or anal fin roof (as Figs E and F) and strike immediately the float goes.

When float trailing deadbaits, which are particularly effective in thickly coloured water with a visibility of mere inches, work two prongs of the top treble into the fish's eye socket and just the barbed prong of the bottom treble midway down the flank. If trailing alone using two rods, one over each side to avoid tangles, work one bait on a short line, say 10 yards behind the boat, and the second 20–30 yards away or even further if the water is clear and the pike well educated. Specialist rod rests are essential for trailing, whether you use a simple shepherd's crook and U, or an automatic Down-East rod rest (see Method 29, 'Trolling for Pike'). These should be fixed on to the gunnel within 2 feet of the stern, so that each rod is angled out and upwards in order to keep much of the line between float and rod tip above the surface.

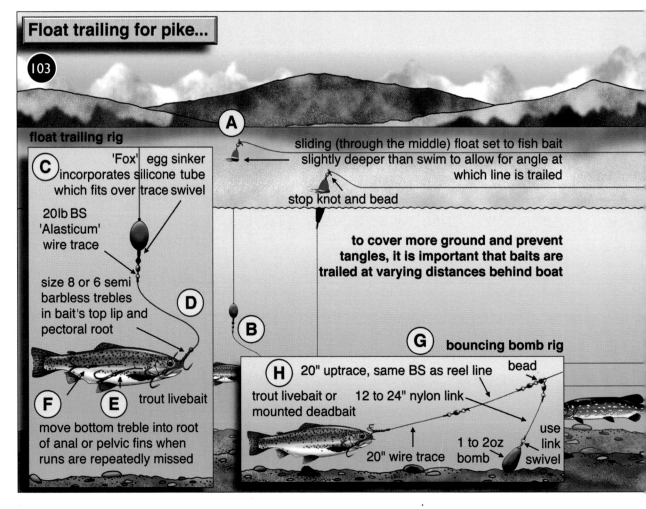

Float trailing for pike...

103

float trailing rig

C 'Fox' egg sinker incorporates silicone tube which fits over trace swivel

20lb BS 'Alasticum' wire trace

size 8 or 6 semi barbless trebles in bait's top lip and pectoral root

D

F E trout livebait

move bottom treble into root of anal or pelvic fins when runs are repeatedly missed

A

sliding (through the middle) float set to fish bait slightly deeper than swim to allow for angle at which line is trailed

stop knot and bead

to cover more ground and prevent tangles, it is important that baits are trailed at varying distances behind boat

B

G bouncing bomb rig

H 20" uptrace, same BS as reel line bead

trout livebait or 12 to 24" nylon link
mounted deadbait

use link swivel

20" wire trace 1 to 2oz bomb

With two anglers sharing a boat, two rod rests on each side is not a problem, indeed being able to work a combination of four rigs set at varying distances behind the boat really does maximize on potential. But you do need to be well disciplined within the confines of a boat and decide in advance who does what. For instance, one can take care of the rowing or working the electric motor whilst studying the fish finder read-out for changes of depth, snags or fish-packed features, while the second attends to the rods, reels and baiting up whilst also keeping his eye on the sonar and the floats of course. It's a great team effort, for in truth who knows which bait will be taken next?

You'll find you need plenty of room when trailing

four outfits behind a moving boat in popular pike fisheries, so be sure to allow plenty of time to manoeuvre a turn, and give all other craft (particularly when river fishing) a wide berth. It may be elementary but don't forget the rule of flowing water is that you drive on the right.

Another way of presenting deadbaits, and livebaits of course, dispenses with the float altogether. This is shown in Fig. G and is called the bouncing bomb rig, because the bomb literally bounces along the bottom ensuring that the live or deadbait is worked through that taking depth band just above bottom (within 2 feet anyway) of where the pike are lying.

This rig works best when trailed reasonably close

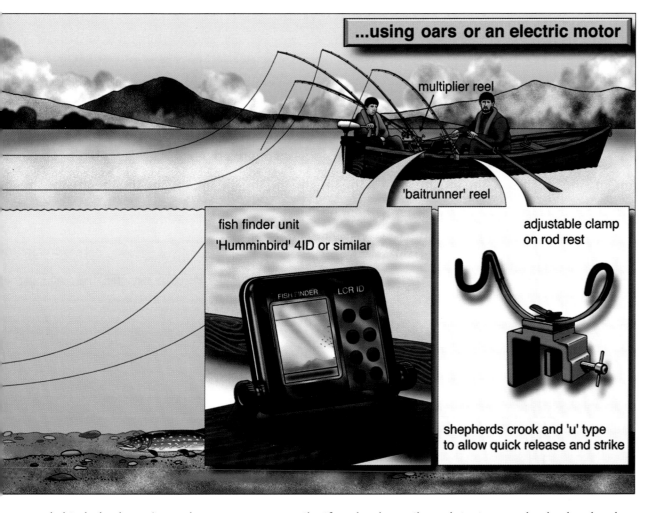

...using oars or an electric motor

multiplier reel

'baitrunner' reel

fish finder unit
'Humminbird' 4ID or similar

FISH FINDER LCR ID

adjustable clamp
on rod rest

shepherds crook and 'u' type
to allow quick release and strike

you have the chance of quickly confirming which is likely to be the most productive rig on the day and in the conditions prevailing.

BAITS

In reservoirs that for most of the year are trout fisheries, and which allow pike fishing only throughout the winter, the most effective bait by far is a live trout. Forward-thinking fishery managers actually sell suitable-sized trout (6–10 inches) on site for pike fishermen and I wish many more would follow suit. Their winter trade in renting out boats would, I am sure, increase tenfold.

Where trout are not available however I rate roach as probably the most durable livebaits. They make ideal deadbaits for trailing too, as do herrings, smelt, mullet and large sand eels, freshness being the key word here. So take your frozen deadbaits along in a coolbag or box, and to ensure livebaits stay active, hang them over the side of the boat in a plastic bucket well drilled with holes (for the water to pass through) and secured at the top with a circle of old netting held in place with heavy duty elastic. It's well worth the trouble.

behind the boat (it tends to snag more easily if worked too far behind) and consists of a 12–24-inch mono bomb link with snap swivel (to facilitate quick bomb changing) at the bottom and a size 10 swivel at the top running on the reel line (with a bead between) above the swivel of the 20-inch mono uptrace (Fig. H). A 20-inch, 15lb braided alasticum or seven-strand wire trace with size 8 or 6 semibarbless trebles completes the rig. The reason for a separate uptrace is that it helps wonderfully in averting would-be tangles and ensures the bait is sufficiently far enough behind the bomb link. Incidentally where snags are commonplace, construct the bomb link from just 4–5lb test so it

breaks easily and jettisons only the bomb when caught up.

You can bump and bounce the bait along at a slow oar or engineer speed, pausing every so often to allow a deadbait for instance to flutter attractively downwards, before lifting it up again. Or even stop altogether for several seconds to present a completely static bait, perhaps paying out line from the reel (if actually holding just the one rod throughout) before working it back towards the boat again.

To make pike trailing more interesting any combination of float and bouncing bomb rigs may be used. It's really a horse for a course situation. But at least by simultaneously trying different options

OARS OR ELECTRIC MOTOR?

When trailing throughout an all-day session, keeping the boat moving by oars alone can prove extremely tiring particularly against strong winds. The answer of course though expensive, is to invest (go half each) in an environmentally friendly electric outboard motor, which will run silently all day long on a fully charged heavy duty 12-volt car battery.

Models in the American Minn Kota range are considered to be the best around, due to their variable speed throttle which permits exceedingly slow speeds to be maintained even into the teeth of a strong wind. And with instant reverse and neutral settings, there is

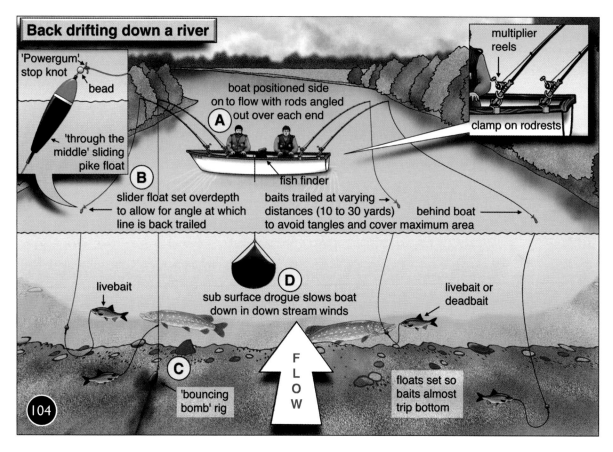

Back drifting down a river

'Powergum' stop knot

bead

'through the middle' sliding pike float

(A) boat positioned side on to flow with rods angled out over each end

(B) slider float set overdepth to allow for angle at which line is back trailed

fish finder

baits trailed at varying → distances (10 to 30 yards) to avoid tangles and cover maximum area

behind boat →

multiplier reels

clamp on rodrests

livebait

sub surface drogue slows boat down in down stream winds

(D)

livebait or deadbait

(C) 'bouncing bomb' rig

F L O W

floats set so baits almost trip bottom

104

no way any petrol-driven engine could even begin to compete. Incidentally, it's worth noting that many fishery owners who ban petrol outboards are sympathetic to anglers using silent electric motors, a situation I am glad to say that exists on several of the Norfolk Broads I fish – not, I hasten to add, for actually trolling or trailing baits on the Broadland system because this is illegal, simply for getting from one spot to another. When out on a 100-acre-plus broad in a cold, blustery wind, the electric motor knocks spots off rowing any day of the week.

Something you will quickly find out when trailing with an electric motor, however, is the temptation to go faster than you actually need to. The result, of course, is that the float-trailed bait rises much higher in the water than is required for pike lying on the bottom to see it. So, if anything, trail slower than

faster, keeping a constant eye on the floats and on the rod tip presenting the bouncing bomb rig, so you can stop the engine and hold steady in position in an instant of a bait being grabbed to minimize resistance.

BACK TRAILING/DRIFTING

I'm not sure whether to call this particular technique back trailing or back drifting, but I am going to opt for the latter because that's what the method is called in Brazil along the fabulous Parana River, near Foz, where I first used it to good effect to catch the legendary golden dourado of South America.

It is a unique technique that requires propulsion neither by oars nor engine, simply the river's current (or a strong wind ripping across a still water) to drift the boat steadily downstream. As can be seen in

Diag. 104, Fig. A, the boat is positioned side on to the flow before commencing a drift, having used the fish finder/sonar to locate a potential pike-holding reach, whereupon the trailed baits on both sliding float (Fig. B) and bouncing bomb rigs (Fig. C) are set at varying distances behind the boat. As with trailing over the stern the rods in this instance are angled, to fish over each end of the boat. Therefore, all rests (assuming two anglers are working four rods between them) are attached to the upstream gunnel.

Incidentally, to slow the drift down when a strong downstream wind is fair ripping the boat (and of course the baits) along too fast, put a reservoir trout-fishing drogue over the upstream side (Fig. D). It will make all the difference and slow the boat right down to current speed.

Another extremely effective method to use when back drifting down a river (or across a large still water in a steady wind) is shown in Diag. 105 and is more or less how the locals in Brazil catch dourado from the mighty Parana River, which incidentally in places is up to ½ mile wide, averages 100 feet deep throughout its centre channel and flows at up to 8 knots. Formidable indeed, yet by using only a small barrel lead above a wire trace and 6/0 hook baited with a live morineta and by casting 20–40 yards upstream, it is possible to get the bait quickly down to the rocky bottom and to keep it within that taking depth band in depths of up to 40–50 feet by paying out a little line every so often throughout a drift covering at least several hundred yards. One reason why I prefer to use a multiplier for back drifting is that line is instantly paid out simply through gentle thumb pressure on the free spool release bar, whereas with a fixed spool you need to be constantly opening and closing the bale arm.

Having enjoyed this Brazilian back drifting method, I have since used it (with a few changes) to good effect on all my local tidal rivers such as the deep and coloured Yare, Waveney and Bure, for twitching a deadbait along close to the bottom. As can be seen from Fig. A, the deadbait is mounted on a 16-inch 15lb test alasticum wire trace and two trebles as you would for wobbling (see Method 30, 'Wobbling Deadbaits') with between two and four swan shot pinched on the trace immediately below the swivel. I find the best baits are silver-sided fish, like herrings, roach and smelt which, being oval in cross section, are also not over-heavy. Round bodied fish, such as mackerel, are size for size much heavier and consequently do not flutter so attractively, in addition to sinking faster and possibly fouling bottom more easily.

The cast is made 20–40 yards upstream (as in Fig. B) and the bait allowed to sink with the reel's bale arm open (or the multiplier in free spool) until it touches bottom (Fig. C). You then engage the reel and gently twitch the bait upwards using rod-tip movement only

(do not wind) and allowing it to pause for between one and three seconds, before gently twitching it again (as in Fig. E). This erratic, wobbling action is repeated throughout the drift (as in Fig. D) until you feel that sudden bang or jerk on the rod tip of a pike grabbing hold. Now at this point my advice is to wind down until all is tight and strike instantly. OK, so you'll lose some jacks and maybe even the occasional better-sized pike which haven't quite got the hooks far enough inside their jaws but I find that even more fish will be missed if line is given and you wait for a positive traditional-type run to develop as though presenting a static deadbait. A fair proportion will in fact not run off and upon feeling resistance promptly drop the bait.

In readiness for a take remember to have a mudweight (with the rope tied up) close to hand which, upon striking and getting the pike under

control, can be immediately lowered single handed down to the bottom, assuming you are alone. This accomplishes two things: it stops you passing over an area yet to be worked and, after with luck landing and unhooking the first pike, it allows you to cover the bottom more thoroughly where it grabbed hold, on the assumption that there might be others around. I have in fact enjoyed some bumper hauls under exactly these circumstances and it provides a puzzle as to why so many pike are all grouped up within such a small area of river. No doubt a large concentration of bait fish has been situated close by. For this reason keep your eyes glued to the fish finder throughout the drift for dense shoals of small bait fish and for any sudden change in depth or snags. It is then a simple matter to adjust the working of the bait accordingly.

Back drifting a wobbled bait in this way calls for holding the rod throughout and much concentration. So unless working a really sluggish river where constant attention to either a float-trailed or bounced bait on a second sleeper outfit is not required, keep with just the one rod. You'll probably account for more pike by the end of the day as a result.

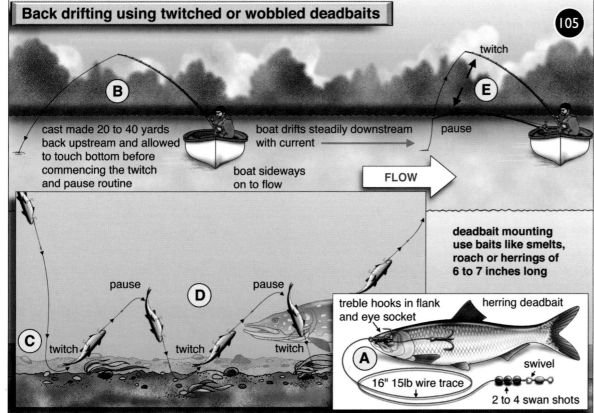

Back drifting using twitched or wobbled deadbaits

105

twitch

B

E

pause

cast made 20 to 40 yards back upstream and allowed to touch bottom before commencing the twitch and pause routine

boat drifts steadily downstream with current

boat sideways on to flow

FLOW

deadbait mounting use baits like smelts, roach or herrings of 6 to 7 inches long

pause

D

pause

C

twitch

twitch

twitch

treble hooks in flank and eye socket

herring deadbait

A

16" 15lb wire trace

swivel

2 to 4 swan shots

Note how Jason Davies can keep an eye on the floats and sonar/fish finder unit while slowly trailing with an electric motor. A heavy duty battery is essential.

LEDGERING LIVE AND DEADBAITS FOR PERCH, EELS, CATFISH, ZANDER AND PIKE

There are numerous occasions when ledgering either a live or deadbait is far more effective than float fishing. Use this method when fishing at extreme range (say 60 yards plus) and especially when fishing into strong facing or cross winds which make any kind of surface float rig not only a waste of time but a liability in that the bait will consequently be dragged away from the intended area. And of course it is useful in rivers, when float fishing any further out than stret-pegging range becomes impracticable. There are occasions (for presentation over bottom weed, for example) which demand the use of a subfloat when ledgering livebaits and one of the most effective rigs is the sunken float paternoster which is rather like the bottom end of the running float paternoster. For this reason it is included in Method 26, 'Float Paternostering for Predators' (see page 197, Diag. 102).

POP-UP SURFACE/LEDGER CATFISH RIG

Now an extremely versatile and quite unique rig can be seen in Diag. 106, but I cannot take the credit for

thinking this one up. It was passed on to me by catfish expert Richard Bowler of Dunstable in Bedfordshire who regularly fishes during darkness for wels catfish in deep clay and sand pits at distances of up to 60 yards using small livebaits.

Casting out livebaits is of course completely out of the question when fishing beyond say 10–15 yards, as the impact alone would kill them. But with this clever rig, which allows you to wind the livebait out gently to wherever you wish, the problem of bait attractiveness and condition is solved completely.

It works like this. First of all make up the end rig (shown in Fig. A) by threading on to the 15lb reel line a 3oz bomb to which a ½-inch diameter plastic curtain ring is attached via a snap link clip. Next, using a needle, make a centre hole through a ½-inch diameter poly ball and thread the line through before

As Paul Curtis is experiencing, it is often easier to catch pussies than hold them. This 10 pounder fell to ledgered mussel but, for night owls, the pop-up surface rig is the business.

tying on a snap link swivel. Incidentally, don't be tempted into using a bomb lighter than 3oz, as it might become dislodged and make the following routine impossible to implement.

Now, and here's the clever part, don't clip on the specialized braided hook trace shown in Fig. B just yet. Have an extra rod (butt end only) at the ready (Fig. C), the reel filled with just 4lb test, and tie on a snap link swivel. Clip this to the link on the catfish rod and whack out the 3oz lead (so that both lines go out over the lake) to the desired spot, ensuring the additional 4lb line has a free path during the cast and doesn't tangle. A friend can hold this second rod, or it can be propped up with the butt ring facing the direction of the cast.

Once the lead has settled, place your catfish rod

on two rests and open the bale arm. Now slowly wind in the 4lb line on the second (butt section) rod and watch line peel from the catfish reel as you reel in the snap link swivel tied to the 15lb test. When the snap link swivel has been retrieved, simply clip on your baited trace and pick up the catfish rod, winding the livebait slowly out into the lake and up to the 3oz bomb.

As you can see from Fig. B, the trace itself is constructed from 20 inches of 35lb braid (quick silver or similar) which has greater abrasion resistance than monofilament against the bristle-pad teeth of wels catfish. To the shank of a size 1 Drennan boilie hook is tied several inches of 15lb test mono and, using a needle, two ¾-inch diameter poly balls are threaded on and tied (around the top ball) to secure. As an

extra precaution a BB shot is pinched on below the lower ball so it fits tight on what is actually a mono hair. Note that a short length of narrow-diameter silicone tubing is sleeved along the hook shank covering both eye and the mono hair knot. Use a barrel-type spade end knot for this (see Diag. 41, page 95).

The best baits are 4–6-inch roach, bream or hybrids which are hooked on immediately below the dorsal fin root. To ensure against it coming off, simply slip on a ⅓-inch section of wide elastic band over the barb. And for viewing the bait's movement during darkness a luminous, chemical element is pushed into the top poly ball.

When slowly winching the bait out (through the large curtain ring on the bomb) it's worth taking

time so it remains lively and when directly over the bomb tightening up so that only one poly ball shows on the surface. If you allow the bait too much freedom, catfish may well miss as they lunge to swallow it in that glorious tail-slapping eruption. At this point a delay will be noticed between seeing the float disappear (often in an appreciable swirl) and a run developing whilst the cat returns back down to the lake bed. So be ready for winding down to the fish and a powerful sweepback strike in order to bang that hook home. Incidentally, if you do actually witness the float zooming under it's better from this point on to disregard the rod indicator by pulling it off, lifting the rod and simply feeling what's happening by holding the line gently between thumb and forefinger.

Now there is no reason whatsoever why this unique method of literally winching out the livebait (or a heavy deadbait too weighty for casting) to any distance within the range of a 3oz bomb cannot be employed when seeking other predators, particularly pike. Indeed its applications are endless and for those far-off hotspots which for various reasons cannot be reached by drift fishing or by boat I can foresee enormous potential. Simply swap the braided hook length and poly ball set-up for a live or deadbait mounted in the usual way on a duo of trebles and wire trace. Obviously a small poly ball or subfloat can be used above the trace to keep a livebait working over bottom weed or debris.

BASIC RUNNING LEDGER RIG FOR EELS AND CATFISH

Whether ledgering large baits such as a small whole squid, swan mussel or perhaps a freshly killed deadbait for these two species (and I cannot stress the importance of freshness enough) you will need the following set-up.

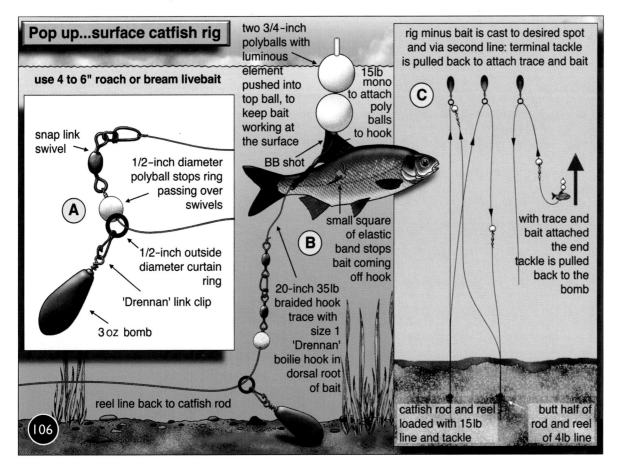

Pop up...surface catfish rig

use 4 to 6" roach or bream livebait

snap link swivel

1/2-inch diameter polyball stops ring passing over swivels

A

1/2-inch outside diameter curtain ring

'Drennan' link clip

3oz bomb

106

reel line back to catfish rod

two 3/4-inch polyballs with luminous element pushed into top ball, to keep bait working at the surface

BB shot

15lb mono to attach poly balls to hook

small square of elastic band stops bait coming off hook

B

20-inch 35lb braided hook trace with size 1 'Drennan' boilie hook in dorsal root of bait

rig minus bait is cast to desired spot and via second line: terminal tackle is pulled back to attach trace and bait

C

with trace and bait attached the end tackle is pulled back to the bomb

catfish rod and reel loaded with 15lb line and tackle

butt half of rod and reel of 4lb line

This running ledger deadbait rig for pike benefits from a small (black-painted) poly ball wired on to the bottom treble which tantalizingly raises the mackerel tail.

Tackle

Suitable reel line strength varies between 12 and 15lb. This largely depends upon the size of fish expected or which are known to exist in the water being fished and the presence of, or lack of, any nearby snags like sunken trees where that extra strength in reserve may be required to stop fish from reaching them. If in doubt, fish heavier rather than lighter.

A powerful through-action 11–12-foot pike-carp rod with a test curve of around 2¼–2½lb, coupled to a fixed-spool reel in the 3000 size format, is the ideal combination for subduing the backwards gyrating fight unique to eels and catfish. As you can see from Diag. 107 the rod is set low to the water on two rests pointing directly at the bait with an electronic bite alarm as the front rod rest.

Bite Indication

Upon casting out and gently tightening up to the ledger bomb, open the reel's bale arm and fix a lightweight coil-type indicator (silver kitchen foil is perfect) around the line and slip over a long (monkey climber) needle pushed into the ground, angled towards the bite alarm. Whenever really gusty conditions or a strong surface drift continually move the indicator along the needle and register false bites, simply retain a small loop of line beneath a tiny run clip or an elastic band on the rod just ahead of the alarm. This permits an eel or pussy to pull the line out when running off with the bait without feeling undue resistance.

See how my running ledger consists of a 20-inch section of mono (same as reel line) above the hook trace with a swivel at each end. This stops the running bomb ledger, cushioned by a small bead against the top swivel, from wanting to tangle with the hook trace and causing a fish to eject the bait. When fishing close to snags, make the 5-inch bomb link from much weaker line (4–5lb test) as it will instantly break if snagged and permit a hooked fish to be landed. Otherwise use slightly heavier line for this link as lines of the same size tend to tangle more easily. Covering the mono link with fine-diameter stiff rig tubing will help enormously.

Traces

As for the hook trace, the choice lies between braid or wire for eels and braid or mono for pussies. Overall, the best choice has to be braid. Modern non-stretch braided lines are so incredibly supple and of considerably less diameter than monofilament of the same test, meaning you can use an abrasion resistant 35–45lb hook trace that is actually thinner than 20lb monofilament. The choice is yours. But do remember to use a compatible knot when tying braid to both swivel and hook. Consider the clinch-uni

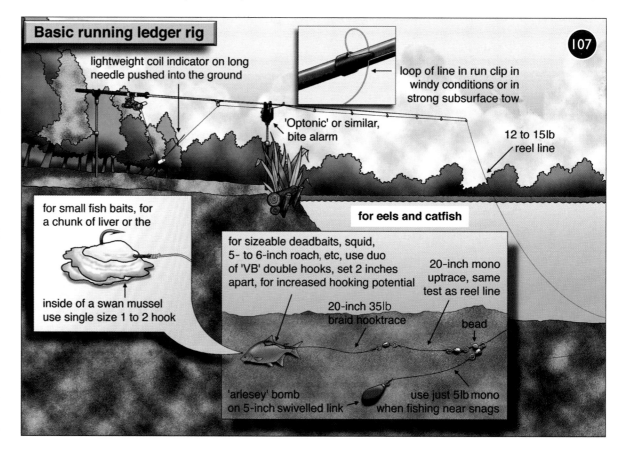

Basic running ledger rig

lightweight coil indicator on long needle pushed into the ground

loop of line in run clip in windy conditions or in strong subsurface tow

'Optonic' or similar, bite alarm

12 to 15lb reel line

107

for small fish baits, for a chunk of liver or the

inside of a swan mussel use single size 1 to 2 hook

for eels and catfish

for sizeable deadbaits, squid, 5- to 6-inch roach, etc, use duo of 'VB' double hooks, set 2 inches apart, for increased hooking potential

20-inch mono uptrace, same test as reel line

20-inch 35lb braid hooktrace

bead

'arlesey' bomb on 5-inch swivelled link

use just 5lb mono when fishing near snags

knot in Diag. 87, for instance, which unlike all the blood knots does not constrict under heavy pressure and create inexplicable fractures.

Baits

With small baits like a minnow or gudgeon, a chunk of liver or the insides of a swan mussel, a single size 1–2 eyed hook suffices. However, for sizeable fish deadbaits like a 5–6-inch dace or roach or a smallish whole squid, a duo of VB double hooks set 2 inches apart offers increased hooking potential.

RUNNING LEDGER LIVEBAIT/DEADBAIT RIG FOR PERCH, PIKE AND ZANDER

The versatile rig shown in Diag. 108 can be adapted to present baits on the bottom for perch, pike, zander and, to a much lesser degree, even chub, the main difference being between various combinations of rod, reel and lines for ensuring maximum enjoyment.

Tackle Combos

For pike the ideal outfit is an 11–12-foot 2–2¼lb test curve medium-tip actioned rod coupled to a 3000 format fixed-spool reel well filled with 10–12 test. For perch (and chub) I step down to an 11–12-foot Avon-actioned rod with a 1¼lb test curve and a 2000 format fixed spool loaded with 6lb test. In most situations the Avon combo also suffices for zander fishing except perhaps where snags or the possibility of a big pike exists. Then I'll step up to an 8lb reel line and a 1½lb test curve light carp/heavy Avon-action rod. But frankly if you wish really to enjoy playing zander, which let's face it are not the greatest scrappers, don't use standard pike gear. Similar to perch the zander is a species which is extremely

sensitive to any kind of resistance, so employing heavy tactics inevitably results in far fewer pick-ups and a greater proportion of dropped runs. (See Method 17, 'Bobbin Ledgering', pages 126–131.)

The running ledger rig shown here is similar to the eel and catfish set-up in Diag. 107 because it too incorporates a 20-inch mono link of reel line above the hook trace with a separate swivel to which the reel line is tied (Fig. B). This ensures the 5-inch swivelled bomb link made of thick mono which runs freely above (with a small cushioning bead in between) does not tangle around the hook trace.

Traces and Baits

For adult perch I use a 15–16-inch monofilament trace made from the 6lb reel line to which is tied a size 2–4 wide gape eyed hook (as in Diag. 108, Fig. A). Small perch deadbaits are best hooked once only through the chin membrane. This not only provides firm hooking when a big stripey grabs hold, but also a secure anchorage for casting. With small livebaits, however, such as stone loach, bleak, gudgeon, perch, roach and dace, hook once only through the top lip from the nose outwards. The large single hook will then fold when the bait is sucked in with the point fully exposed for easy penetration on the strike. As in Diag. 108, Fig. B, for both zander and pike a wire trace is of course imperative. I use 15–16 inches of 10lb test braided alasticum holding a duo of semibarbless size 10 trebles for zander, stepping up to 15–20lb wire and size 8 trebles for pike. With deadbaits such as smelt, herring, Joey, mackerel or half a mackerel or freshly killed roach or small bream, the barbed point of the top hook is worked carefully into the sinewy muscle part of the tail root with the lower treble nicked into the body midway down the flank, again by just the one barbed point.

Though zander do occasionally gobble up sea deadbaits like sprats and herrings, freshly killed

gudgeon, dace, roach and eel sections (just 3–4 inches are invariably more effective. Zander are not silly and can be surprisingly choosy. On the other hand, with pike I would put sea baits slightly ahead of freshwater deads, particularly species possessing a strong and distinct aroma and high oil content, like herrings, mackerel and the cucumber-smelling smelt.

To encourage maximum movement from livebaits like roach, dace, small bream and hybrids in the 5–7-inch range, the barbed point of the top treble goes into the bait's top lip (from the snout out) while the lower treble is gently eased into the root of the pectoral fin again with the barbed point only.

Bite Indication

Although a simple ledger bobbin can be effectively used when coupled to an electronic bite alarm screwed into the front bank stick (see Method 17, 'Bobbin Ledgering' page 126) especially when seeking sensitive species like perch and chub, overall I rate drop-off or drop-arm indicators more practical when ledgering livebaits and deadbaits. Use a simple non-audible drop-arm indicator, which via a terry clip fits on to the rear bank stick and can be fixed on to the line (with the bale arm open) once you have tightened up to the ledger rig. If a predator then swims towards the rod (and dislodges the bomb) the arm will drop down. And if it belts off directly away from the rod the line will pull from the adjustable clip and peel freely from the spool whilst the arm still falls back down – hence the terms 'drop off' or 'drop arm'.

Drop-arm indicators incorporating an electronic alarm and LED (light emitting diode) within the unit are advisable for those lengthy sessions where constant observation of the indicators can prove tiring. The very best in such indicators is represented by the Fox Micron PS Predator Unit that operates on a mercury tilt action which activates both an LED in the buzzer unit (which screws into the rear bank stick

Police officer, Jason Davies, arrested this chunky mid-twenty on a ledgered smelt cast into a deep gully between two islands in a Norfolk gravel pit complex.

literally to become the rear rod rest) and in the high-visibility indicator head itself which incorporates a fully adjustable line clip (as in Diag. 108, Fig. C).

After casting out, tightening up to the rig and opening the reel's bale arm, the indicator head is clipped on to the line immediately below the reel. Due to a sensitive pressure-release button activated by the rod handle whilst resting on the unit, this alarm (which has a volume control) is automatically switched off when the rod is picked up for striking or casting. A great help this.

To stop those frustrating bleeps caused by overactive livebaits, retain a loop of line beneath a run clip or an elastic band fixed around the rod just ahead of the butt ring. But do keep an eye on the angle of line from rod tip to the surface and watch for slack line bites should a predator drag the entire rig towards the rod. Remember that drop-backs won't register when the line is clipped up regardless of the indicator being used.

RIVER FISHING

Clipping up ahead of the drop-arm indicator is also sometimes necessary when ledgering in fast-flowing rivers where by sheer current strength line is still pulled from the adjustable line clip regardless of tension.

Incidentally for those who happen to forget their indicators or young anglers who cannot afford designer units, remember to keep a large folded square of silver kitchen foil amongst your kit plus a few small-diameter elastic bands. It may be old hat but you can then easily manage by slipping a loop of line beneath a band on the rod handle opposite the reel's spool, after opening the bale arm, and then gently folding an oblong of kitchen foil over the line 6 inches in front of the tip ring. If the line is kept tight drop-backs are registered by the foil hanging down, whilst belters see the foil disappearing into the river. I won't tell you for how many years I fished for zander and pike on the Great Ouse Relief Channel during the 1970s using this routine. Suffice to say that it worked, and it still does when the occasion dictates.

Now here's a tip for really attracting zander and pike up to your ledgered deadbait in running water that is a great boon when the river is running high and is the colour of tea. It was passed on to me by fellow predator enthusiast *Angling Times* photographer, Mick Rouse. There is absolutely no reason why this ruse cannot be used when fishing in still waters but it is particularly devastating in rivers for attracting fish lying well downstream of your ledgered bait which, like someone smelling bacon frying in the morning, quickly home in on the source.

You simply use the freezer to make some liquidized fish lollies by putting all your old or unused deadbaits into a blender and pouring the mixture into an ice-cube tray, remembering to push a circle of thick mono into each cube so it can be attached to the bomb link prior to casting out. Upon hitting the bottom the lolly instantly starts to melt,

sending aroma and a continual cloud of liquidized fish particles downstream for several minutes. For transporting these fish lollies, invest in a mini, well-insulated coolbox that will keep the cubes frozen for several hours, and you'll enjoy their pulling power for an entire session. Simple yet so effective.

SWAN SHOTS ONLY

A point to bear in mind, and this obviously applies to ledgering deadbaits in still waters only, is that if you are fishing at really close range when a bomb is simply not required to get the bait out, then don't use one. Tie your wire trace (without the additional mono link) directly on to the reel line and pinch on two to four swan shot 15–20 inches above it. I also choose to fish in this way when out afloat in an anchored boat in a lake or on my local Norfolk Broads whenever wind

velocity makes any kind of float fishing impossible. Bite indication is provided by a loop of line clipped beneath an elastic band or run clip on the handle with the bale arm open. And because the swan shots, which help to keep the bait static on the bottom give just that hint of resistance, a pike usually runs off in the opposite direction and provides a belting run. Drop-backs are, in my experience, quite rare.

One benefit of presenting the bait in this manner is that the line literally follows the route of the pike resulting in few rejections before the hooks are slammed home. When the line passes through a bomb, on the other hand, the angle of line that must be straightened before striking (if the fish runs off at right angles) is acute.

THE STRIKE

Lastly, let's consider the strike itself, because this is when most pike are lost – usually because the hooks are not driven home. Don't simply close the bale arm, pick the rod up and strike. Wait for the line to be tightened fully by the running pike, and if distance fishing hold the rod well out in front so that when all's really tight and you sweep the rod back in a powerful strike the pike's momentum and weight help in setting the hooks. Actually whilst the pike has its jaws clamped tightly I doubt whether the hooks ever penetrate. They only do so when it opens its jaws in that head-shaking, gill-flaring attempt to eject the bait. So don't allow the rod to straighten at any time. Keep winding throughout, before and immediately after the strike, to keep that all-important torque on the line. You'll lose far fewer fish, believe me.

Drop arm indicators incorporating an electronic alarm and LED, such as the Fox Micron PS predator units, operate via a mercury tilt action.

TROLLING FOR PIKE

Sadly, in the majority of English lakes and river systems the technique of trolling is not allowed. In the lochs of Scotland and loughs of Ireland and throughout most countries the world over, trolling in freshwater and in salt is accepted for what it is, probably the most effective method of not only catching predatory species but of maximizing on the amount of territory covered during a day's fishing. It is therefore imperative to enquire at your area branch of the Environment Agency, which encompasses the National Rivers Authority, to ascertain exactly where you may or may not go trolling for pike. In my local waters, the Norfolk Broads, with its interconnecting river system of tidal waterways for instance, trolling is illegal. And for much of the year when the entire area is a hive of activity, often with hired cruisers ploughing three or four abreast up and down the comparatively narrow rivers, who indeed would even want to contemplate the complications bound to arise from trolling lures or a mounted deadbait behind a small boat. The mind boggles! However, to be fair, there are periods lasting for week upon week during cold winter months when hardly another (moving) boat is seen all day by the relatively small band of pike enthusiasts who brave the elements. So I cannot see what harm trolling could possibly do from say, the end of November through until the middle of March. But so it goes.

Compared to being anchored in just one spot or fishing from the bank, trolling is devastatingly effective due to the sheer amount of water covered and consequently the number of pike which actually got to see the lure or bait. The method is therefore particularly suited to large expanses of still water and large river systems, where visibility is good. Chances of sport are definitely reduced when a water colours up and the pike's natural senses veer more towards smell than sight. But before we go any further let's talk tackle.

RODS, REELS, LINES AND TRACES

Long, softish, all-through action rods do not go well with trolling, believe me. The ideal length is around 8–10 feet and the action should be snappy with a reserve of power in the butt section. A medium to fast tip action salmon spinning rod doubles nicely for trolling, particularly when coupled to a multiplier in the 6000–6500 format, which has a smooth clutch and an audible ratchet, loaded with either a reasonably low-stretch 15lb monofilament line, or a gel spun polyethylene braided line of 25–28lb test. With the latter, that has virtually no stretch (which is why it is so effective for slamming the hooks home), you can actually afford to use a rod with a softish tip. I have purposely suggested a higher breaking strain as a safety margin due to the fact that braid is almost devoid of elasticity and until you get used to its unbelievably positive feel, you may just break off on the strike. This could happen when a lively pike starts cavorting near the boat on a short line if the same test as monofilament (15lb) is used. Besides even 25–28lb braid is considerably more limp, abrasion resistant and noticeably thinner than 15lb monofilament which has 25 per cent stretch. Braid has less than 5 per cent stretch, incidentally, which means that you can set hooks firmly even when trolling the bait or lure a long way behind the boat on a flat line or deep down with the aid of a paravane.

It is interesting to note that due to the inherent buoyancy of gel spun polyethylene braided line, when flat line trolling a mounted deadbait or a large spoon, even way back behind the boat, it tends to fish much higher in the water than with monofilament. Obviously vaned-type plugs and other diving lures are not so affected. As an insurance against times when a pike starts crashing and leaping about close to the boat you can always incorporate a monofilament uptrace between the wire trace and your braided reel line. In fact for most trolling situations I use at least a 4–6-foot uptrace of 15lb mono, to act as a shock absorber. Overall it does not dampen the effectiveness of braid but, because just 5 feet of monofilament will stretch a further foot or so when under tension, it's nice to have that safety factor when holding a big fish on a short line ready for netting.

One final point about using braid is to set the reel's clutch noticeably lighter than you would for monofilament. When all becomes instantly tight should the lure or bait foul bottom for instance, with next to no stretch between reel and snag something

Trolling out on massive Lough Corrib in Southern Ireland with Danny Goldrick, where a big spoon usually sorts out the biggest pike.

Success is hard earned when trolling Irish loughs. It is important to locate feature lies on the sonar unit and then cover them thoroughly using artificials.

As can be seen from Fig. B, a large, wide gaped size 3/0-5/0 hook is tied into the mouth and acts like a keel with two trebles along the belly for additional hooking power. Fig. C shows how a baiting needle is used to pull the trace up by the swivel through the bait's throat and out through its mouth so both lips and the eye of the large single are tied together.

Alternatively consider the specialized trace in Fig. D which uses a pair of size 2/0 hooks on a split ring arrangement, both of which press into the eye socket and evenly take the weight of the trolled bait. Size 6 trebles are then mounted on separate (alasticum) wire links and nicked into the bait along each flank (Fig. E shows a top view). There are numerous similar ways of mounting trolling baits so don't be afraid to try anything which just might work and suit or overcome the particular circumstances on the day.

The best deadbaits to use are firm-bodied species like brown or rainbow trout, Joey mackerel, large sand eels, half a freshwater eel (the tail end) or a lamprey. I like freshly caught roach or hybrids too. And as I have mentioned in Method 22, 'Downrigger Trolling for Pike', small whole squid are excellent pike catchers when trolled.

SONAR

The most useful, dare I say indispensable, piece of modern technology that no serious angler trolling for pike should be without is a sonar/fish finder unit. On arrival at any massive sheet of seemingly featureless still water that you intend to troll for the first time, you would indeed be at one hell of a disadvantage without one. This is not so much because of its fish-finding capabilities but more for the all-important continual depth read-out which, together with actual bottom topography, is displayed on the screen. If you do not know the depths, how can you select the type of lure required? It's as simple as that. This problem

has got to give and, as many anglers have experiences to their cost, the rod becomes the weakest link and promptly snaps. So beware.

A trace for presenting lures should be 12 inches long and constructed from 20lb test braided wire, either alasticum or seven-strand with a size 10 Berkeley swivel at the line end and a size 5 Croslok snap swivel at the other to facilitate quick lure changing. For mounted deadbaits increase the length of the trace to 16 inches with a duo or trio of size 6 treble hooks at the business end. That extra treble along the bait's flank (as in Diag.

109, Fig. A) will account for the odd bonus pike which makes a hasty snatch without much intent. Others may make repeated attacks and follow a bait for some considerable distance, until they either become hooked or swim off in disgust to sulk. And as no two days trolling are ever the same, it pays to experiment with various hooking set-ups. Consider actually sewing the bait's mouth up for instance (using elasticated cotton and a large-eyed needle) in order that it looks more lifelike on the troll and holds together better.

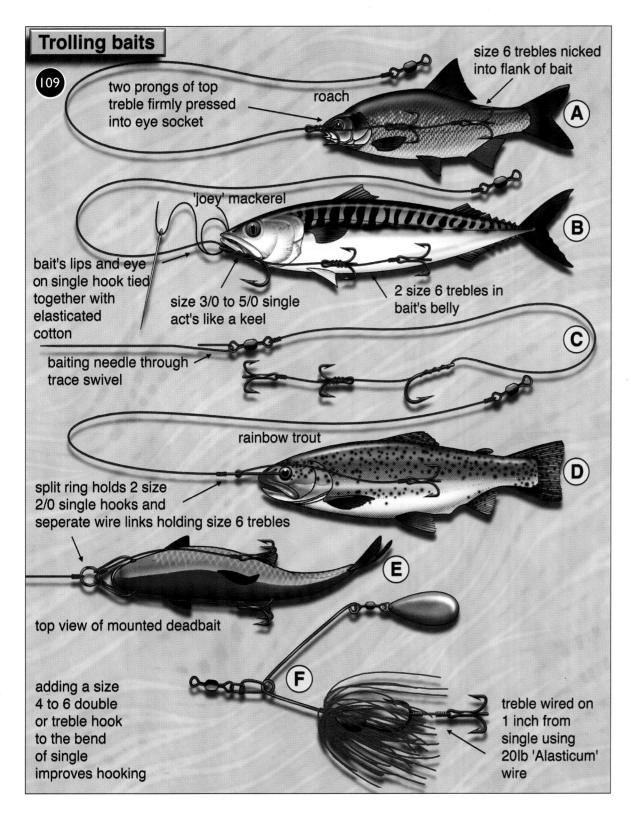

Trolling baits

109

roach

two prongs of top treble firmly pressed into eye socket

size 6 trebles nicked into flank of bait

bait's lips and eye on single hook tied together with elasticated cotton

'joey' mackerel

size 3/0 to 5/0 single act's like a keel

2 size 6 trebles in bait's belly

baiting needle through trace swivel

rainbow trout

split ring holds 2 size 2/0 single hooks and seperate wire links holding size 6 trebles

top view of mounted deadbait

adding a size 4 to 6 double or treble hook to the bend of single improves hooking

treble wired on 1 inch from single using 20lb 'Alasticum' wire

becomes compounded when trolling in deep, cold water when pike are only going to be interested in lures or baits presented through that lowest depth band of all just above the bottom where they lie. Even with all the latest gizmos, state-of-the-art fish finders with side scanning facility, 3D perspective and full colour display, you will still suffer the occasional inevitable blank whilst trolling, as indeed you will with any other method, but by learning to use a fish finder and relating to its read-out by selecting various lures to work certain depth bands, and specifically to search out those pike-holding features, your results can only improve.

Look for the kind of features you would concentrate upon if fishing into deep water from the bank, such as troughs and gullies, sudden drop-offs from shallow into deep water and irregular rock formations and areas of broken or rough ground where the form of a pike lying in wait is all too easily hidden from a shoal of meandering shoal fish until it's too late. Deep and narrow, steep-sided runs between islands or a deep trench running parallel to the shoreline of islands – areas of even-depthed water where a peak, plateau or gravel bar suddenly appears on the screen – are all exactly the kind of subsurface hotspots where shoal fish gather and where predators are bound to patrol. These and many more features are why read-outs from the fish finder are so important. And as I have already mentioned in Method 22, 'Downrigger Trolling for Pike', when exploring the floor of huge man-made lakes and reservoirs created by the damming and subsequent flooding of river valleys, your target pike-holding features might well be cottages, old farm building, stone walls, fences and roads plus numerous tree stumps. Huge areas of woodland were in fact felled before some of our larger reservoirs could be flooded, so just imagine what magnificent feature lies these areas now provide for predators such as pike.

Sometimes the single bleep and mark of a pike lying in wait is displayed on the fish finder screen, sometimes not. In shallow water, especially, fish swim away from a moving boat as it approaches and so cannot be picked up by the unit's transducer clamped on to the transom below the waterline with a rubber suction disc, and registered on the display screen, although hi-tech units with side scanning facilities can help overcome this problem to a degree. But as I mentioned earlier what is of paramount importance is the read-out depicting bottom contours and actual depth because these dictate tactics. Which lure should you use and at what depth should you present it?

So imagine if you will and try to picture in your mind's eye all waters in cross section rather like a giant layer cake (as Diag. 110), which if exceedingly deep contains numerous depth bands. The task of depth selection will perhaps then not seem such an awesome subject, because in reality it is not. As most pike (during the colder months especially) choose to keep very low down in the water often within inches of the bottom, they are perfectly placed for an upwards attack and consequently grabbing a lure or bait trolled within 2–4 feet above them. Consider Diag. 111, for instance, showing in cross section a reservoir fishery where trolling over and within a few feet of all the feature lies will produce the hottest pike action. In trout fishery reservoirs pike are also naturally attracted to the pens or cages in which brown and rainbow trout are reared on pelleted food until they are large enough for release.

FLATLINE TROLLING

Flatline trolling is so called because a lure or bait is allowed to be taken back behind the boat between 40 and 100 feet away (or further) under gentle thumb pressure upon the spool of the multiplier, on a flat

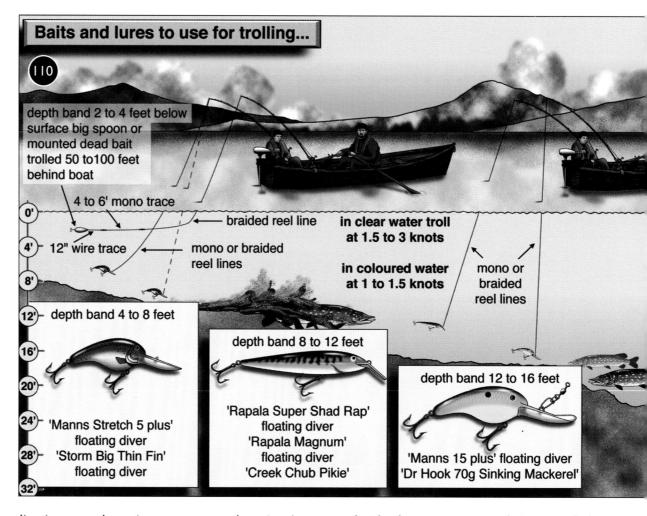

Baits and lures to use for trolling...

110

depth band 2 to 4 feet below surface big spoon or mounted dead bait trolled 50 to100 feet behind boat

4 to 6' mono trace

12" wire trace

braided reel line

mono or braided reel lines

in clear water troll at 1.5 to 3 knots

in coloured water at 1 to 1.5 knots

mono or braided reel lines

depth band 4 to 8 feet

'Manns Stretch 5 plus' floating diver
'Storm Big Thin Fin' floating diver

depth band 8 to 12 feet

'Rapala Super Shad Rap' floating diver
'Rapala Magnum' floating diver
'Creek Chub Pikie'

depth band 12 to 16 feet

'Manns 15 plus' floating diver
'Dr Hook 70g Sinking Mackerel'

line (as opposed to using a paravane or downrigger) before the reel is put into gear and the clutch is adjusted. You may then hold the rod at a 45-degree angle so the tip can be watched for hits or it can be put in a rod rest.

I have already mentioned the shepherd's crook type with G clamp mounting and the lightweight polycarbonate side mounting rod rests in Method 22, 'Downrigger Trolling for Pike', but there are others on the market such as the famous Down-East rod holders, imported from the US by Bob Carolgees, PO Box 223, Northwich, Cheshire. These automatically locking rests made from cast alloy are available with a variety of mounts to fit your boat's

gunnel, side plates, transom or rail. Big Jon tubular rod holders also imported from the US, are available through the same company.

As trolling is an extremely mobile, totally explorative method of searching out pike from huge expanses of water by literally covering as much territory as possible, you should never become bored. There is always something different to try, like varying trolling speed from the normal 1–2 knots, to much faster bursts, or slowing right down every so often especially when trolling around known features, so a heavy lure like a large spoon or a mounted deadbait suddenly begins to free fall before you gun the engine again and the trolled bait bursts

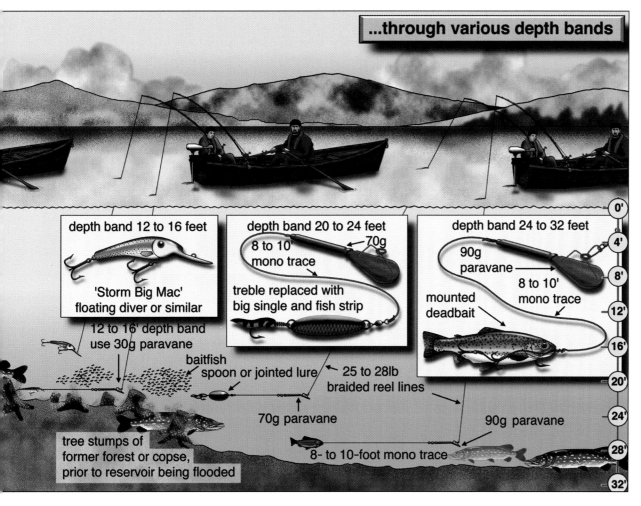

...through various depth bands

depth band 12 to 16 feet

'Storm Big Mac' floating diver or similar

12 to 16' depth band use 30g paravane

baitfish

spoon or jointed lure

tree stumps of former forest or copse, prior to reservoir being flooded

70g paravane

depth band 20 to 24 feet

8 to 10' mono trace

70g

treble replaced with big single and fish strip

25 to 28lb braided reel lines

depth band 24 to 32 feet

90g paravane

8 to 10' mono trace

mounted deadbait

90g paravane

8- to 10-foot mono trace

0'
4'
8'
12'
16'
20'
24'
28'
32'

gathered. For working in depths of between 8 and 20 feet there is a host of superb big lipped plugs from which to choose in the floating/diving format, and also amongst sinking divers. The manufacturers of quality floating/divers usually provide guidelines as to the depths at which their various plugs will work effectively. For instance the famous Manns' depth control range of deep diving floaters are actually marked in feet, like the 10+, 15+, 20+, 25+ and believe it or not the 30+ whose lip is almost the size of its body, but then to dive straight down to over 30 feet even on a slow troll its diving vane needs to be large. Unless actually marked, this is the best way of deciding which plug does what: the bigger the lip the deeper it will dive.

I can thoroughly recommend Normark's Rapala range of plugs and, in particular, the Rapala Magnums which are fitted with extremely strong split rings and trebles, so they are perfect for trolling. Both the floating and sinking magnums will dive to around 10 and 15 feet respectively (depending upon trolling speed) and the floating diver is particularly useful when trolling over known shallow peaks or structures well above the general bottom contours. You simply slow right down whenever shallow areas appear on the fish finder allowing the plug to float upwards and clear the bar, peak, snag or structure before accelerating back to normal speed once well past it.

Incidentally, don't be in too much of a hurry to cut engine speed completely when a pike does grab hold, particularly if using monofilament because, due to its enormous stretch, a firm hook hold is not always achieved on the strike. Only when the pike opens its jaws and flares its gills in that lovely head-shaking routine will the hooks find purchase, so it is essential that torque is kept on. With braid, however, cut the engine to tick over as soon as the reel's ratchet starts screaming. A point worth mentioning here,

into life. Should any pike be following, an aggressive hit is almost guaranteed.

With flatline trolling even heavy lures designed without diving vanes such as spinner baits and large heavy spoons, plus mounted baits of course, won't work much lower than a few feet below the surface even when trolled slowly. Working a really long line in excess of 100 feet behind the boat may add an extra foot, but generally speaking only the upper water layer is explored. This is fine in relatively shallow rivers and still waters averaging, say, less than 8 feet deep. However to explore deeper water it is imperative to use lures incorporating an angled diving vane or a lip sufficient to go down quickly and

work within the depth band at which pike are most likely to be lying. After all, it's pointless trolling a spoon just 3–4 feet beneath the surface in 30 feet of water when the pike are lying on the bottom. During the warmer months pike will periodically hunt within the upper water layers because their staple diet of small shoal fishes will themselves be feeding upon emerging aquatic insects close to the surface.

For the greater part of the pike fishing season however, and especially during winter conditions, both lures and mounted deadbaits are most effectively fished within that lowest depth band within 2 to 4 feet of the bottom or the top of any feature or structure around which their prey is

If working two outfits, place one in a rest and hold the second, dropping the mounted deadbait or lure every so often before re-engaging the clutch. Multipliers are the reels to use.

particularly with those large lipped plugs, is to start at a slow troll during the descent and increase the throttle slowly to around 1½–2 knots trolling speed. Either start with the plug 75–100 feet behind the boat or watch it dive down on a short line and

steadily give line from the reel on demand until it is working deep enough and far enough behind. Always give line and increase the throttle speed smoothly or the plug will suddenly turn turtle and skip up to the surface.

Other floating divers that work effectively within the 8–20-foot depth band are Rapalas Fat Rap Deep Runner, Rattl'n Fat Rap, Super Shad Rap and the Shad Rap Deep Runner. There is in fact enormous choice within this particular depth range and I suggest either a visit to your local specialist tackle shop, or send away for a specialist artificial lure company's brochure. The Harris Angling Company of Blacksmith House, East Ruston, Norfolk, for instance, stock an unbelievable range of top-quality American lures from the stables of Heddon, Manns, Bagley, Aarbogast and Rebel.

PARAVANE TROLLING

For exploring depths below 20 feet I have already mentioned Manns' huge lipped 20+, 25+ and 30+ but in truth there are few models that work effectively below 20 feet. What you can do however is to use a diving paravane as the vehicle for diving down deep. I use models by Kuusamo of Finland, which incidentally are available in the UK only from The Friendly Fisherman, 25 Camden Road Tunbridge Wells, Kent. There are in fact three different sizes which dive on the troll to 12, 24 and 36 feet respectively and weigh 33g, 70g and 90g. So unless you are contemplating catching pike from water in excess of 40 feet deep (a rarity in British fisheries) every depth band can be worked effectively, not only with mounted baits and spoons but also with diving plugs (which obviously work a little deeper still) and even surface lures. You attach a Croslok snap swivel on the reel line (preferably braid) to the split ring on the paravane's angled head, and to the swivel at its other end you add up to a rod's length (say 8–10 feet) of monofilament plus wire trace and lure or mounted bait. Obviously monofilament trace length depends on the length of

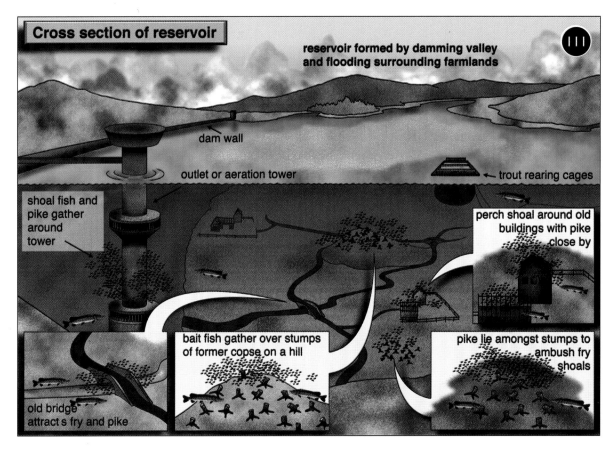

Cross section of reservoir

reservoir formed by damming valley and flooding surrounding farmlands

dam wall

outlet or aeration tower

← trout rearing cages

shoal fish and pike gather around tower

perch shoal around old buildings with pike close by

bait fish gather over stumps of former copse on a hill

pike lie amongst stumps to ambush fry shoals

old bridge attracts fry and pike

your rod because if any longer hand lining would be necessary to land a fish.

Kuusamo also produce paravanes that incorporate a directional trolling vane which, through moving a hinged lip to one side or the other, allows the unit to troll your bait or lure not in a straight line but well away from the boat to the right or to the left. This is a crafty dodge which fools those extra-spooky fish living in crystal-clear water that might otherwise be put off by the boat passing directly overhead, and one that makes trolling with more than two rods more pleasurable.

There is no hard-and-fast rule as to actual trolling speed, other than to start by motoring along slowly at say 1 knot and progressively increase speed (up to a maximum of 3 knots) until bites materialize. In clear water especially pike often want a chase,

whereas in levels of low visibility slow speeds invariably work best. If using monofilament reel line, gunning the engine an extra few knots when the rod buckles over, just for a few yards or so, helps to promote firm hooking on days when pike repeatedly grab but instantly let go.

In Method 22, 'Downrigger Trolling for Pike', I have explained how spoons or plugs can be doctored by swapping the rear treble for a large single which is then baited with fresh fish strip. Another ruse for increasing the hooking power of single hook lures such as spinner baits is shown in Diag. 109, Fig. F. Using 20lb alasticum, which is easily twisted, you simply wire on to the bend of the large single, a size 6 or 4 double or treble hook. It accounts for numerous pike that just nibble without intent or come short.

WOBBLING DEADBAITS FOR PIKE AND ZANDER

As a roaming working technique for predatory species like pike and zander, and to a much lesser extent chub and perch, the art of wobbling deadbaits is perhaps one of the least used. This is a great pity really because wobbling will account for predators in all types of waters from narrow Fenland drains to wide expanses of shallow flats such as my local Norfolk Broads. And it works in flowing water too. Our forefathers aptly called wobbling 'sink and draw' which I guess is more accurate, because you do indeed allow the mounted deadbait to sink before drawing it forwards. But I prefer the modern terminology because the bait actually wobbles attractively when worked on the retrieve due to the slightly off-set way in which it is mounted as opposed to the old traditional way of mounting on an archer-type flight.

The trace is rigged (as in Diag. 112) with the upper treble (wind the trace wire around the shank a few times at the desired distance away) firmly embedded into the bait's eye socket with two barbed points of the hook. The bottom treble is then worked into the bait's flank midway down, with one barbed point, leaving two barbless prongs showing for good hooking purchase. This is why I prefer to use standard trebles and crunch the barbs down gently, as opposed to purchasing semi-barbless models. You can then use exactly the pattern and strength of hooks required, perhaps a small point (no pun intended) but an important one nonetheless.

When presenting 2–3-inch dace or sprats for chub, perch or zander, use a brace of size 12s or 10s to match the size of the bait. For pike, however, a duo of size 8s should suit all but the largest baits, going up a notch to size 6s only if large baits are all that is on offer. You cannot always catch natural baits of the exact size, neither is it possible to rely upon the local wet-fish shop always having exactly the right-sized sprats or herrings.

When perch and chub are the target species the trebles are tied direct to a 6lb reel line, but for all zander and pike fishing use a reel line of around 10–11lb test with the hooks mounted on a 16-inch swivelled trace made from 15lb test braided alasticum. The only addition (just below the swivel) is to squeeze on gently between one and four or five swan shots in order to get the bait down to the desired depth band and keep it there throughout the retrieve regardless of speed. Obviously you need more shots

John mounts a dyed golden herring for wobbling through the shallow reed-lined waters of famous Horsey Mere, which produced Peter Hancock's 40lb 1oz pike that once held the British record.

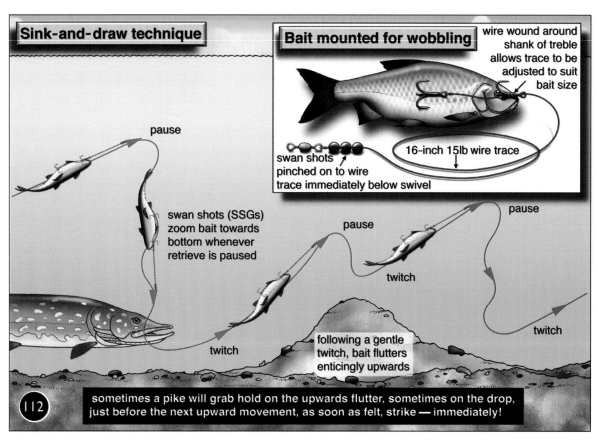

Sink-and-draw technique

pause

swan shots (SSGs) zoom bait towards bottom whenever retrieve is paused

pause

twitch

twitch

following a gentle twitch, bait flutters enticingly upwards

pause

twitch

Bait mounted for wobbling

wire wound around shank of treble allows trace to be adjusted to suit bait size

swan shots pinched on to wire trace immediately below swivel

16-inch 15lb wire trace

112

sometimes a pike will grab hold on the upwards flutter, sometimes on the drop, just before the next upward movement, as soon as felt, strike — immediately!

on the trace for a fast retrieve through gin-clear water and fewer for a slow search close to the bottom in really soupy conditions, where you need virtually to bump a pike on the head for it to grab hold.

When wobbling over areas of really shallow water where even in the depths of winter subsurface weeds or cabbages clog that bottom layer or zone where pike lie, the bait can usually be more efficiently worked without any shots on the trace. And when wobbling baits literally through or above dense surface greenery the most wonderfully aggressive attacks occur from pike lying up in clearings which must make an instant grab or allow a meal to escape.

Some of the most spectacular action I have ever experienced whilst wobbling deadbaits came (fortunately for me) during the filming of one of my 'Go Fishing' TV programmes, fishing in the Upper Thurne group of Broads which even in early October were still carpeted in stoneworts, marestail and hornwort, virtually from top to bottom. With an average depth of less than 4 feet, freelining static deadbaits which was how I started the programme, proved to be a complete waste of time. So no other option existed than to wobble deadbaits and I selected the lightest, thinnest smelts in the coolbag so they wouldn't sink down and catch up during the retrieve on weed which in places was actually sprouting through the surface film.

Though we only had enough screen time to feature the two largest pike caught, beauties of 20¼lb and 27½lb respectively, I did in fact catch several others that afternoon on smelt wobbled across the surface and all from water so weeded any other sort of pike fishing would have, at first glance, seemed totally impractical, save for weedless surface lures or poppers. But as lures were not permitted in the particular Broad I fished it was wobbled deadbaits or go home. Whilst smelt are an ideal general bait choice (sand eels are worth a try too) particularly in shallow water, they are

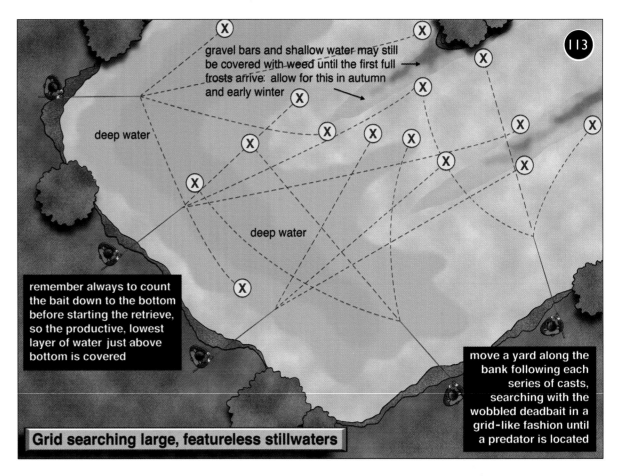

gravel bars and shallow water may still be covered with weed until the first full frosts arrive: allow for this in autumn and early winter

deep water

deep water

remember always to count the bait down to the bottom before starting the retrieve, so the productive, lowest layer of water just above bottom is covered

move a yard along the bank following each series of casts, searching with the wobbled deadbait in a grid-like fashion until a predator is located

Grid searching large, featureless stillwaters

prone to breaking up after a few long casts so for sheer durability small freshly killed roach or roach/bream hybrids take some beating. These and any other small deadbaits may be easily coloured using powdered carp bait dye dissolved in water (1 teaspoon to a cupful) and put into a 2-pint bait tin. Hold each bait by the tail with forceps and swish about until evenly coloured. The baits can then be put into polybags and into the freezer for future use.

Now if you fancy trying a real oddball wobbling bait, pop along to your local wet-fish shop and buy some baby calamari squid. These hand-sized baits can be mounted as you would a 6-inch fish – and their trailing tentacles flutter tantalizingly. Squid are excellent in coloured water in particular and most durable when casting.

Overall, taking most situations into account, the ultimate baits in my opinion are small brown and rainbow trout which can usually be bought quite cheaply from most trout fisheries that rear on their own stock or from actual trout farms. I find it is best to purchase in bulk and freeze down in packs of say eight to twelve fish for later use. As for size, I like fish in the 5–6-inch range and no larger which permit an instant strike with a good chance that one of the trebles will find purchase.

Whilst on the subject of when to strike I do so immediately when wobbling, just as though lure fishing, as opposed to slackening off and waiting for the bait to be turned like a livebait or static deadbait. It has been my past experience that far too many pike simply spit a wobbled bait out when you open the bale arm and wait for a traditional run to develop. So bang those hooks home posthaste.

It is most important to continue winding as the rod buckles over and heave the tip upwards against the solid resistance in order for the hooks to find purchase while the pike flares its gills and violently shakes it head from side to side. Obviously any slackening of tension at this stage will help the pike in its attempt to get away, so keep the pressure on and enjoy the subsequent fight once it starts to run realizing that the irritation is not going away. As the pike nears the bank on an ever-reducing length of line it is wise to slacken the clutch off a little. At this point there will be less stretch to play with or, put another way, a shorter elastic band to act as a cushion and you don't want to lose a whopper or a lively double that somersaults across the surface when held on a short line. Should a fish come off, then look at it philosophically in that it was probably small anyway. This is why I choose to wobble with modest-sized baits. The only exception is when using whole small eels and these I freeze down as I catch them during the summer months for use later on in the year. Eels in the 8–10-inch range are perfect, being heavy enough to cast with the addition of a swan shot or two. And when wobbled, eels can drive pike absolutely wild. I'm sure it's that tantalizing tail wiggle.

Taking wobbling as a whole, from late summer through until the end of the season, many situations will call for shots to be added to the trace in order to achieve the right action and the correct depth. So be prepared to juggle about and experiment with trace shots and the rate of retrieve until strikes are induced. Some days pike will follow and only grab hold when

Just 2lb short of 30lb, this Broadland pike took a wobbled smelt in shallow water and produced some fantastic action for the cameras during a 'Go Fishing' TV programme.

you cannot wind any faster but more often they will respond to that tantalizing wobbling, fluttering action imparted to the deadbait by rod tip action. Incidentally to this end I prefer to use a 9–9½-foot crisp-actioned spinning rod for wobbling. You can use longer rods but the bait's action does tend to be dampened somewhat. This is why American anglers use such short rods for their lure fishing – to impart as much action as possible (see Method 3, on 'Working Top-water Lures').

I have often experienced with pike that by wobbling a real fish, as opposed to an artificial, they invariably respond more aggressively. This is particularly so if the bait is missed as they lunge even if the hooks are felt. So quickly get that bait out and working through the same area again.

Just as though working a big spoon (having first counted the deadbait down to the bottom) allowing approximately 1 foot of descent for every second, start the retrieve so it jerks upwards when between 1 and 2 feet from the bottom. In clear water conditions

work it up a couple of feet before pausing and allowing the bait to flutter down again (pulled by swan shots on the trace) as in Diag. 112, before repeating the sequence. Sometimes a pike will grab hold on the upwards flutter, sometimes on the drop just before the next upward movement and, as I mentioned earlier, the time to strike is straight away.

STILL WATERS

When working open water devoid of features such as reed lines, islands or promontories, the best plan of action is to search large areas, grid fashion, by making a cast either to the extreme left or right and moving across a yard or so on each successive cast (as in Diag. 113). Always remember to count the bait down and when it reaches bottom, having provided you with the approximate depth, commence the retrieve. Whether the trebles come back weeded or completely clear you will instantly know what the bottom is like and if the bait grounds halfway in, you will know the

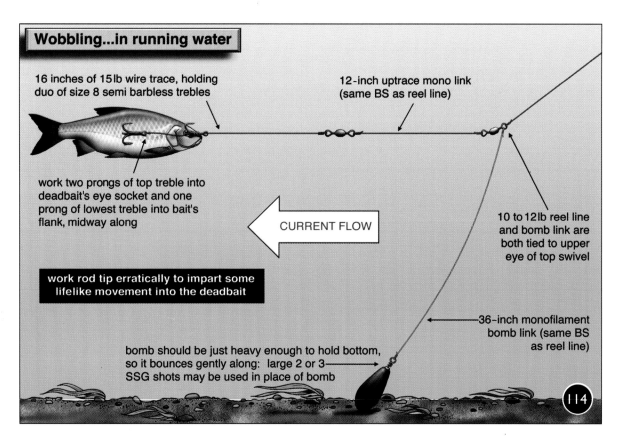

Wobbling...in running water

16 inches of 15lb wire trace, holding duo of size 8 semi barbless trebles

12-inch uptrace mono link (same BS as reel line)

work two prongs of top treble into deadbait's eye socket and one prong of lowest treble into bait's flank, midway along

CURRENT FLOW

work rod tip erratically to impart some lifelike movement into the deadbait

10 to 12lb reel line and bomb link are both tied to upper eye of top swivel

36-inch monofilament bomb link (same BS as reel line)

bomb should be just heavy enough to hold bottom, so it bounces gently along: large 2 or 3 SSG shots may be used in place of bomb

114

tied a small bomb that will gently bounce along the bottom (a couple of 2 x SSG or 3 x SSG shots will do at a pinch) while the wobbling trace has an additional mono link of 12 inches between swivel and reel line to avoid tangles.

This is a great rig for catching pike in deep wide rivers and especially from weir pools. Simply cast downstream and across, eventually working the bait into the margins by bouncing the bomb slowly along the bottom. Take a pace downstream and repeat the procedure, cast after cast, until you strike gold. Remember to work the rod tip erratically throughout to impart lifelike action to the bait.

In cold, clear conditions wobble the bait slowly and just above bottom if you want to boat beauties like this.

position of a shallow bar. Get the message? When exploring really huge waters it sometimes helps to make a simple drawing of the lake or pit and to write in the various depths as you fish, for reference in a future session. Remember almost to point the rod at the bait throughout the retrieve.

Provided the reel's clutch is set forgivingly yet firmly even if a real monster should go screaming off in the opposite direction (a rarity) snapping up on the strike is most unlikely. But you will hook a large per centage of hits cleanly. Although I strike through instinct when the bait is grabbed, it is the fish's own weight which really pulls the hooks home. So keep a tight line at all times.

When wobbling in really clear waters, even in the depths of winter, remember to wear Polaroid glasses so that pike giving chase but failing to grab hold can be observed and the retrieve or action altered to induce a

reaction. Often is it simply a case of speeding the retrieve up as the bait nears the bank which triggers off a last-minute grab by the pike lest its meal gets away. If you are continually slowing up at the end of each retrieve because you need to gauge the amount of line out enabling the next case to be made, this means you will consistently miss out on a whole pile of action. If you were not wearing Polaroids, you might never have known what was on the cards anyway.

FLOWING WATER

I mentioned at the beginning that wobbling can prove rewarding in flowing water, which is perfectly true. If four or five swan shots, say, are insufficient to keep the bait working down near the bottom and counteract current pull then make up a simple rig (as in Diag. 114). As you can see, to the 36-inch link is

INDEX